Coyote Cafe

Foods from the Great Southwest

Recipes from Coyote Cafe,
Santa Fe, New Mexico

Mark Charles Miller

Ten Speed Press

🍍 Ten Speed Press
Post Office Box 7123
Berkeley, California 94707

Edited by John Harrisson.

Book design and typography by Fifth Street Design, Berkeley, California.

Coyote logo by Harry Fonseca.

Photography by Brenton Beck, Glen Craley, Lois Ellen Frank, Terry Husebye, Peter Macchia, Michael McConeghy, Mark Miller, and John Vaughan.

Illustration on pages ii-iii by Elizabeth Read/Read Ink., San Francisco.

Pre-press and printing by Ringier America, Phoenix and New Berlin Divisions, respectively.

A portion of the royalities from this book is being donated to Share Our Strength, a national organization based in Washington, D.C., dedicated to feeding the homeless, and to the Dominican Mission in Chiapas, Mexico.

Library of Congress Cataloging-in-Publication Data

Miller, Mark 1949-
    Coyote Cafe.
    Includes index.
    1.   Cookery, American—Southwestern Style.
2.   Coyote Cafe (Santa Fe, N.M.)   I.   Title.
TX715.M6477   1989   641.5979   882099

ISBN 0-89815-244-5

Manufactured in the United States of America

90   91   92   93   —   5   4   3

To Marie, my mother, and John, who are always there.

Acknowledgments

So many people over the years have helped me and believed in me. If this is a long list, there are still many more whom I consider friends and allies in the pursuit of good food and providing good food for others.

The first friends I want to mention are those who gave me my culinary education in the Bay Area during those exciting years from the 60's to the 80's: Alice Waters ("taste everything" and "best is what's good enough"); Jean Pierre Moullé, who was my culinary academy and who taught me all the professional techniques that I use every day in the restaurant; Thomas Royal Guernsey, my constant travelling companion to faraway exotic places ("the best style in life is to enjoy it" and "let's have another"); Paul Bertolli, who is so gifted, and provided me with some of the most memorable meals — a true concert artist in the kitchen; these people I remember with fondness and miss them. It took a long time to get from there to here. There are many unsung heroes of that era; for example, the vendors who provided the raw materials for that great transformation. I spent many pre-dawn hours with them at the produce market and many more rushing to pick up the freshest and best ingredients for Chez Panisse or Fourth Street Grill: from the old Italians at the Oakland Produce Market, to Chinatown for duck, to North Beach for salt cod and prosciutto, to Tomales Bay for oysters and Amador County for spring lamb.

Among the individuals are Paul Johnson and Tom Worthington, who worked so hard to bring us the most perfect fish; Vince at C & M and George at Ninth Street, who understood that great meat and poultry dishes begin with great meat and poultry; Judy Rodgers, an honest cook whose soul is always on the plate; Bill Wallace and Tom Taylor from the Old 24th Street Cheese Company who, before it became chic, knew more about cheeses of the world than anyone; Steve Sullivan of Acme Bakery, who makes bread the way it should be; Bill Fujimoto and his family at Monterey Market, who make a produce market a true treasure hunt, with the ripest, the rarest, and the most exotic; Patty Unterman and Tim Savinar, who were always so excited about my cooking and who supported it with great reviews and great appetites.

My other Bay Area culinary friends with whom I shared many good meals include Barbara Tropp, Bradley Ogden, Carlo and Lisa Middione, Joyce and Evan Goldstein, Kathy and George Wolf, Christopher Chung, Narsai David, Marion Cunningham, Shirley Sarvis, Lonni Kuhn, James Nassikas, Mary Risley, Billy Marinelli, Sam Duval and Carolyn Chandler, and Laura Chenel.

Then there are my special friends in the Wine Industry: Bruce and Barbara Neyers, whose hospitality and champagne never run out; Robert Mondavi and Margarit Beiver, who constantly amaze me with their knowledge and enthusiasm for learning; Joseph Phelps, who always goes out of his way to support the chef and the restaurant; Audrey, Barry and Joy Sterling and Forrest Tancer at Iron Horse Vineyards, who have a gentility and grace in presence and in their wines; and Tor and Susan Kenward at Beringer, who have provided longtime support and interest in Southwestern cooking.

I can even claim to have some Special Texas Friends who are the best down-home bunch, and who have adopted a New Englander not only because I love to eat chile, but more important, because I also enjoy a good time: Robert and Mimi Del Grande, Dean Fearing, Stephen Pyles, John Dayton, Anne Greer, John Makin, Anne Clark, Elizabeth and Mike Hughes, Bruce Auden, Lucinda Hutson, Susan and Ed Auler, and Paula Lambert.

I am fortunate in having many other fond friends scattered about, who feed me wonderful food and who listen to my restaurant woes with a kind ear: Jonathan Waxman, Larry Forgione, Wolfgang Puck and Barbara Lazaroff, Nancy Silverton and Mark Peal, Jasper and Nancy White, John Sedlar, Steve Garcia, Jimmy Schmidt, Ricardo Solares, Michel Richard, Mary Sue Milliken and Susan Feininger, Michael Roberts, Sally Clarke, Lydia Shire, Frank and Francis Stitt, Zarela Martinez, Marcel Desaulniers, Patricia Quintana, and Rick and Deann Bayles.

Among the food writers I would like to thank for their support and encouragement are Donna Warner, Ruth Reichl, Coleman Andrews, Jan Weimer, Karen MacNeil, Bill Rice, Ellen Brown, John Mariani, Stanley Dry, Marion Burros, Barbara Kafka, and John Shoup.

No such list would be complete, of course, without mentioning my mentors and teachers, who inspired me to start cooking and to keep going. I particularly respect their taste and their efforts to educate on the subject of food and how to enjoy it: James Beard, Richard Olney, Chuck Williams, Diana Kennedy, Paula Wolfert, and Jack Lirio.

Last, but not least, are the staff of Coyote Cafe and friends in Santa Fe — people who have made the doors stay open for every performance possible: Bucky Harris, Sam Skarda, Reed Hearon, Chris Galvin, Kim Peoples, Kimberley Sweet, Debbie Slutsky, Paul Perret, Lyn and Larry Sisson, Terry Peay, Elizabeth Berry, Susan Dunshee, Jett and Jennifer. A number of people worked tirelessly on the design of Coyote Cafe: Harry Fonseca, Stephen Samuelson, Harry Daple, Dewayne Youts, Kit Carson, Juan and Patty Navarette, Leroy Ortega, Fred Prescott, Frank Rolla, and Robert Stanfield. The printed graphics and artwork for the restaurant are the work of Steve Lowe and his design staff at Casa Sin Nombre. Special thanks to John Harrisson and Andrea Jarrell for their sterling work in editing this book; to Phil Wood and Ten Speed Press, my superb publishers, and the ever-patient and supportive George Young and Jackie Wan; and to Brent Beck at Fifth Street Design for the wonderful, colorful artwork. Finally, special thanks to all my partners who believed in me and Coyote Cafe and who made it all possible.

Table of Contents

Acknowledgments, v

Preface, xi

Introduction, xiv

Cocktails I

Tips for Making Great Cocktails, 2

Bloody Maria, 3

Brazilian Daiquiri, 3

Sunburnt Señorita, 3

Coyote Cocktail, 4

Coyote Margarita, 4

Chimayo Cocktail, 4

Pisco Sour, 5

Planter's Punch, 5

Tamarindo, 5

Señor Playboy, 8

Champagne Padre, 8

Liquados, 9

Salsas II

Pico De Gallo Salsa, 13

Roasted Tomato and Mint Salsa, 13

Tomatillo Salsa, 13

Roasted Corn Salsa, 14

Roasted Serrano Salsa, 14

Poblano Pesto, 15

Black Bean Salsa, 16

Black Bean Corn Salsa, 16

Chile Mignonnette, 16

Chimayo Chile Salsa, 17

Nopales Salsa, 17

Pineapple Salsa, 18

Melon Salsa, 18

Squash Salsa, 19

Gazpacho Salsa, 19

Mango Salsa, 20

Green Chile Chutney, 20

Hot Corn Relish, 20

Sauces & Soups   23

Red Chile Sauce, 25

Mark's Red Chile Sauce, 25

Green Chile Sauce, 26

Tomatillo Chipotle Sauce, 26

Smoked Tomato and
Jalapeño Sauce, 27

Tamarind Chipotle Sauce, 27

Manchamantel Sauce, 28

Ranchero Sauce, 28

Mole Rojo, 29

Mole Verde, 30

Pipián Rojo, 30

Pipián Verde, 31

Peanut Chipotle Sauce, 31

Black Bean Soup, 32

Yellow Squash Soup, 34

Southwest Painted Soup, 34

Green Gazpacho Soup, 35

Yucatán Lime Soup, 36

Roasted Corn Soup, 36

Green Chile & Oyster Chowder, 37

Albóndigas de Camarónes, 38

Posole, 38

Clam Soup with Sausage, 39

Appetizers & Salads   41

Black Pepper Yucatán Oysters, 43

Oyster Empanadas, 43

Salpicón of Texas Blue Crab, 44

Crab Cushions, 44

Swordfish en Escabeche, 45

Scallop Ceviche, 46

Manila Clams, 46

Southwest Spicy Steak Tartare, 47

Carpaccio of Venison, 47

Barbecued Duck Cakes, 48

Wild Chanterelle Sopes, 49

Carnitas Raviolis, 51

Queso Fundido, 52

Squash Blossoms, 52

Mérida-style Octopus Salad, 53

Pickled Shrimp and Corn Salad, 54

Sonora Salad, 54

Lobster and Corn Salad, 55

Mark's Caesar Salad, 55

Tamales   57

General Instructions, 59

Tamale de Elote, 61

Chicken Tamale, 61

Yucatán Chicken Tamale, 62

Black Bean Tamale, 62

Mincemeat Tamale, 63

Carnitas Tamale, 63

Confit of Duck Tamale, 64

Blue Corn Tamale, 65

Blue Corn Shrimp Tamale, 65

Lobster and Salmon Tamale, 68

White Truffle Tamale, 68

Wild Morel Tamale, 69

Goat Cheese and Mint Tamale, 70

Currant and Canela Tamale, 70

Sweet Blackberry Blue Corn
Tamale, 71

Seafood & Fish 73

Red Chile Pesto Clams, *75*

Red Chile Risotto Clams, *76*

Curried Oysters, *77*

Chipotle Mussels, *78*

Lobster Enchiladas, *79*

Lobster and Scallops, *80*

Texas Blue Crab Cakes, *80*

Spicy Soft-shell Crab, *82*

Scallop Hash, *82*

Shrimp Brochette, *83*

Paillard of Salmon, *83*

Salmon Fillet, *84*

Brook Trout, *84*

Blue Corn Trout, *85*

Grilled Tuna, *86*

Tuna Tartare Rellenos, *86*

Cumin Swordfish, *87*

Huachinango, *88*

Santa Fe Seafood Stew, *88*

Caribbean Seafood Stew, *89*

Game & Fowl 91

Tips on Cooking Game and Fowl, *93*

Venison Chile, *94*

Grilled Venison, *94*

Grilled Texas Axis Venison, *95*

Roasted Venison, *96*

Pan-fried Quail, *96*

Red Chile Quail, *97*

Pan-roasted Quail, *99*

Hibiscus Quail, *100*

Cumin Squab, *100*

Braised Duck, *101*

Sautéed Duck, *102*

Duck Carnitas Rellenos, *102*

Pheasant, *103*

Chicken Roulade, *104*

Grilled Breast of Chicken, *104*

Yucatán Stuffed Wild Turkey, *105*

Smoked Rabbit Enchiladas, *106*

Horno-style Goat Leg, *107*

Meat 109

Cowboy Steak, *112*

Fillet of Beef, *112*

Beef Fillet, *113*

Seared Tenderloin, *113*

Oaxacan Rellenos, *114*

Yucatán Lamb, *115*

Rack of Lamb, *116*

Pecan Crust Rack of Lamb, *116*

Papantla Pork, *117*

Brazilian Pork, *117*

Tenderloin of Pork, *120*

Pork Tacos, *120*

Pork Loin, *121*

Tamarind Barbecued Ribs, *122*

Desserts & Breads 125

Chile Corn Bread, *127*

Cinnamon Buckwheat Bread, *128*

Orange Cumin Bread, *129*

Ibarra Chocolate Cake, *130*

Anise Pound Cake, *130*

Almond Polenta Pound Cake, *131*

Christine's Venison Mincemeat, *132*

White Chocolate Buttermilk Tart, *133*

Rhubarb Anise Crisp, *133*

Coyote Churros, *134*

Kathy Wolf's Chocolate Kumquat Helado, *135*

Vanilla Helado, *135*

Cajeta Caramel, *136*

Cajeta Caramel Sundae, *136*

Cajeta Tart, *138*

Cinnamon Shortcake, *139*

Blackberry Cinnamon Shortcakes, *139*

Mango Raspberry Brûlée, *140*

Pie Pastry, *141*

Tart Shell, *141*

Coyote's Bag of Tricks 143

Red Chile Rice, *146*

Spicy Green Rice, *146*

Sweet Cinnamon Rice, *147*

Pecan and Wild Boar Bacon Waffles, *147*

Green Chile Corn Muffins, *148*

Huevos Rancheros, *148*

Green Chile Stew, *149*

Chipotle Shrimp, *149*

Grilled Cheese Sandwich, *151*

Oyster Po' Boy, *151*

Chorizo, *152*

Yucatán White Sausage, *152*

Chiles Rellenos, *153*

Blue Corn Black Bean Rellenos, *154*

Refried Black Beans, *155*

Glossary, 157

Chiles, 171

Special Techniques, Equipment, and Terms, 177

Wine, Beer, and Spirits, 181

Sources, 185

Index, 187

Preface

This book and its recipes are a reflection of my own personal taste in food. Most of the recipes are traditionally Southwestern, while others introduce personal touches, new ideas, or techniques derived from other cuisines. Many of these recipes have been adapted from my travels and from other cookbooks — some are recognizable and others are not. Other sources of inspiration include my friends and peers in the restaurant business, and the food heritage of New England that I grew up with.

This book contains a broad sampling of Southwestern dishes arranged in chapters ranging form cocktails, salsas, sauces and soups, through appetizers, entrées, desserts, and a final chapter that is a potpourri of particular favorites. Each chapter in the book is designed as a lesson, with the individual recipes serving as examples of what can be created in the style of Southwestern cuisine. As you become familiar with the recipes in this book, you will begin to understand and appreciate Southwestern cuisine and learn to use the essential ingredients — herbs, spices, and especially chiles — creatively. In time, you will be able to form your own style or interpretation of this food. The glossary that follows these chapters defines and describes the ingredients, terms, techniques, and equipment used. A source list provides a starting point for the cook in obtaining many of the ingredients commonly used in Southwestern cuisine, especially those that may be harder to find in other regions.

Southwestern food is an indigenous regional cuisine. It has evolved over a long period of time, and has been molded and shaped by a variety of influences, including Native American, Hispanic, Mexican, Tex-Mex, and the neighboring Cajun and Creole cuisines. It is characterized by straightforward cooking techniques and defined by bold, strong, flavors. The essential techniques and tastes can be grasped if you have basic cooking skills, and your early results will be rewarding. At the same time, a mastery of the subtle composition and myriad flavors will take a little effort to refine and become fully accustomed to.

It is best to start slowly; for example, if you are unsure whether you like cilantro, use only a little at first. I remember the first time I tasted cilantro, I pulled it out of my mouth because I thought it had a "soapy" flavor; now I eat whole bunches. This is a food to experiment with, and to become involved with. It takes care and time, but in general, is relatively inexpensive and straightforward to prepare. It is extremely healthy food: most dishes contain large amounts of fresh ingredients which are high in nutritional value and use little salt or fats. It is most of all robust, flavorful, and sensual food that is immensely satisfying.

Coyote Cafe is keeping alive old traditions, but at the same time, it is creating a new form of cuisine for a new audience. I encourage you to try the many other wonderful restaurants of the Southwest. Some of my favorite places are Cafe Annie in Houston, The Mansion on Turtle Creek, Routh Street Cafe and Baby Routh in Dallas, and St. Estephe in Los Angeles. Others I like are Vincent's on Camelback in Phoenix, and Janos in Tucson. They are all exciting places where you can taste and learn about the food of the Southwest. This book will show you what we do at Coyote Cafe in Santa Fe and help you recreate some of the dishes that so many people have enjoyed at the restaurant.

"More Is Better"
(more chiles are better still)

Abundant dark clouds I desire

An abundance of vegetation I desire

An abundance of pollen,
abundant dew, I desire.

Happily may fair white corn,
to the ends of the earth, come with you,

Happily may fair yellow corn, fair blue corn,
fair corn of all kinds, goods of all kinds,
jewels of all kinds, to the ends of the earth,
come with you,

With these before you,
happily may they come with you,

With these behind, below, above, around you,
happily may they come with you,

Thus you accomplish your tasks.

From: A Prayer. Songs of the Southwest.
In *American Indian Poetry:*
An Anthology of Songs and Chants.
George W. Cronin, ed. Liveright, New York, 1934.

Introduction

I'm often asked why I came to Santa Fe to open Coyote Cafe, far from my roots in New England and later, Berkeley, and the highly developed food culture of the Bay Area. Besides my love for this place, I have always had a love for the people and the culture of the Southwest. As a youngster growing up in the Boston area, I was exposed to many foreign cultures. My parents had numerous friends who came from other parts of the world to study at the universities in Boston. One family friend in particular influenced me greatly: his name was Sergio and he was from Guadalajara, Mexico — an exotic, far-off sounding place to an impressionable teenager who lived in puritan New England and whose family was French-Canadian. Sergio would make chorizo for breakfast on Sundays, which was very exciting considering our Sunday dinner was usually a pot roast or a simple boiled meal. I was enchanted by spices which always seemed magical to me, with their power to transform everyday materials into something foreign and wonderful.

Sergio would take me to New York to see soccer games, to buy spices at Latin American markets, and to eat at the great restaurant Fonda del Sol, one of the most beautiful places I have ever been in. The hot pinks of the cushions and the handmade Mexican plates on the tables were in such contrast to the pewter and maple of the New England restaurants I had known. I took to spicy food like a fish to water: this was true excitement, much better than Disneyland, but this was reality, not fantasy.

This dawning awareness of other culinary traditions coincided with a series of events which were to shape my future. At about this same time I visited one of the art museums nearby to see an exhibit of aboriginal bark paintings from Australia and was immediately caught by their power and vitality. That afternoon, at the museum, I heard a lecture on the Cosmology of the Dream Time, a formal philosophical system explaining the origins of the universe. I learned that the aborigines, for example, with their nonmaterial culture, possess highly developed theories on this subject. Right then I decided to become an anthropologist, and study the creators of the paintings I had seen. I had always been interested in history, and was captivated by the power and expressiveness of other cultures, which I preferred to study rather than historical facts. Besides, I figured that as an anthropologist I could see all the wonderful art and taste the magical foods which came from other parts of the world. For the next ten years I pursued that goal, ending up at the University of California at Berkeley, studying cross-cultural aesthetics, and later, teaching.

While I was at school, I used to cook as a hobby (I liked to eat well, even then). I needed this outlet as a balance to my intellectual work, and enjoyed involving myself with a practical activity, where I could use unusual and interesting food products and ingredients. I learned as much about food as I could and became an adept cook. After five or six years of academic life, my need to work with food plus a growing dislike of academic politics pushed me in new directions, and so I began writing a private newsletter on foods called "The Market Basket." This was a consumer report on gourmet products and sources which, as it turned out, was about ten years ahead of its time — today's larger, more aware, and more receptive audience supports a number of similar publications.

I also worked for Williams-Sonoma, which was right on the cutting edge of the food revolution, and took wine and cheese classes and as many cooking lessons from itinerant teachers as I could find. I had also done some part-time work for friends in restaurants and a charcuterie shop; I was just glad to be part of a kitchen and working with food. I would stop by different kitchens and shops and talk to the owners, looking for food leads. While I was talking to them, I would help bone out pork loins, peel garlic, whatever — it was satisfying work and I was learning. During one of my visits to Chez Panisse, Alice Waters asked me if I wanted to help out in the kitchen for a few weeks as a member of the staff was going on a wine tour with Richard Olney. It was my big chance! I fit right in immediately, and the two weeks became three and a half years.

At Chez Panisse I learned the ways of a professional kitchen. Besides cooking every day, I was buying all the produce and foodstuffs for the restaurant, everything from freshly picked wild mushrooms to salmon just hours out of the water, to wine and garlic. At this time, food in general was moving away from staid Continental or French styles, and American cuisine was beginning to define itself in its regional roots and heritage. By 1976, regional menus had been presented at Chez Panisse, and the importance of cooking with regional products was becoming firmly established. Alice Waters played a major role in this transition with her emphasis on use of fresh local ingredients obtained from local suppliers. My years at Chez Panisse were exciting ones: the social and political aftermath of the '60s had also helped spawn a food revolution. Among the factors responsible for this were the backlash against institutionalization, big business (especially agribusiness), and food technology; an increasing consciousness of healthy ingredients and of the link between diet and disease; the trend towards more natural foods and farming techniques; the growing interest in health and fitness; and more widespread travel. This period also saw the beginning of a food community — people who shared a common goal of producing great food for themselves and for their friends. For the first time, an educated, creative elite was entering the cooking profession, experimenting with innovative techniques and ingredients.

The first time I traveled through the great Southwest and to Santa Fe was on a cross-country car trip in 1975, and it was love at first sight. I made a promise to myself right then that I would live here someday. After that trip, I returned to the Bay Area with a fresh enthusiasm, fired by New Mexican chiles. For the next few years I often returned to Santa Fe to visit, to ski, to take photographs, and to ride in the mountains. The land and I were courting each other — exploring that first love.

In 1979, I took a leap and left Chez Panisse to open a restaurant in Berkeley with Susan Nelson as my partner. We called it the Fourth Street Grill. I had wanted to cook spicier, more rustic food drawn from ideas gained from my travels through Central America, North Africa, and Southeast Asia, among other places. I also wanted to experiment more with a mesquite grill: this was the founding period of what became known as the mesquite grilling fad and "California Cuisine."

The simple grill at Fourth Street was visited by James Beard, Elizabeth David, and other famous food celebrities who helped me and the restaurant gain recognition. Fourth Street Grill became a remarkably successful and very busy little restaurant. Our policy was not to take reservations because it was a diner, but before we knew it there were more people lined up outside the doors before opening than we had seats. Some of them waited patiently for hours, sipping our house wine while anticipating our simple food.

In 1980, feeling a little cramped for space, I opened up a second restaurant, the Santa Fe Bar and Grill, again in Berkeley. Given my love of the Southwest, the name of the restaurant was an obvious choice for me, but it was doubly appropriate because the restaurant was built on the site of the old Santa Fe Railroad depot station which dated from around 1910. The menu here featured Southwestern, Caribbean, and Cajun food exclusively. It was here and at this time that I dedicated myself to cooking Southwestern food and learning about the ingredients and techniques of that region. As time went by, I gradually dropped most of the Caribbean and Cajun items from the menu and concentrated on Southwestern recipes. I began to think that the logical place to further develop this cuisine was in the Southwest and I started to seriously look at the possibilities in New Mexico and Santa Fe in particular.

On one of my trips here at about this time, I bought some wonderful land outside of Santa Fe overlooking the Rio Grande Valley and the Jemez Mountains. During the following years, I worked hard on the two restaurants but kept a picture of that land over my desk to remind me of my dream of moving to New Mexico and building a house there.

After a while, running two restaurants became too hectic and I relinquished my interest in the Santa Fe Bar and Grill to concentrate on cooking at Fourth Street Grill and to spend more time traveling to the Southwest and to Central America. Finally, in 1985, I could not resist any longer — I decided to move on a permanent basis to Santa Fe and to open a restaurant there. I wanted to concentrate on developing my style of Southwestern cuisine and to establish an identity for it in a particular place and time.

As it turned out, the project took over two years to complete. I am grateful to all the food writers who wrote about the Coyote Cafe long before it ever opened. Coleman Andrews of the Los Angeles Times said that I had the most famous nonexisting restaurant. I told people it was the newest thing — a conceptual restaurant! When the big day finally arrived and we were ready to open our doors, people just had to come out to see what we were all about. It was a great party. We had about 500 friends and food people from all over the U.S. who came to offer their support. One reviewer wrote that if a bomb were dropped on that party, American food would be set back twenty years!

I have now finished the plans to build my dream house on the land I bought so many years ago and am getting closer to realizing that dream. Until then, I'm living ten miles outside of town in a very quiet house overlooking the Sandia Plains with my horse out back. It's a great home for me and my food, and whenever I return from a trip that takes me out of town, I'm always glad to be home again.

Another question I'm invariably asked is how Coyote Cafe got its name. Long before the restaurant opened, I bought a carved cottonwood coyote on one of my trips to Santa Fe. He was about four feet tall and an original made by Leroy Ortega, a local Hispanic artist who has created other animals for the restaurant since then. I shipped the coyote back to Berkeley and set him up in a corner of the dining-room at the Fourth Street Grill. Like a friend from the Southwest, he served as a constant reminder that the two of us would be going back there one day. Years later, go back he did, howling all the way to his new home in Santa Fe, Coyote Cafe.

Since then I have collected half a dozen or so coyotes, and have learned quite a bit about what the coyote represents in the Native American culture. According to legend, he is one of the progenitors of the beginning of time, and he is the symbol for the trickster and the merrymaker (he may have had something to do with why it took so long to open the restaurant, who knows?). His main purpose is to prevent the world from taking life too seriously. The Indians say that Coyote has many guises and it's true. Sometimes he likes to dress up and go out on the town. We've snapped pictures of him enjoying himself: you can see these likenesses etched on the glass panels near the entrance of the restaurant. If you see someone really enjoying themselves at Coyote Cafe — eating, drinking, laughing and especially telling jokes — look carefully because it might be Coyote dressed up in one of his disguises.

We describe the food we serve at Coyote Cafe as modern Southwestern cuisine. It is expressive, simple in spirit, and robust, and does not hide its character. The recipes I have created are derived both from my passion for cooking and my anthropological background. Modern Southwestern cuisine comes out of the traditions which have created pre-Columbian pottery, Hispanic folk art, eyedazzlers, sand paintings, and the indigenous Hispanic architecture of New Mexico. Just as the Navajo eyedazzlers of the 19th century were created by using new European dyes and traditional weaving processes, so new food products and different techniques applied to traditional ingredients and recipes have given rise to modern Southwestern cuisine. This food, by introducing new elements to an established cuisine, creates a bridge between the old and the new, encompassing and yet preserving the historical spirit of the Southwest. In a technological age, this food meets the need — in part unconscious — to connect with the earth and a simpler time. Modern Southwestern cuisine reflects a wonderful balance between tradition and the present. It incorporates all the elements of the region's long and diversified cultural and culinary heritage. It also reflects the influence of other culinary traditions that are geographically close, such as Creole, Cajun, and of course, Mexican cuisines. Like the culture of the region, modern Southwestern cuisine is alive — constantly evolving and redefining itself.

Many of the dishes we serve at the restaurant, and whose recipes are included in this book, are derived from traditional food and compositions; some, like the Wild Morel Tamales, date from pre-Columbian times. I have studied, and continue to collect, books that document the histories of the ancient foods and techniques of the Southwest. This cuisine involves recreating food in a new form, derived from an old aesthetic; I feel it is important to remain true to this heritage. I think of it as modern food which honors the ancient spirits.

COCKTAILS

More than any other sensual experience, I associate drinking a cocktail with place. When I taste a perfectly made Pisco Sour, I am immediately transported to Machu Picchu, while a Señor Playboy puts me in the Oriental Hotel in Bangkok amidst English colonials dressed to the nines and beautiful Thai women wearing gold and green threaded sarongs who seem to glide rather than walk over the marble floors.

Unlike drinking a glass of wine, which I see as an analytical experience, having a cocktail is pure enjoyment. But the art of making a good cocktail and, for that matter, the art of appreciating one, have been all but lost. Part of the enjoyment of drinking cocktails is sitting in a lounge or at an elegant bar, preferably one with a patina of age, watching the artistry and craftmanship of the resident bartender as creative and attractive cocktails are custom-made before you. It helps if, as with our own Timothy LeBlanc at Coyote Cafe, the genius behind the swizzle stick is a character with a style of his own. It used to be that the cocktail hour indicated a respite, almost a lull after the work of the day and before the adventure of the night. At Coyote Cafe we try to bring back that age — in Coyote's spirit of good fun we want to transport our guests to faraway places and the ways of another time.

TIPS FOR MAKING GREAT COCKTAILS:

✳ *Premium alcohols and flavorings are essential to making wonderful cocktails. Additives found in lower grades dilute your drinks, muddying the flavor.*

✳ *You can add fresh spices and flavorings to rum, vodka, and tequila, and let them soak in a sealed container for at least 48 hours (longer is better). For a wonderful tropical flavor try adding vanilla beans (Tahitian are best), anise seeds, or cocoa beans to rum. For spicy cocktails, try cumin seeds, citrus rinds, or jalapeños with tequila.*

✳ *If cocktails include fruit juices, always use freshly squeezed juices as they are more acidic and are less likely to be bitter or give drinks an off flavor.*

✳ *Always use superfine sugar because it dissolves more easily than regular sugar.*

✳ *If possible, keep liquor in the freezer before serving. This is a trick from Harry's Bar in Venice. The cold temperature changes the viscosity of the liquor, giving it a thicker texture. The very cold temperature also will give you purer cocktails because the ice won't melt as quickly. (Don't worry about exploding bottles — the high alcohol content will keep liquor from actually freezing.)*

✳ *For drinks that do not require ice, but that should be served cold, glasses should be chilled. You can do this either by placing ice in the empty glass and then dumping the ice out before pouring in the beverage, or by chilling glasses in the refrigerator or freezer. The latter frosts glasses however, which some people don't like.*

✳ *For blended drinks, ice should be in the smallest pieces possible to avoid having to blend drinks for too long. Over-blended drinks can be too cold. For stirred drinks, on the other hand, ice should be in large pieces to prevent the ice from melting and diluting the cocktail.*

✳ *In general, I prefer cocktails chilled or strained of ice.*

✳ *To add another festive dimension to the experience of the drink, use colored stemware. Blue or pink martini glasses are perfect for tropical cocktails.*

✳ *To salt a glass, moisten the rim with a wedge of lime and dip the rim in salt.*

✳ *Measurements for drinks*
   ½ ounce = **1 tablespoon**
   1 ounce = **2 tablespoons**
   1 ounce = **1 pony**
   1½ ounce = **1 jigger**

BLOODY MARIA

For me, breakfast means one of three things: Huevos Rancheros, accompanied by hot, steamy tortillas fresh off the griddle, fresh oysters on the half-shell, or smoked salmon with fresh cracked pepper and a drop of lemon juice. Bloody Marias go particularly well with all three. And tangy serrano chiles, the fresh cilantro, and spiky tequila mixed with the subtle acidity of the tomato juice has the magical effect of bringing one's soul back to life after a late night full of fun.

Yield: 12 cocktails

3 to 5 serrano chiles

¾ cup gold tequila, chilled

1 can (46 ounces) tomato juice

1 teaspoon salt

1 bunch cilantro, chopped

juice of 1 to 2 limes (about ⅓ cup)

Soak the chiles in tequila for 5 to 10 minutes. Mix all of the ingredients in a blender with some ice. (If your blender can't handle it all at once, do it in two batches.) Serve in 4½- or 5-ounce wine or martini glasses. Garnish with lime circles if desired.

BRAZILIAN DAIQUIRI

This cocktail brings to mind images of warm light breezes, and the sound of waves lapping on the shore. Even its color is that of bronzed beauties tanning on the sand. Two or three of these daiquiris will soon bring out a distinctly carnival feeling!

Piloncillo is unrefined brown sugar that comes in small cones. You can substitute regular brown sugar.

Yield: 12 cocktails

1 cup Bacardi light rum

1 cup Bacardi dark rum

¾ cup Myers's rum

1 Mexican vanilla bean, split lengthwise

1 large sweet ripe pineapple, peeled, cored, and cut into eighths

2 ounces piloncillo (or 3 tablespoons light brown sugar)

juice of two limes

Place all ingredients except lime juice in a clean glass jar, cover tightly, and let sit at room temperature for 48 hours. Strain out the pineapple and vanilla. (Don't throw away the pineapple — it's wonderful served with vanilla ice cream.) Put the rum mixture in the freezer until very cold. Add lime juice and serve in shot glasses or martini glasses.

SUNBURNT SEÑORITA

Also known as a Watermelon Margarita, this light and refreshing cocktail is very popular at Coyote Cafe. Its beautiful pink hue reminds me of the color of the skirts worn by the Mexican folklorico dancers. I am also taken back to the flower markets of Mexico, and their bright, warm pinks. The Sunburnt Señorita combines the heat and ripeness of summer with the refreshment of cold tropical fruit.

Yield: 1 cocktail

½ teaspoon superfine sugar (not necessary if a very ripe watermelon is used)

1 teaspoon fresh lime juice

⅓ cup juice from a sweet watermelon (extract juice by putting watermelon through a food mill)

1 ounce gold tequila

Half fill a shaker glass with ice. Add all ingredients and shake together until well blended. Strain into a martini glass and garnish with a lime wedge.

COYOTE COCKTAIL

Guaranteed to make you howl!

1 liter Herradura gold tequila

3 serrano chiles split lengthwise

Add chiles to tequila in the bottle and let sit for 48 hours or more at room temperature. Put the tequila in the freezer until thoroughly chilled. Serve straight from the freezer in chilled shot glasses. Garnish with a lime wedge, if desired .

Note: This can also be used to make Coyote Martinis, substituting the serrano-tequila for gin or vodka.

COYOTE MARGARITA

The once proud margarita has been demoted to a dubious place on the drinks scene. It has been shuffled to the back of Yuppie bars where it emerges from a machine, looking more like a snow cone than the wonderful King of the Tropical Cocktails that is served at the finest haciendas. Here at Coyote Cafe we give the margarita the recognition it warrants and return it to its just position in the Cocktail Universe. It is the perfect accompaniment to all hot Southwestern hors d'oeuvres.

Yield: 1 cocktail

1½ tablespoons superfine sugar

3 tablespoons fresh Mexican lime juice

1½ ounces Herradura gold tequila

1 teaspoon Marie Brizard triple sec

Half fill a shaker glass with ice. Shake all ingredients together. Strain into a chilled martini glass with a salted rim. Garnish with a lime wedge, if desired.

CHIMAYO COCKTAIL

When I was growing up in New England, I used to go to the apple orchards in the fall to buy fresh McIntosh cider that had been made with old-fashioned presses. I used to enjoy these excursions, and I was pleasantly surprised when I later discovered that the Chimayo apple cider from northern New Mexico is just as good. I love late Indian summer in New Mexico. It signals the return of quietude, and the time for long horseback rides through the mountains. After watching the sunsets and the golden colors of the aspen and cottonwood trees beside the Rio Grande, I like to stop at the Rancho de Chimayo for one of these cocktails.

Yield: 1 cocktail

½ cup unfiltered premium organic apple cider

1 ounce Sauza gold tequila

½ ounce cassis

1 teaspoon fresh Mexican lime juice

Fill a 10-ounce highball glass with ice. Transfer ice and all of the ingredients into a shaker. Shake until just blended. Pour back into the highball glass and garnish the rim with an apple wedge, if desired.

Note: Unfiltered cider is preferable; however, if it is unavailable, filtered cider or unfiltered apple juice will do. Gravenstein cider, which is generally available only on the West Coast, also makes a very good base for this cocktail.

PISCO SOUR

To truly appreciate this cocktail you must make the trek through the Andes, through tropical rain forests and magnificent stone out-croppings of ancient Inca cities, tent out under planetarium-like skies, and rough it through heavy rains for three days. Only then will you have arrived at Machu Picchu to look down on the hidden jewel of the Inca civilization. It's at the Hotel Machu Picchu that they serve the best Pisco Sours. Sitting on the terrace at sundown, you look over the spectacular sanctuary of another time and claim your deserved prize.

Yield: 1 cocktail

1 ounce Pisco or light rum

1½ tablespoons superfine sugar

juice of 2 limes (about ⅓ cup)

1 egg white

1 dash bitters

Half fill an 8-ounce wine glass with ice. Transfer ice to a blender, add all the ingredients except the bitters, and blend until smooth and frothy. Pour back into the wine glass and top with a dash of bitters.

Note: This is a very popular drink for parties and barbecues. Make sure you have plenty of egg whites on hand!

PLANTER'S PUNCH

The first time I had a great Planter's Punch was on a visit to the Caribbean island of Tobago. I felt as though I was in some kind of time warp — I was staying in an old English plantation house which had been converted into a grand hotel, complete with magnif-icent gardens. Its own private bay was perfect for snorkeling and watching the myriad colors of thousands of tropical fish and exploring the reefs. After a day in the salty water, beneath bright blue skies, I would relax on the verandah (in whites, of course!) and look out over the idyllic scene with a Planter's Punch at my side.

Yield: 1 cocktail

2 dashes bitters

½ teaspoon vanilla extract

1 tablespoon fresh pineapple juice

2 teaspoons grenadine syrup

2 tablespoons fresh lime juice

2 ounces Bacardi light rum

1 ounce Myers's rum

Shake all ingredients together and pour into a 12-ounce Collins glass, two-thirds filled with ice.

TAMARINDO

This Mexican drink uses a paste made from the sticky pods of the tamarind tree. The paste, which forms the base for most cola drinks, has a distinctly mellowing effect! It can be obtained from most Middle Eastern or Southeast Asian grocery stores. This cocktail goes very well with hot and spicy food.

Yield: 1 cocktail

3 tablespoons puréed mango (or mango juice)

1 ounce Lemon Hart Demarrera rum

2 teaspoons fresh orange juice

1 tablespoon fresh tamarind paste

3 or more cubes of ice

Blend all the ingredients together in a mixer until smooth. Serve in a chilled martini glass and garnish with a small slice of mango, if desired.

SEÑOR PLAYBOY

When you go to Bangkok — and you must go sometime — head straight for the bar at the Oriental Hotel. This is one of the four greatest cocktail bars in the world (the other three are Harry's Bar in Venice, Trader Vic's in San Francisco, and Boadas in Barcelona). Every year in Bangkok they hold a bartender's competition, and seven times the winner has been the bartender at the Oriental Hotel. The Señor Playboy is one of this consummate bartender's finest creations. How exactly it got its name I never did find out!

Yield: 1 cocktail

¾ ounce Bombay gin

1 ounce Remy Martin cognac

½ ounce Cointreau

1 teaspoon fresh lime juice

3 tablespoons fresh orange juice

1½ teaspoons superfine sugar

1 teaspoon fresh pineapple juice

Quarter fill a shaker glass with ice. Add and shake together all the ingredients, and serve in a chilled martini glass. Sit down before drinking, preferably not on a tall stool!

CHAMPAGNE PADRE

Here's another liquid Latin masterpiece. It originates from the Lima Country Club, where I stayed on my travels en route to Cuzco, Machu Picchu, and the Upper Amazon. After a day of visiting the varied museums of Lima, including the incredible Gold Museum with its thousands of pieces of pre-Columbian artifacts, I would remove myself to the bar at the country club and enjoy a Champagne Padre. This recipe is my personal adaptation (the original contains Benedictine). I like the combination of champagne and bitters, and find it much more stimulating to the appetite than sweeter champagne cocktails.

Yield: 1 cocktail

1 teaspoon superfine sugar

2 dashes bitters

1 ounce cognac

3 ounces champagne

lemon peel

In a champagne glass, stir together the sugar, bitters, and cognac until the sugar dissolves. Add the champagne and stir once. Garnish with a long spiral of lemon peel.

LIQUADOS

Liquados, fresh fruit drinks, are the staple liquid refreshment of Mexico. Everywhere you go, you will find them in large ribbed glass jars, beckoning with their mysterious contents. Vendors at pushcarts or stalls will offer liquados of all flavors: tamarind, mango, coco, papaya, melon . . . . No two liquado stands are alike, and this drink represents, for me, the infinite variety and vitality of Mexican cuisine. If you go to Mexico, be sure to try the local liquado since each region and locality has its own special tropical fruits and ingredients. I recall a late spring evening in Cuernavaca, listening to the competing mariachi bands in the zócalo (town square) at night, and sipping the local zarzamora (wild blackberry) liquado — a heavenly experience.

Yield: 1 large glass per recipe

LIME LIQUADO
2 large ripe Mexican limes
2 handfuls ice
1 cup water
3 tablespoons superfine sugar

Cut the limes in half. Squeeze the juice into a blender. Add the remaining ingredients, including the lime rinds. Blend for 10 seconds and immediately strain through a fine sieve into a glass. Drink while still foamy and cold.

Note: Follow this basic technique for all the following recipes. Have your stopwatch handy since timing is very important: overblending pulverizes the bitter pith into the drink, making the liquado too acidic. You don't win any medals for underblending either!

TAMARIND LIQUADO
2 tablespoons tamarind paste
1 cup water
3 tablespoons superfine sugar
2 handfuls ice

Blend 15 seconds and strain.

KUMQUAT LIQUADO
12 kumquats
1 cup water
3 tablespoons superfine sugar
2 handfuls ice

Blend 10 seconds and strain.

ORANGE LIQUADO
2 oranges cut into eighths and juiced
1 cup water
2 handfuls ice
2½ tablespoons superfine sugar

Blend everything, including the peel, for 4 seconds and strain.

STRAWBERRY LIQUADO
10 strawberries
1 cup water
2 handfuls ice
2 tablespoons superfine sugar

Blend 15 seconds and strain.

MANGO LIQUADO
¼ cup puréed mango
1 cup water
2 handfuls ice
2 tablespoons superfine sugar

Blend 15 seconds and strain.

SALSAS

Salsas always put me in a South-of-the-Border mood. Their cool yellows and greens mixed with hot pinks and bright reds make me think of a brilliantly costumed mariachi band. And as for flavors, salsas are like a mini-fiesta for the taste-buds: they are at once sharp and sweet, hot and cool. Certain qualities marry to form the essence of a salsa. They include the zingy green flavors of cilantro and fresh herbs like basil, mint, Mexican mint marigold, and epazote, the warmth of rich ripe tomatoes or sweet fruit, the tang of a lime, and the heat of a chile. Together, these flavors light up the senses like fireworks exploding in the night.

At the Symposium on American Cuisine, a couple of years ago, an important food writer declared that chefs should concentrate on the basic sauces like the classic béchamel or hollandaise sauces, rather than serve salsas on everything. He was implying that salsas are an easy escape, and a fad, and that they are not always suitable. I jumped up and asked him why he thought sauces were more important than salsas. I argued that it's a different way of eating and to my mind a better way. With a salsa, nothing is hidden, as in a sauce — you can taste the individual characters of ripe tomatoes, roasted chiles, sharp cilantro. So you get something that is a little rich, a little sweet, and a little crunchy all at the same time. In a great salsa, no one note is excluded from the melody; you can hear all of them at the same time, although one note may be louder than the others at certain times. The idea is to weave all of the sounds together and not to lose any one of them.

I can't think of a time when I wouldn't choose a salsa over a sauce. Maybe salsas are a little brassy and brash, but I think it's better to be bold than to roll over and play dead. Butter and cream, or heavy reductions with smooth rich textures are sleeping pills for the palate, luring us into dangerous hidden pounds for the hips.

To me, the increasing popularity of salsas means that American chefs are waking up. They are exploring a world of different ingredients, and learning that the technique of putting strong flavors together allows for greater expression and leads to wonderful taste discoveries.

In general, the salsas in this chapter are best used after they have been allowed to sit for at least 30 minutes, so that the flavors can marry. The recipes include serving suggestions but there are no firm rules, so that you can mix and match as you wish, and choose your own combinations. Remember Rule One of Southwestern Cuisine: There are no rules! This is closely followed by Rule Two: Next time you think sauce, try salsa instead!

PICO DE GALLO SALSA

This is one of the standard South-western salsas, sometimes called Salsa Fresca, that is a familiar feature of Mexican and Tex-Mex cuisine, used on everything, everyone, anytime, anywhere, no fail! (Actually, this may be a slight exaggeration, as it doesn't go too well with hot fudge sundaes.) This salsa is so easy to make, don't even think about buying the horrible jarred versions. It will happily accompany anything from red meats to tortilla chips.

Yield: About 2 cups

2 tablespoons diced onion

2 cups tomatoes chopped into ¼-inch cubes

2 serrano chiles, finely chopped

2 tablespoons finely chopped cilantro

2 teaspoons sugar

¼ cup Mexican beer

2 teaspoons salt

juice of 1 lime

Put onion in a strainer, rinse with hot water, and drain. Combine all ingredients and mix well. Let sit in the refrigerator for at least 30 minutes before serving. Feel free to consume the rest of the beer while waiting!

Note: More sugar may be used if the tomatoes are acidic, but make sure the salsa does not taste of sugar.

ROASTED TOMATO AND MINT SALSA

Ripe red tomatoes roasted on a hot steel comal until the skins blacken are a basic element of many Mexican salsas. The smoky flavor adds a complexity to the taste of ripe tomatoes. Mixing fresh mint as a counterpoint to this cooked flavor creates the combination of raw and cooked which is one of the classic taste motifs of Southwestern cuisine. This salsa goes particularly well with the wild Churro lamb that we serve at Coyote Cafe because it does not mask the Churro's unique taste. It can also be served with venison chops, grilled pork, grilled marlin, and that faithful standby, tortilla chips.

Yield: About 1½ cups

6 large Roma tomatoes with tops removed

1 clove garlic, minced, not crushed

juice of 1 Mexican lime

3 tablespoons extra virgin olive oil

1 to 2 serrano chiles, minced, with seeds

1½ tablespoons minced cilantro

3½ tablespoons minced spearmint

½ teaspoon lime zest

½ teaspoon orange zest

pinch of salt

With a comal or black iron skillet over medium-high heat, cook the tomatoes until blackened all over. While still warm, pulse the tomatoes with the garlic in a food processor until roughly chopped. Let cool to room temperature and add the remaining ingredients. Mix together and let sit at least 30 minutes before using.

TOMATILLO SALSA

The tomatillo has a bright sharp flavor akin to that of green plums or rhubarb. It is best understood raw. In the winter months, when it's sometimes hard to get fresh red tomatoes, we use tomatillos, which are available all year round. Select tomatillos that are firm and hard, with a clean, straw-colored husk (never use one with a blackened, sticky, or wet husk). The outside husks can be removed and saved for blanching cactus; this is an old Mexican kitchen trick. I don't know exactly how it works, but it does prevent the cactuses from becoming slimy and discolored. The garden green color of the Tomatillo Salsa is just as interesting as that of a tomato salsa. This salsa goes especially well with all simple seafood, such as grilled tuna or scallops. I also like to serve it with cold seafood such as chilled shrimp that has been poached in a spicy broth, or with raw oysters or clams.

Yield: About 2½ cups

1 pound fresh green tomatillos

3 tablespoons finely chopped sweet red onions

1 serrano chile, finely chopped

juice of 1 Mexican lime

1 bunch cilantro, roughly chopped

1 to 2 tablespoons virgin olive oil (optional)

Husk the tomatillos and wash them under very hot water, or blanch them in boiling water for 15 seconds; do not let them cook. Cool under cold water and purée in a food processor. Add red onions, serrano chile, lime juice, and cilantro. Add a touch of sugar if the tomatillos are too sour and a little olive oil if you wish.

ROASTED CORN SALSA

The idea for this salsa recipe, which combines roasted, slightly smoky corn with dried tomatoes and wild mushrooms, came from a corn crêpe dish I once ate in a Tijuana restaurant. That dish was made with huitlacoche, a delicious, exotic-looking grayish fungus that grows on corn and tastes like wild morels. The combination used here creates a salsa of intriguing flavor and complexity, and with more sophistication than a regular Mexican cantina salsa. Roasted Corn Salsa goes well with grilled chicken, venison sausage, chile rellenos, cheese enchiladas, and corn crêpes with goat cheese.

Yield: About 3 cups

5 ears corn in the husk

⅜ cup fresh morels or other wild mushrooms, cleaned and diced

5 tablespoons extra virgin olive oil

¼ cup diced sun-dried tomatoes, with 1 tablespoon of their oil

2 large poblano chiles, roasted, peeled, seeded, and diced

2 tablespoons minced cilantro

2 teaspoons minced marjoram

3 cloves garlic, roasted, peeled, and chopped

1 tablespoon adobo sauce from canned chipotle chiles in adobo sauce

½ teaspoon sherry vinegar

½ teaspoon fresh lemon juice

1 teaspoon fresh Mexican lime juice

½ teaspoon kosher salt

Roast ears of corn on a baking sheet in a 400° oven until the husks begin to blacken (about 15 minutes). Set aside to cool. Meanwhile sauté morels in ½ tablespoon of the oil until well cooked, about 10 minutes. Shuck the corn, brush with ½ tablespoon of the oil, and grill or broil until the exposed kernels turn a light mahogany, about 10 minutes. Let cool and cut the kernels from the ears shallowly enough to cut through the milky part of the kernels but not through the cob. You should have about 1½ cup kernels. Mix corn, mushrooms, remaining oil, and the rest of the ingredients together. Serve salsa hot or at room temperature.

ROASTED SERRANO SALSA

This is a hot relish that will warm you up during those cold winter months! We served this salsa at Coyote Cafe's second anniversary party which we held up at the Santa Fe Ski Area. As the snow flurries fluttered gently around the assembled throng, we consumed a good number of delicious Hog Island oysters accompanied by the Roasted Serrano Salsa, and no one seemed to notice the weather! This salsa also goes well with fish dishes.

Yield: 3 cups

6 serrano chiles

1 pound ripe Roma tomatoes, finely diced

2 tablespoons minced sweet red onion

¼ cup fresh orange juice

2 tablespoons sweet yellow pepper, very finely diced

2 tablespoons minced cilantro

1 tablespoon unseasoned rice vinegar

½ teaspoon salt

½ teaspoon sugar

With a comal or black iron skillet over medium-high heat, cook the serranos until blackened. Remove about half of the blackened skin, and then chop finely. Mix together with all the remaining ingredients. Let stand for 1 hour. Cover, and refrigerate.

POBLANO PESTO

Poblano chiles provide the dark pine-green color and texture for this salsa. After they have been roasted and peeled, they have a rich, hot, smoky flavor that is sometimes piquant and sometimes not. But be warned — once you've tasted their unique, subtle flavor, you may never use regular sweet peppers again! As the name indicates, the poblano originates from Puebla in Mexico, and their increasing availability means that you won't have to drive down to Puebla to get them! I use this recipe for a number of dishes here at Coyote Cafe: angel hair pasta with grilled shrimp, grilled scallops, or one of our great favorites, Southwestern-style Oysters Rockefeller (oysters grilled on an open fire and served with Poblano Pesto). It can also be used as a topping for canapés or enchiladas, with any pasta, or spread on a roast pork sandwich. Use this salsa the same day it is made or it will lose its bright clean flavors.

Yield: About 1½ cups

6 tablespoons pine nuts

6 medium-sized poblano chiles, roasted and peeled

1 small clove garlic

4 to 6 tablespoons virgin olive oil

1 bunch cilantro, leaves only

sea salt, to taste

juice of 1 to 2 Mexican limes

1 large sweet red pepper, roasted, peeled, seeded, and diced

Lightly roast pine nuts in oven at 350°, and let cool. In a food processor, pulse together the pine nuts, poblano chiles, garlic, olive oil, and cilantro into a rough paste. Add salt and lime juice to taste. Stir in diced red peppers. There should be enough red pepper pieces to contrast with the color of the rest of the salsa.

BLACK BEAN SALSA

The idea for this recipe came from one of the most requested soups at the Fourth Street Grill in Berkeley — a black bean soup flavored with bacon and an orange crema. Earthy black beans mixed with a confetti of sweet red and yellow peppers, orange zest, and a dash of tequila provide a great color combination and flavor contrast. The success of this recipe depends on the beans being cooked in a very flavorful stock until they are soft but not too mushy. The individual elements must keep their own separate identities. This salsa goes well with lighter, sweeter dishes. It is a very attractive accompaniment to grilled poultry or bluefin tuna.

Yield: About 3 cups

3 cups cooked black beans (see Black Bean Soup, page 32)

4 tablespoons minced canned jalapeños en escabeche

1 medium sweet red pepper, roasted, peeled, and diced

1 medium sweet yellow pepper, roasted, peeled, and diced

4 tablespoons sautéed minced wild boar bacon with its fat (or Amador, Smithfield, or Harrington's corn cob smoked bacon)

1 teaspoon orange zest

2 teaspoons gold tequila

2 teaspoons fresh Mexican lime juice

2 tablespoons extra virgin olive oil

2 cloves garlic, roasted, peeled, and minced

2 tablespoons minced cilantro

1 tablespoon minced marjoram

Make the Black Bean Soup, but cut cooking time to about 1½ hours. (The beans should be firm and just tender.) Drain in a sieve until very dry. Put the beans in a bowl and fold in remaining salsa ingredients, being careful not to crush the beans. Serve hot or at room temperature.

BLACK BEAN CORN SALSA

Here's a slightly different black bean salsa. It, too, is the perfect accompaniment for fish or poultry. Try it with sautéed chicken or grilled halibut or salmon.

2 cups fresh corn kernels

4 tablespoons diced sweet red pepper

2 teaspoons diced serrano chile

pinch sugar

¾ cup water

2 cups cooked black beans (see Black Bean Soup, page 32)

½ cup light fish stock (or clam juice)

4 tablespoons diced Roma tomatoes

3 tablespoons balsamic vinegar

2 tablespoons olive oil

4 tablespoons basil, julienned

juice of 1 lime

Cook corn, pepper, serrano, and sugar together with the water in a covered pan over medium heat for 2 to 3 minutes. Add beans, stock, and tomatoes, and cook until warmed through. Add the vinegar and oil and cook over low heat for 2 minutes. Remove from heat. Toss in basil and lime juice immediately before serving.

CHILE MIGNONNETTE

This is a simple adaptation of the classic French mignonnette which consists of red wine, shallots, and pepper, and is served with oysters. This recipe, which originated at the Santa Fe Bar and Grill, substitutes cilantro, rice vinegar, white wine, and, of course, chiles — remember, chiles make everything better! It can be made hotter by adding more chiles, or sweeter by adding a little sugar, although the rice vinegar makes the salsa naturally sweeter than would a regular vinegar. Chile Mignonnette should be served with fresh raw oysters or clams on the half-shell.

Yield: About ½ cup, enough for 2 dozen oysters

2 tablespoons minced shallots

2 tablespoons finely chopped assorted peppers and chiles (sweet red and yellow peppers, and poblano, jalapeño, fresno, or serrano chiles)

2 tablespoons chopped cilantro

2 tablespoons unseasoned rice wine vinegar (or champagne vinegar)

1 tablespoon dry white wine

In a small strainer, rinse and drain shallots. Combine all the ingredients and chill. Serve about 1 teaspoon per oyster.

NOPALES SALSA

Although it may seem strange to eat cactus, nopales, the flat pads of the prickly pear cactus, are delicious, and are a traditional food of the Southwest. In flavor they are somewhere between green beans and okra. Some people object to their so-called slimy texture, but if blanched quickly in boiling water for a maximum of 1 minute, preferably with tomatillo husks, the cactus will retain its firmness. (The husks are also said to prevent the cactus from getting discolored.) Firm Roma tomatoes can be substituted for the tomatillos, but then you won't have the tomatillo husks for blanching the nopales. If prickly pear syrup is unavailable, pomegranate juice can be used. This salsa can be served cold with chilled roasted meats as a salad, or hot on tortillas to accompany grilled meats (it is especially good with lamb). It is also wonderful mixed with cold poached shrimp or served as a garnish for barbecued meats.

Yield: About 2½ cups

1½ cups small nopales

3 tomatillos

¼ cup diced sweet red peppers

¼ cup diced sweet yellow peppers

2 serrano chiles, minced (optional)

1½ tablespoons juice from canned
   jalapeños en escabeche

¼ cup prickly pear syrup (or
   pomegranate juice)

2 tablespoons minced cilantro

2 tablespoons roasted corn kernels,
   cut from the cob

1 tablespoon minced spearmint

Remove needles from cactus paddles. Blanch for 1 minute in boiling water with tomatillo husks. Next, cut blanched cactus paddles into ¼ x 1-inch strips. Combine all ingredients and let sit for 1 hour before using.

CHIMAYO CHILE SALSA

This classic New Mexican salsa comes from the northern part of the state. Try it with grilled brochette of shrimp, or with satay-style grilled strips of pork or grilled duck breasts.

Yield: 3 cups

½ pound (about 25) dried Chimayo
   or New Mexico red chiles

2 quarts water

5 cloves roasted garlic

1 teaspoon salt

1 tablespoon roasted ground Mexican
   oregano

Remove stems and seeds from chiles. With a comal or black iron skillet, or in an oven at 250°, dry roast chiles for 3 to 4 minutes. Shake once or twice and do not allow to blacken. Add to the water in a covered pan and simmer very low for 20 minutes to rehydrate. Strain, reserving chiles and water, and allow to cool.

Place the chiles in a blender and add 2 cups of the chile water if it is not bitter (otherwise use plain water). Add garlic and salt to blender and puree. Strain, reserving liquid and discarding solids. Add oregano to liquid and combine. Serve warm, not hot.

PINEAPPLE SALSA

For this recipe, canned pineapple will not do. When selecting a fresh pineapple, be sure to smell and feel it. It should have a strong pineapple aroma, feel a little soft, and you should be able to pull leaves out of the crown.

This recipe was one of our great standby favorites at the Fourth Street Grill. I've had variations of this in the Mexican Caribbean and in Thailand. Both used ripe, perfumed pineapple, mixed with chiles, cilantro, lime, and sugar to create salsas for grilled fish. A food processor makes this salsa a snap to make. You can also cook it if you want to make it ahead of time (it doesn't keep well uncooked). If piloncillo is unavailable, use dark brown sugar. Ripe mangoes or peaches can be substituted for the pineapple. This is a great sauce for pork, grilled chicken, or fish.

Yield: About 2 cups

1 cup very ripe peeled, cored, and diced pineapple

2 teaspoons grated piloncillo (or dark brown sugar)

1 teaspoon unseasoned rice vinegar

2 serrano chiles or 2 canned chipotle chiles in adobo sauce, minced

¼ cup finely chopped sweet red peppers

juice of 1 Mexican lime

1 tablespoon finely minced cilantro

Mix all ingredients together. Taste and add more lime and chiles as needed. To cook it, mix all ingredients together except the lime and cilantro. Bring to a boil and simmer 20 minutes. Cool and add lime juice and cilantro. Serve at room temperature.

MELON SALSA

This is a perfect recipe for late August days when the markets seem to have melons by the truck-load. Until I moved to California I never realized how many types of melon there are: from ordinary cantaloupes to sweet, pink and green honeydews, Persians, Crenshaws, and the smaller, more intensely flavored European varieties. Using two or three different kinds of melon in this recipe enhances the contrast in color and texture. If the melons are very sweet, add a little pineapple for crunch and acidity. Other tropical fruits such as mangoes, papaya, or mamey make wonderful salsas and can be substituted for the melon. This is an easy salsa to prepare and goes fabulously well with empanadas, grilled tuna, and cold shellfish.

Yield: About 2¼ cups

1 ripe cantaloupe (about 2 pounds)

½ sweet red pepper, seeded

2 serrano chiles, finely minced

2 tablespoons finely chopped cilantro

1 tablespoon unseasoned rice vinegar

juice of 1 lime

sugar to taste

Cut melon and red pepper into ¼-inch dice. Combine with chiles, cilantro, vinegar, and lime juice. Add sugar, if necessary. Let sit for 30 minutes in refrigerator before serving. This recipe should be used the same day it is made.

SQUASH SALSA

This salsa is a great way to deal with all those squashes that miraculously multiply by the score in the garden. The first squash salsa I had was in Zarela Martinez's restaurant in New York City, and it was marvelous. Squash salsa makes a pleasant change from tomato salsa, and is less acidic. Select young, tender squash, and be sure that everything is very finely and evenly diced: the salsa should be crisp and crunchy, not squashy in texture! At Coyote Cafe, we use it as a vegetable accompaniment with sautéed salmon, grilled chicken, and pasta. Served at room temperature, or cold with tortilla chips.

Yield: About 2 cups

1 small zucchini

1 small yellow summer squash

1 small carrot

2 tomatillos

1 medium tomato

1 clove garlic

3 serrano chiles

½ small red onion

1 tablespoon finely chopped fresh marjoram

4 teaspoons extra virgin olive oil

1 tablespoon unseasoned rice vinegar

sugar to taste

salt to taste

Trim the ends of the squashes, peel the carrot, and husk and rinse the tomatillos. Finely dice (⅛ inch or less) the squashes, carrot, tomatillo, tomato, garlic, and serranos. Dice the onion equally finely, put in a strainer, rinse with hot water, and drain. Then combine all the ingredients. Add more serranos or 2 diced canned chipotle chiles for an extra-hot salsa. Let sit for at least 1 hour at room temperature before serving.

GAZPACHO SALSA

A great salsa can be made by using similar ingredients as for gazpacho soup. It is important to keep the vegetables cold and crisp (don't salt them), and to remove some of the excess tomato juice. Gazpacho Salsa goes great with grilled fish, and on eggs for brunch. A large spoonful will top off your Bloody Maria perfectly (see page 3), and it can even be made into a fantastic sorbet if semi-pulsed in a blender and frozen.

Yield: About 2 cups

¼ cucumber

1 large ripe tomato

½ medium red onion

2 cloves garlic

1 poblano chile

½ sweet red pepper

½ sweet yellow pepper

2 tomatillos, husked and rinsed

2 tablespoons chopped cilantro

2 tablespoons extra virgin olive oil

1 tablespoon imported Spanish sherry vinegar

salt to taste

Cut all the vegetables into ¼-inch dice and mix them together with the remaining ingredients. Let sit at least 1 hour in the refrigerator. Strain off some of the excess juice before serving.

MANGO SALSA

Make this one when mangoes are in season. Serve it with tuna.

Yield: 1 cup

1 large ripe fragrant mango

2 tablespoons each sweet red and yellow peppers cut in small dice

1 tablespoon minced serrano chiles

1 tablespoon minced cilantro

juice of 1 ripe Mexican lime

Peel the mango and cut the flesh away from the seed. Chop finely, and mix with the remaining ingredients, adding a few drops of lime juice to temper the sweetness of the mango.

GREEN CHILE CHUTNEY

This is very easy to make, and it goes particularly well with crab cakes (we always seem to run out of both when we serve them at Coyote Cafe!). It also goes well with eggs, pork, chicken, and sautéed trout or salmon. It can be served warm or cold. In short, it makes sense to have this chutney around, just in case! (Store it in the refrigerator—it keeps very well.)

Yield: 4 cups

2 pounds fresh New Mexico green chiles, roasted, peeled, and diced (or roasted Anaheim chiles, with 2 or 3 roasted jalapeños)

2 cups sugar

1 tablespoon roasted ground Mexican oregano

⅔ cup cider vinegar

1 teaspoon salt

Mix the ingredients together and cook for 10 to 15 minutes over medium heat in an enamel or stainless steel pan. Allow to cool, and serve cold. For a hotter chutney, add 6 diced roasted jalapeños (or increase the number accordingly if using Anaheims and jalapeños).

HOT CORN RELISH

This is an adaptation of an old New England corn relish that always seemed to be on the table at holiday time. The original recipe was sweeter, but this version is ideal for Southwestern food — Barbecued Duck Cakes, scallops, or grilled chicken in particular.

Yield: 3½ cups

2 cups fresh corn kernels

5 cups brown poultry stock (or chicken stock)

2 teaspoons finely minced serrano chile

2 tablespoons diced sweet red pepper

2 tablespoons chopped fresh marjoram

1 teaspoon salt

4 tablespoons softened sweet butter

cilantro leaves for garnish

Cook corn in stock with chile, sweet pepper, marjoram, and salt over medium heat until reduced to about 3½ cups. Remove from heat and whisk in the butter. Garnish with cilantro.

HOW COYOTE BROUGHT THE CHILES

Unlike Beaver or Squirrel, Coyote has never been known for his industriousness. Instead, he revels in being clever, and you can bet that if ever there was a schemer, it's Coyote. The good thing is that oftentimes Coyote's self-serving plans backfire, and sometimes the result is wonderful. This is just such a story.

It all happened back before the world was really up on its feet and all that existed were a few animals and the seasons. One winter, as he lay on a rock cursing the cold wind that continually rifled through his fur, Coyote came to the conclusion that winter just wasn't working out. Spring, summer, and fall were fine, but winter, he thought, was just a bad idea that should be done away with. He decided that the thing to do was to convince the Goddess of the Seasons, who had carelessly created this thing called winter, to rid everyone, but mainly Coyote, of this heartless time of year.

So from where he sat on his rock among the last bit of remaining brush, he pointed his nose up to the sky and howled to the Goddess of the Seasons. When he'd gotten her attention, he said, "You must have realized by now that you made a big mistake with winter. Look at Deer searching for grass through the frost on the ground, and Bear—Bear got so hungry he just went to sleep. Doesn't it just break your heart?" he whimpered, faking a tear. "It's not fair that once a year our very world is stripped away from us. At least Bear has hibernation and Squirrel has his way of collecting all those acorns. But what about me? I have nothing to do to make the winter any easier."

Now work was not something that Coyote wanted to become familiar with, but in his zealousness to convince the Goddess of the Seasons, he had let the words slip out that he wanted something to do. Quickly he asked if she couldn't just do away with winter altogether. The Goddess of the Seasons answered that she could definitely see his side of the situation and that she did know of a way to make the sun shine throughout the winter if Coyote was willing to work a little. Coyote didn't want to do anything but play—that was clear—but he also could not bear the thought of knowing that the harshness of winter was here to stay, so he agreed to do whatever it took. The Goddess of the Seasons pointed over her shoulder to several rows of plants that Coyote had never noticed before. She told him to wait until the pods on each plant became deep red in color and then to pick them and hang them to dry.

So Coyote waited (not an easy thing for him). Then when the plants were a beautiful dark red, he worked well into the night picking every last one of them. Next, just as the Goddess of the Seasons had instructed him, he threaded these pods onto strings so that they hung in bunches like red bananas. With care, Coyote hung the bunches so that the sun shone down on them all day. From his rock where he was enjoying the sun himself, Coyote watched over his treasure through the fall, but to his distress he noticed that, just as they had the year before, the days were getting shorter and shorter. Soon the sun shone less and less, and Coyote was afraid that he had done something very wrong.

As Coyote watched Bear head to his den for his annual three-month nap and Squirrel scurry off with the last few acorns she could find, he could stand it no longer. "Goddess of the Seasons," he howled. "You promised me. What's gone wrong? Where are you? Come down here," he continued to bellow.

Suddenly she appeared before him as he had never seen her before. She had taken the form of a beautiful woman and was dressed in blue and gold with a crown of brilliant red and yellow feathers. "Coyote, stop howling this instant," she cried. "I did not promise you that winter would not come. I promised that the sun would shine on you this winter and all winters from now on. Calm down and listen to me. Go to the hanging red bundles that you have made. You'll see that the pods have grown very dry and brittle. Break off one of them and crush it between two stones. This will make a fine red powder."

As she spoke, Coyote followed her instructions. "Now touch your tongue to the powder." Coyote did this, and suddenly all was clear to him. His mouth was filled with a sweet warmth. The wind was blowing just as it had been a minute before, but he was no longer cold. He could actually taste and feel the summer sun even though it was long gone. That winter, Coyote stayed warm, and every fall in the years that followed, he would dry the red pods in preparation for the bitter winter to come. As people came to the earth, they learned to do the same. Coyote's pods we now call chiles which we still hang in bunches or "ristras." After they are hung, the chiles dry and are preserved for the winter months. And sure enough, the sun's warmth is captured in all its glory in each chile pod. At Coyote's hangout, Coyote Cafe, we feel you can never have too much of a good thing, which is why our motto is simply, "More Chiles."

SAUCES & SOUPS

If salsas are the mariachi band of modern Southwestern cuisine, then the sauces are its symphonic orchestra. Just as the orchestra provides unity for the musical composition, weaving together the various themes, and building up to the grand finale, so the sauces blend together the various seasonings and ingredients from which they are made, and provide the background for the main player — the entrée.

Southwestern sauces tend to be intense, lean, and strong. Most are made with a base of puréed chiles combined with roasted tomatoes and garlic, and onions, corn, tomatillos, fruits, epazote, cumin, cilantro, oregano — the whole repertoire of earthy Southwestern flavors.

To make a really good sauce, you need to have a few high notes or "treble on the chord." While earthiness provides the bass notes, it is the added high notes that give the sauce a "racy" style or lightness. This is best achieved with natural acidity, as can be obtained from fruit such as lemons, limes, and tomatoes (yes, tomatoes are members of the fruit family), or from vinegar. When using vinegars, try unflavored varieties such as rice vinegar or high-quality cider vinegar; or use a Southwestern flavored vinegar like Mexican mint marigold. Other wonderful sources of acid are cooked tomatillos, tamarind, or a mixture of grapefruit and lime juice. All these can really perk up a sauce and make it dance a little bit.

It is also important that there be a balance between sweet and hot. Sweetness comes naturally from the chiles themselves; in their dried state, chiles taste akin to dried fruits such as plums or prunes. The sense of sweetness is also derived from such spices as anise and cinnamon. This sweetness balances the fire of the chiles.

Finally, the elements should all blend together. To achieve this, some sauces are puréed and others may be simmered for lengthy periods of time. Some recipes specify that the sauces be "refried" to finish them off — this helps smooth out the sharp edges and bring everything together.

If a sauce has a base of dried chiles, the chiles should be dry-roasted and then rehydrated. Avoid overroasting or blackening the chiles, or the sauce will be bitter. Taste the water in which the chiles are rehydrating before adding it to the sauce. If it tastes bitter, use plain water or chicken stock instead. Consult the section on chiles in the back of the book for more information on selecting or preparing chiles.

Many of the sauces require charring or blackening the skins on tomatoes, and roasting garlic and tomatillos. These techniques for creating a roasted flavor play an important role in the traditional compositions that have been perpetuated over the centuries. Don't throw away any of the blackened portion because this contains the part with the flavor you want. Sauces keep very well: with few exceptions, they will keep a week in the fridge, and indefinitely in the freezer.

Because soups and sauces are closely related in Southwestern cuisine, they are placed together in this chapter. Many of the ingredients, flavors, and techniques, such as roasting and smoking, are the same for both, and some soups can almost be used as sauces: for example, Green Gazpacho Soup makes a great sauce for crab cakes. Likewise, sauces can be adapted to make delicious soups: Ranchero Sauce or Tomatillo Chipotle Sauce, combined with chicken stock or water make wonderful soups.

In Southwestern cuisine, soups are generally used as main courses for large brunches, or as centerpieces for a light supper. They are essentially homely, hearty, and filling. At Coyote Cafe, soups are especially popular in the fall and winter when the cold brisk air and the high altitude seem to stimulate the appetite for hearty and comforting food. In summer, light refreshing soups such as the Green Gazpacho Soup with a chilled garden vegetable garnish, or Yellow Squash Soup with Red Chile Crema, bring out the simplicity and fullness of fresh ingredients.

RED CHILE SAUCE

This is the most famous of all the New Mexican sauces. In fact, just as a great batting or golf swing makes the player, so the quality of the red chile sauce defines the quality of the cooking. To a great extent, the success of the sauce depends on the freshness of the chiles, which should be used in dried or powdered form (I like to use whole dried New Mexico red chiles). There are many versions of this sauce — this one is round, smooth, and deep. It has no sharp edges, and provides the setting and support for dozens of dishes, both simple and complex. It particularly complements tamales, enchiladas, red meats, and grilled food.

Yield: 4 cups

½ pound (about 25) whole dried New Mexico red chiles or red ancho chiles (or ½ pound dried New Mexico red chile powder)

2 quarts water

1 pound Roma tomatoes

½ cup chopped white onion

1 tablespoon olive oil

5 large cloves garlic, roasted, peeled, and finely chopped

1 teaspoon roasted ground cumin

1½ teaspoons roasted ground Mexican oregano

1 teaspoon salt

2 tablespoons peanut oil (or lard)

Remove stems and seeds from chiles. With a comal or black iron skillet, or in an oven at 250°, dry roast chiles for 3 to 4 minutes. Shake once or twice and do not allow to blacken. Add to the water in a covered pan and simmer very low for 20 minutes to rehydrate. Allow to cool. Blacken tomatoes in a skillet or under a broiler (about 5 minutes). Sauté onion in the oil over low heat until browned.

Put chiles in a blender. Add blackened tomatoes, onion, garlic, cumin, oregano, and salt. Add 1 cup liquid. (Taste the chile water first. If it is not bitter, use chile water, otherwise add plain water or chicken stock.) Purée to a fine paste; adding more chile water, water, or chicken stock if necessary.

Add oil or lard to a high-sided pan, and heat until almost smoking. Refry sauce at a sizzle for 3 to 5 minutes, stirring continuously. Do not allow sauce to get too thick; add water if necessary.

MARK'S RED CHILE SAUCE

I like this variation of Red Chile Sauce because the combination of different types of red chile gives it more dimensions. It goes better with more complex, heartier dishes such as venison.

Yield: 4 cups

4 ounces whole dried New Mexico red chiles

2 ounces whole dried ancho chiles

2 ounces whole dried cascabel chiles

2 whole dried or canned chipotle chiles in adobo sauce

1 teaspoon adobo sauce

2 quarts water

1 pound blackened Roma tomatoes

½ cup chopped white onion

1 tablespoon olive oil

5 large cloves garlic, roasted, peeled, and finely chopped

1 teaspoon roasted ground cumin

1½ teaspoons roasted ground Mexican oregano

1 teaspoon salt

2 tablespoons peanut oil (or lard)

To prepare, follow the same instructions as for the Red Chile Sauce (see preceding recipe).

GREEN CHILE SAUCE

While Green Chile Sauce is usually hotter than its red counterpart, it can vary from mild to scorching. The green chiles for this sauce are always roasted, and this process provides one of the great fall aromas in these parts: large burlap bags of New Mexico chiles are emptied into butane-fired drums, and turned by hand so that torches flame and char the skins. The air is thick with fiery oils that are enough to clear the head! Native New Mexicans then freeze the chiles for use through the winter. In my opinion, the best green chiles grown anywhere come from New Mexico, due to the altitude and climate. Unfortunately, the rest of the country does not have a comparable supply of uniquely hot yet sweet chiles. If New Mexico green chiles are unavailable, use a combination of Anaheim and jalapeño or serrano chiles. This sauce goes well with the simple flavors of eggs, potatoes, chicken, or trout, and makes a base for a great Green Chile Stew. If using this sauce with fish, or some other light entrée, blister the chiles in oil but do not blacken, or the sauce will be too acrid.

Yield: 4 cups

4 pounds fresh New Mexico green chiles (or Anaheim chiles, with 3 or 4 jalapeños)

8 cloves garlic, roasted, peeled, and finely chopped

4 cups water

4 teaspoons roasted Mexican oregano (rubbed between the fingers, but not too fine)

1 teaspoon roasted ground cumin

2 teaspoons salt

Roast the chiles under the broiler for about 5 minutes, until lightly blackened. Place in a plastic bag or closed container and allow to steam until cooled. Remove the blackened parts without washing (to preserve the oils). Place the chiles and the rest of the ingredients in a food processor and chop at a medium setting (do not purée). Warm before serving.

TOMATILLO CHIPOTLE SAUCE

This is one of the most versatile sauces in my repertoire. It can be served hot or cold, added to mayonnaise, spread on roast pork sandwiches, used to complement grilled fish, pork, rabbit, lamb, or chicken, and is perfect with enchiladas. It is less acidic and softer in the mouth than sauces using regular tomatoes. If this sauce is served warm, do not let it sit for too long as the cilantro tends to lose its color and gets tired in flavor. If you like cilantro as much as I do, put in a little extra — remember, more is better!

Yield: 4 cups

25 large tomatillos (about 2 pounds)

3 cloves garlic, unpeeled

1 medium white onion, finely chopped

3 tablespoons olive oil

4 canned chipotle chiles in adobo sauce

2 teaspoons adobo sauce

1 bunch cilantro, leaves only (about 1 packed cup)

1 teaspoon salt

juice of 1 lime

Husk and wash the tomatillos under hot water. With a comal or black iron skillet cook the tomatillos for 20 to 25 minutes over medium-high heat until soft and blackened all over — do not allow to dry out. Shake pan every couple of minutes. Roast the garlic until soft but not burnt (about 20 to 25 minutes), peel, and remove blackened parts. Sauté onion in 1 tablespoon olive oil until soft and browned (about 15 minutes). Place the tomatillos, garlic, onion, and remaining ingredients (except lime juice) in a blender. Blend until combined; consistency should be even, with no lumps. Add water if necessary. Add lime juice and blend for a few seconds. Add more cilantro, if, desired. Serve warm, at room temperature, or chilled.

SMOKED TOMATO AND JALAPEÑO SAUCE

Smoky flavors are one of the basic trademarks of Southwestern cuisine. Ideally, sweet fruit wood such as apple should be used to smoke the tomatoes and jalapeños; oak, hickory, and mesquite are more acrid, so only a tiny amount should be used, and for a shorter period. Though the results will not be as good, you can also use "liquid smoke." This sauce is easy to make and is very versatile. It goes on almost anything, including grilled chicken, scallops, soft-shell crab, pork, eggs, and enchiladas, or it can be served cold with vegetables or cold beef. We use it at Coyote Cafe to accompany our Lobster and Salmon Tamale — the combination of colors and textures is wonderful.

Yield: 4 cups

2½ pounds Roma tomatoes, cut in half lengthwise

7 jalapeño chiles, cut in half lengthwise and seeded

1½ cups finely chopped white onion

2 tablespoons olive oil

6 cloves garlic, roasted and peeled

2 tablespoons brown sugar

1 teaspoon salt

¾ cup softened sweet butter

1 tablespoon balsamic vinegar

Using a fruit wood, smoke the tomatoes and jalapeños, cut-side up, for approximately 1 hour. Slowly sauté the onion in the oil until brown. Place in a blender together with the tomatoes, 4 of the jalapeños, garlic, sugar, and salt. Purée to an even consistency and strain through a medium sieve. Transfer to a pan, warm gently, and stir in the butter and vinegar. Garnish with the remaining 3 jalapeños, cut into julienne strips.

If using liquid smoke, sauté the onions. Add 1½ teaspoons liquid smoke and the remaining ingredients, and simmer 35 to 40 minutes.

TAMARIND CHIPOTLE SAUCE

I created this recipe one evening while cooking ribs over an outdoor barbecue; it goes perfectly with any pork dish, barbecued or not, and also with sautéed soft-shell crab or other seafood, especially when combined with a little mint. It can also be used as an interesting variation on Chinese plum sauce. This is not a traditional sauce, but I really like the sourness of tamarind combined with the smoky hotness of chipotle. Fresh tamarind pods are usually available from Latin American or Southeast Asian grocery stores.

Yield: 3 cups

2 pounds whole fresh tamarind

6 quarts water

⅔ cup piloncillo (or ½ cup brown sugar)

2 cloves garlic, roasted and peeled

2 canned chipotle chiles in adobo sauce

2 teaspoons adobo sauce

juice of 1 lime

Clean the tamarind pods and discard the brittle outer shell. Place in a large pot with the water, cover, and simmer slowly for at least 2½ hours. Allow to cool; place in a food mill and using a medium mesh, strain the water and extract (approximately 9 cups). Transfer to a pan and reduce further, until about 3 cups are left. Place in a blender and purée together with the sugar, garlic, chipotle, and adobo sauce. Then add the lime juice and blend in. Serve slightly warmed.

MANCHAMANTEL SAUCE

Literally, manchamantel means "tablecloth stainer." This sauce with its red chile is likely to stain a few palates along the way! It is a classic fruit-and-chile sauce from Central Mexico that goes wonderfully well with pork and shrimp dishes, and tamales. It is very popular at Coyote Cafe because of its natural sweetness and hotness, and in form and texture is akin to an old-style Cantonese sweet-and-sour sauce. While this recipe contains bananas and pineapple, other combinations of ripe fruit, such as apples and peaches, can also be used. If you can't get canela, which is the form of cinnamon commonly used in Mexico, ordinary cinnamon can be substituted, but cut the amount in half.

Yield: 6 cups

½ pound whole dried ancho chiles

2 quarts water

½ pound Roma tomatoes

2 cloves garlic, roasted and peeled

1¾ cups diced fresh pineapple

½ pound ripe bananas

1 large green apple (Granny Smith or pippin), peeled, cored, and chopped

3 teaspoons canela (or 1½ teaspoons cinnamon)

1 tablespoon cider vinegar

pinch ground clove

¼ teaspoon ground allspice

2 teaspoons salt

1 tablespoon sugar

3 tablespoons peanut oil (or lard)

Remove stems and seeds from chiles. With a comal or black iron skillet, or in an oven at 250°, dry roast chiles for 5 minutes. Shake once or twice and do not allow to blacken. Add to the water in a covered pan and simmer very low for 30 minutes to rehydrate. Allow to cool. Blacken tomatoes in a skillet or under a broiler (about 5 minutes). Place chiles, tomatoes, and the remaining ingredients in a blender and purée. If necessary, add a little liquid. Taste the chile water first. If it is not bitter, use chile water; otherwise add plain water. Strain.

Add the oil or lard to a high-sided pan, and heat until almost smoking. Refry sauce at a sizzle for 3 to 4 minutes, stirring continuously.

RANCHERO SAUCE

*This is one of my favorite sauces, and I associate it with a little restaurant called Capri in San Cristóbal de las Casas, in southern Mexico. This sauce is simpler than some but is usually misunderstood, misinterpreted, and poorly executed by most restaurants. It is a rustic-style sauce that traditionally is cooked in the morning and is used throughout the day. It is **the** original tomato sauce, and can be considered the granddaddy of the most widely used sauce in the world today! This version provides the primitive quality and expressiveness that I appreciate but find lacking in some of its more sophisticated cousins. Ranchero Sauce goes naturally with eggs, chicken, pork, tamales, and seafood.*

Yield: 8 cups

5 pounds Roma tomatoes

6 serrano chiles

2 cups finely chopped white onion

2 tablespoons finely chopped garlic

2 tablespoons peanut oil (or lard)

6 poblano chiles, roasted, peeled, seeded, and cut into julienne strips (about 1½ cups)

1 bunch cilantro, tied

2 teaspoons salt

Lightly blacken tomatoes and serranos in a skillet or under a broiler (about 4 to 5 minutes). Chop together and set aside. Sauté onion and garlic in the oil over low heat until soft but not brown (about 10 to 15 minutes). Combine all ingredients in a saucepan (reserving a few strips of poblano chiles for garnish). Cook partially covered over low heat for 20 to 30 minutes, adding water if necessary. Remove cilantro. Garnish with the reserved julienned poblanos.

MOLE ROJO

People tend to have strong feelings about mole sauces: they either like or dislike them, and there is little middle ground. Some people object just to the thought of a Hershey-type sauce on their chicken or duck. But moles really bear no resemblance to chocolate syrups you would serve on ice cream or cake. The chocolate used more nearly resembles cocoa than a candy-style ingredient, and it is balanced by the sharp acidic flavors of the tomatoes and tomatillos. The dry fruit ingredients also enhance the plum or prune flavors of the ancho and mulato chiles. Cooking moles in a clay pot will give the sauce a smoother taste; putting them through a strainer helps gives them a finer texture and helps weave the flavors more closely together. Mole Rojo, or Red Mole Sauce, originates from Puebla, in central Mexico, and is traditionally used with fowl — turkey in particular. Do not be daunted by the length of this recipe — it is not as complicated as it may appear!

Yield: 5 cups

6 whole dried chiles negro (or pasillas)

10 whole dried ancho chiles

8 whole dried mulato chiles

2 quarts water

4 tomatillos

5 Roma tomatoes

½ cup raisins (or dried plums or dried cherries)

⅓ cup sesame seeds

½ cup whole almonds, unskinned

1 tablespoon peanut oil

2 corn tortillas, dried in the oven and chopped

6 cloves garlic, roasted and peeled

2 cups brown duck stock or chicken stock

4 teaspoons canela (or 2 teaspoons cinnamon)

⅛ teaspoon ground cloves

½ teaspoon ground black pepper

½ teaspoon ground allspice

1 teaspoon salt

3 ounces Mexican Ibarra chocolate

2 ounces unsweetened chocolate

3 tablespoons duck fat (or peanut oil)

Remove stems and seeds from chiles. With a comal or black iron skillet, or in an oven at 250°, dry roast chiles for 5 minutes. Shake once or twice and do not allow to blacken. Add to the water in a covered pan and simmer very low for 30 minutes to rehydrate. Strain, and allow to cool. Husk and wash the tomatillos under hot water. Blacken the tomatillos and tomatoes in a skillet or under a broiler (about 5 minutes). Soak the raisins in warm water until soft (about 20 minutes); discard the water. Dry roast sesame seeds in a sauté pan for about 5 minutes until they have finished popping; do not allow seeds to burn. Sauté the almonds in the oil over low to medium heat until browned. Purée the tomatillos, tomatoes, sesame seeds, almonds, and tortillas in a blender to form a paste. Add the chiles, raisins, garlic, stock, spices, and salt, and purée together. Melt the chocolate and blend into the mixture.

Add the duck fat or oil to a high-sided pan, and heat until almost smoking. Refry sauce over medium heat for 5 to 15 minutes, stirring constantly. Add more stock, if necessary — do not allow to get too thick. Strain the sauce through a sieve, and serve warm, not hot.

MOLE VERDE

Mole Verde, or Green Mole Sauce, originates from Oaxaca, in southern Mexico. Unlike its cousin, Mole Rojo, it is rarely seen in restaurants in this country. This is a shame, because Mole Verde is light, tasty, and delicate. It always receives rave reviews from diners who are trying it at Coyote Cafe for the first time. It is excellent with seafood, poultry, and pork.

Yield: 4 cups

6 tomatillos

1 cup rich poultry stock

2 cups chopped Romaine lettuce leaves (no stems)

½ cup cilantro leaves

6 poblano chiles, roasted, peeled, and chopped

½ teaspoon cumin seed, roasted and ground

1 teaspoon coriander seed, roasted and ground

pinch anise seed, roasted and ground

½ teaspoon salt

1 corn tortilla, dried in the oven and chopped

2 tablespoons chopped fresh epazote (optional)

2 tablespoons duck fat (or peanut oil)

Husk the tomatillos and wash under hot water. Dry roast in a skillet or under a broiler for about 4 or 5 minutes. Place in a blender with stock, romaine, cilantro, poblanos, spices, salt, tortilla, and epazote, and purée together.

Add duck fat or oil to a high-sided pan, and heat until almost smoking. Refry sauce at a sizzle for 3 to 5 minutes, stirring continuously. Strain the sauce, and serve warm, not hot.

PIPIÁN ROJO

Pipiáns are sauces made with ground nuts or seeds — sort of like Southwestern pestos. They date from pre-Colombian days: the conquistador Cortés recorded that pipiáns were served at some of Montezuma's court feasts. The flavor of pumpkin seed is foreign to most American palates. It does not have the richness of pine nuts; instead, the taste is more like that of the vegetable itself. Raw pumpkin seeds are available at most health food stores. Pipiáns are a very versatile element in the Southwestern repertoire, and can be used for appetizers, or as a sauce or garnish for grilled meats. Pipián Rojo, or Red Pipián, gets its color from the dried ancho and guajillo chiles, and from the tomatoes.

Yield: 5 cups

2 ounces whole dried ancho chiles

2 ounces whole dried guajillo chiles

1 quart water

¾ pound Roma tomatoes

½ cup finely chopped white onion

2 tablespoons olive oil

4 ounces green unroasted pumpkin seeds (about 1 heaping cup)

6 cloves garlic, roasted and peeled

2 canned chipotle chiles in adobo sauce

1 teaspoon adobo sauce

½ cup dry roasted peanuts

½ teaspoon ground allspice

2 teaspoons canela (or 1 teaspoon cinnamon)

pinch ground clove

1 teaspoon sugar

1½ teaspoons salt

1 tablespoon duck fat (or peanut oil)

Remove stems and seeds from chiles. With a comal or black iron skillet, or in an oven at 250°, dry roast chiles for 5 minutes. Shake once or twice and do not allow to blacken. Add to the water in a covered pan and simmer very low for 30 minutes to rehydrate. Allow to cool. Blacken tomatoes in a skillet or under a broiler (about 5 minutes). Sauté onion in the oil over low heat until slightly browned. Dry roast pumpkin seeds in a sauté pan for about 5 minutes until they have finished popping. Place in a blender and purée together with tomatoes to form a paste. Add the chiles, about ½ cup of chile water if it is not bitter (otherwise use plain water), onion, garlic, chipotles, adobo sauce, peanuts, spices, sugar, and salt, and purée further.

Add duck fat or oil to a high-sided pan, and heat until almost smoking. Refry sauce at a sizzle for 3 to 5 minutes, stirring continuously. Serve at room temperature.

PIPIÁN VERDE

This green pipián sauce contains a base of fresh greens and herbs, instead of the dried red chiles used in the Pipián Rojo (see recipe above). In Mexico, Pipián Verde, or Green Pipián, is made with the yerba santa leaf, which has a strong sassafras-like flavor, similar to root beer; this recipe uses anise seed instead. Epazote can also be used as the flavoring. Pipián Verde is a wonderful accompaniment for sautéed pork or scallops, or toss it with pasta. Classically it is served with roast duck or duck enchiladas. Serve it together with Pipián Rojo to create an attractive combination of flavors and colors.

Yield: 4 cups

4 ounces green unroasted pumpkin seeds (about 1 heaping cup)

½ cup finely chopped white onion

2 tablespoons peanut oil

1 cup rich chicken stock

1½ cups cilantro

2 cloves garlic, roasted and peeled

8 large leaves Romaine lettuce, chopped (no stems)

1 bunch watercress

1 bunch radish tops

1½ teaspoons roasted anise seed (or ¼ cup loosely packed chopped epazote)

1 teaspoon salt

1 teaspoon sugar

1 tablespoon duck fat (or peanut oil)

Dry roast pumpkin seeds in a sauté pan for about 5 minutes until they have finished popping. Set aside a few seeds for garnish. Sauté onion in the oil over low heat until slightly browned. Process the pumpkin seeds and stock in a blender to form a paste. Add ½ cup of cilantro and the remaining ingredients, except for the duck fat or oil, and purée.

Add duck fat or oil to a high-sided pan, and heat until almost smoking. Refry sauce at a sizzle for 3 to 4 minutes, stirring continuously; do not overcook or the sauce will lose its greenness. Return to blender, add the remaining cup of cilantro, and purée together. Garnish with the reserved pumpkin seeds. Serve at room temperature. (The sauce can be gently warmed, if you wish, but be careful not to bring it to a boil or it will lose its color.)

PEANUT CHIPOTLE SAUCE

Peanuts originated in the New World, and were used as thickening and flavoring agents for pipiáns. The same flavorful combination of peanuts and hot chiles are also to be found in the satays of Indonesia and Southeast Asia. High-quality, chunky-style peanut butter should be used, preferably ground fresh by a health food store. This relatively simple sauce should be used with pork or chicken, or with skewered shrimp.

Yield: 4 cups

2 Roma tomatoes

½ cup finely chopped white onion

3 tablespoons peanut oil

1 cup chunky peanut butter

8 cloves garlic

1 cup warm water

6 canned chipotle chiles in adobo sauce

3 teaspoons adobo sauce

1 cup Mark's Red Chile Sauce (see page 25)

1 teaspoon salt

juice of 1 lime

1 cup chicken or pork stock (optional)

Blacken tomatoes in a skillet or under a broiler (about 5 minutes). Sauté onion in 2 tablespoons of the oil over low heat until dark and caramelized. Place the peanut butter in a food processor together with the tomatoes, garlic, and water, and blend. Add the onion, chipotles, adobo sauce, red chile sauce, salt, and lime juice, and blend further.

Add the remaining tablespoon of peanut oil to a high-sided pan, and heat until almost smoking. Refry sauce at a sizzle for 3 to 4 minutes, stirring constantly. Thin with stock if desired. Serve at room temperature or warm.

BLACK BEAN SOUP

Since I grew up in Boston, I have eaten my share of homemade baked beans, and I still have a fondness for beans of any type. It was on my first trip to Guatemala that I acquired a taste for black beans, in particular. There they are served as a side dish with almost every meal. Back in Berkeley at the Fourth Street Grill, I began developing my own recipes for black beans. This soup is one of them. The first month this soup was on the menu, James Beard came in, really liked it, asked for the recipe, and published it in his nationally syndicated column. It is a favorite of my customers, and is, in fact, a basic recipe which will be referred to throughout this book.

Yield: 8 servings

1 pound dried black beans

1 teaspoon cumin seed

1 teaspoon coriander seed

1 teaspoon roasted Mexican oregano

½ large onion, peeled, with root fibers attached

4 large cloves garlic, slightly smashed

2 jalapeño chiles, cut lengthwise

1 bunch cilantro, tied

2 bay leaves

½ teaspoon dried thyme

1½ teaspoons peppercorns

6 quarts water

½ cup tomato purée

1½ teaspoons salt

Spread the beans out on a cookie sheet and remove any foreign particles. Look out for small black stones that resemble the beans. Rinse the beans in cold water two or three times, stirring by hand. Do not soak, as the new varieties of beans do not need it. Roast cumin, coriander, and oregano together and crush or roughly grind them in a spice mill. Tie them up together with the onion, garlic, jalapeños, cilantro, bay leaves, thyme, and peppercorns in cheesecloth and simmer in water for 15 minutes. Add the beans, tomato purée, and salt to the water and simmer very low for 3 hours, or until the beans are completely soft and just starting to fall apart. Add water as necessary. Remove the cheesecloth bag. To make a thicker soup, you can purée 1½ cups beans and stir them back into the soup.

YELLOW SQUASH SOUP
with Red Chile Crema

Here is a simple soup to make late in summer. Ideally, squash should come from your own garden: the homegrown variety tends to be tastier and less starchy. I prefer yellow crookneck squash, which is sweeter than yellow zucchini. When sweating the vegetables, ensure that the heat is low and the pan covered: this way, none of the sweet perfume flavors escape. This soup can also be served cold.

Yield: 6 servings

3 pounds yellow crookneck (or summer squash or yellow zucchini), cut into large dice

1½ cups finely chopped white onion

2 tablespoons butter

6 sprigs fresh marjoram

2 cups water

1 cup heavy cream

½ teaspoon salt, or to taste

Red Chile Crema

4 whole dried red chiles

1 cup water

Put the squash, onion, butter, marjoram, and 2 cups of water in a saucepan. Cover and cook over low heat for about 25 minutes. Allow to cool, remove marjoram, and purée in a blender. Heat the purée with the cream and season with salt, adding a little water if necessary to prevent the mixture from becoming too thick.

To make the Red Chile Crema, place the dried chiles on a baking sheet and roast in oven at 325° for 5 minutes. Remove seeds, and boil in 1 cup of water until soft. Purée in blender and season with a pinch of salt.

Ladle soup into bowls and decorate with Red Chile Crema on top in a Southwestern zigzag design.

SOUTHWEST PAINTED SOUP

This red and green soup is visually very striking. The trick with this soup is to make both parts of the same consistency so they don't merge into each other. This recipe calls for a soup made of cherry tomatoes and shallots on one side, and of blanched and puréed greens on the other; however, roasted red and yellow tomatoes or roasted red and green chiles can be used just as well. This latter combination won accolades when I prepared it for a dinner at The Mansion on Turtle Creek in Dallas, although it was a bit too hot for some of the Texans present; I find the New Mexican palate has a little more tolerance for green chile!

Yield: 4 servings

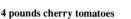

4 pounds cherry tomatoes

6 large shallots, finely minced

2 tablespoons butter

1 head butter lettuce

1 head Romaine lettuce

1 bunch green chard, stems removed

6 green chiles (or 6 Anaheim and 2 jalapeño chiles), roasted, peeled, seeded, and chopped

2 cups water

1 tablespoon virgin olive oil

salt to taste

Cut the tomatoes in half, place on a baking sheet and roast in oven at 350° for 45 minutes. Sauté shallots in 1 tablespoon butter over low heat until soft (about 10 to 15 minutes); do not allow to color — add water if necessary. Purée the tomatoes and shallots in a blender and sieve finely. Set aside.

Blanch the lettuces and chard in lightly salted boiling water for 1 minute. Rinse under cold water to preserve color, and finely purée in blender with chiles and water.

Heat the red and green soups separately. Add 1 tablespoon of butter to the red soup and stir in. Whisk the oil into the green soup after it has heated through. Add salt to taste, and water if necessary, to keep both soups at a similar consistency. Ladle out about ¾ cup of each mixture simultaneously into opposite sides of a rimmed soup bowl. The soup can be garnished with Red Chile Crema on top in a Southwestern zigzag design (see preceding recipe).

GREEN GAZPACHO SOUP
with Mexican Crema

The inspiration for this recipe came from a soup I had in Spain while I was on a horseback riding holiday through the rolling hills of Andalusia. Each town and district there has its own particular style of gazpacho, and this one is made from green tomatillos. I find this soup very refreshing and cooling both in color and flavor. It can be garnished with shrimp or crab meat and served as a light lunch entrée.

Yield: 4 servings

25 to 30 tomatillos

1 medium red onion

2 cloves garlic

1 English cucumber (or 2 regular cucumbers)

2 poblano chiles, roasted, peeled, and seeded

20 sprigs cilantro, leaves only

3 or 4 serrano chiles

1 tablespoon sugar

salt to taste

½ cup Mexican Crema (see recipe below) or sour cream

8 lime wedges

Husk the tomatillos and wash them under hot water. Coarsely chop tomatillos, saving 4 unblemished ones for the garnish, and place in blender. Chop three-fourths of the onion, and all of the garlic, the poblanos, and the cilantro, and add to the tomatillos. Chop three-fourths of the cucumber. (If regular cucumbers are used, peel and seed them first. English or hothouse cucumbers can be used as is.) Add the chopped cucumbers to the tomatillos. Purée, adding ice water to thin if necessary, and add salt. Chill thoroughly.

For the salsa garnish, mince very finely the remaining tomatillos, onion, cucumber, and the serranos. Combine with sugar and salt to taste. Chill.

To serve, taste again for salt and check for consistency. Place in chilled bowls and add a dollop of Mexican Crema or sour cream, and a tablespoon or more of the salsa. Garnish with lime wedges.

MEXICAN CREMA

Crema, the Mexican equivalent of crème fraîche, is often served with Southwestern dishes as a relief to spicy food, as well as to provide a richness — for example, with refried black beans or a spicy stew. The crema, which should be prepared 24 hours in advance, is very simple to make. This basic crema can serve as the base for other flavored cremas. You can also whip it with a little sugar and use it as a dessert topping. The touch of sourness gives fresh fruit or chocolate a great edge.

Yield: 1 cup

1 cup heavy cream (preferably unpasteurized)

1 tablespoon buttermilk (preferably raw)

Heat cream in saucepan to warm (approximately 70°). Do not over-heat. Remove from heat and pour into clean container. Add butter-milk, cover with cheesecloth, and place overnight in warm location (75°) to set. The consistency of the crème fraîche the following day should be of a loose sour cream. If any mold has developed, toss the mixture out and start again. Once set, the crema should be stored in the refrigerator in a clean covered container (it will keep for at least one week).

YUCATÁN LIME SOUP

On the whole, I prefer soups that are brothy and have a country feeling to those that are creamy or puréed. This is, without doubt, my favorite soup of all. It's my version of chicken soup, and it incorporates all the things I love in Southwestern food: the clean, bright flavors of cilantro, the sparkling sour taste of lime, the smoky flavor of grilled chicken, the crunch of tortilla strips, the hearty, simple wholesome richness of chicken stock, and the distinct weedy flavor of oregano. This soup should be served in colorful soup plates, rather than in bowls, so the ingredients don't sink beneath the surface and disappear out of view! Make sure the lime juice goes in at the very end, as it loses its sharpness if it's boiled, and never allow any pith to find its way into the soup, as that will make it bitter. This dish, with homemade tortillas, or bread and salad, makes an excellent lunch or après-ski meal.

Yield: 4 servings

½ pound boneless chicken breast, skin removed

1 pound Roma tomatoes

6 cups rich chicken stock

10 cloves garlic, roasted, peeled, and finely chopped

4 serrano chiles, chopped in rings

1 bunch cilantro, tied (remove 12 sprigs for garnish)

4 rings white onion, ¼ inch thick

1 poblano chile, roasted, peeled, and julienned

8 teaspoons fresh lime juice

1 tablespoon roasted ground Mexican oregano

thin strips of deep-fried tortilla (¼ x 3 inches)

4 lime wedges

Grill or broil the chicken until brown but still moist, and shred by hand into ¼ x 2-inch strips. Set aside. With a comal or black iron skillet over medium-high heat, cook the tomatoes until blackened all over, and chop roughly. Place tomatoes in a saucepan with the stock, garlic, serranos, and cilantro. Simmer over low heat for 20 to 30 minutes. Remove the cilantro.

Divide the chicken equally between the soup plates. Broil the onion rings until cooked but not blackened and add to the plates together with the poblano chile. Then ladle the soup over, and stir in 2 teaspoons of lime juice per plate. Garnish each plate with cilantro sprigs, a pinch of oregano rubbed between the fingers, tortilla strips, and a lime wedge. You could also serve the soup in a large tureen surrounded by the garnishes, and ladle it out at the table.

ROASTED CORN SOUP
with Smoked Chiles and Cheese

I remember many corn soups from my past. There were corn chowders from New England, and Diana Kennedy's Sopa de Elote, which Alice Waters liked to make at Chez Panisse. (The recipe for that soup appears in Diana's superb book The Cuisines of Mexico, which was one of my early bibles; my copy is now very well-thumbed.) Alice would use Silver Queen corn, an especially sweet corn that was grown in the Livermore Valley and delivered to the restaurant the same day it was picked. At Coyote Cafe we use Platinum Lady corn which grows on the high plain in New Mexico, and is even sweeter than the Silver Queen. The roasted corn in this soup complements the smoky flavor of the chipotle chiles and the feta cheese particularly well.

Yield: 6 servings

10 ears corn in the husk

5 cups water

4 dry (or canned) chipotle chiles, deveined, seeded, and julienned

salt to taste

4 ounces feta cheese (or *queso fresco*)

Roast the corn on a cookie sheet in a 400° oven for 45 to 60 minutes; the outside of the husks should be dry and dark brown. Cool the husks, shuck the corn, and cut the kernels from the ears. Purée 3 cups of the corn with 3 cups of water in a blender. Cook the purée in a pan together with the chipotle chiles and remaining water for 10 to 15 minutes over low heat. Add the reserved whole corn and salt. Pour the soup into bowls and crumble the cheese over the top.

GREEN CHILE
& OYSTER
CHOWDER

Once again, this recipe reflects my Northeastern background, where homemade chowders made from onions, milk, potatoes, and clams were ever-present. This is a Southwestern adaptation of one of my favorites. The ingredients are precooked and added at the last minute so they retain their flavor and identity. Use whole large oysters as smaller ones will dry out and not have the plump, rich center that you want. Shucked oysters are likely to be freshest at the local fish market; fresh scallops can be used as an alternative. In this soup you do not want any hint of smokiness, so the chiles are blistered in hot oil, not roasted or grilled. For a richer chowder, use heavy cream instead of half-and-half.

Yield: 4 servings

1 pound red potatoes, cut into ½-inch dice

1 medium onion, finely chopped

2½ cups fish stock (or clam juice)

1 bay leaf

½ pound fresh green chiles

2 cups peanut oil

½ cup fresh corn kernels

16 shucked oysters in their liquor

1 large sweet red pepper, roasted, peeled, and cut into ½-inch dice

2 cups half-and-half

salt to taste

1 tablespoon butter

1 teaspoon fresh marjoram, chopped

Gently boil the potatoes for about 4 minutes in salted water, rinse, and cool. Cook the onion with 1 cup of stock and the bay leaf over low heat for 15 to 20 minutes, until cooked through, but not browned. Discard the bay leaf and cool. Fry the green chiles in the oil for about 4 or 5 minutes until the skin is blistered, but not blackened. Skin the chiles, remove seeds, and cut into ½-inch dice. Steam the corn in ¼ cup water in a covered pan for 2 minutes until tender.

In a large pan, combine the oysters with their liquor, the remaining stock, and the green chiles. Heat for 2 minutes, then add the potatoes, onion, and red pepper, and bring to a boil. Add the half-and-half, keeping the mixture below a boil to keep the half-and-half from separating. Add salt, corn, and butter. Pour into soup bowls and garnish with the marjoram.

ALBÓNDIGAS DE CAMARÓNES

Every culture seems to have its dumpling soup, and this is the Mexican version — I rate it as one of the great soups of that cuisine. It also happens to be the Coyote Cafe staff's favorite soup! Albóndigas de camarónes, or shrimp dumplings, roasted tomatoes, smoked chile sauce, and the surprise taste of canela are a wonderful combination. This is a great wintertime seafood soup which can be served as the centerpiece of an evening meal along with toasted Chile Corn Bread, or soft corn quesadillas with cheese and rajas. The dumplings can be made and poached ahead of time, and the broth heated at the last minute. Rice and vegetables can be added to make a delicious stew.

Yield: 4 servings

½ pound shrimp, peeled and deveined

3 tablespoons cooked fresh sweet corn

1 tablespoon minced white onion

1 tablespoon minced peeled and seeded tomato

1 teaspoon canela (or ½ teaspoon cinnamon)

½ teaspoon roasted ground Mexican oregano

¼ teaspoon salt

1 tablespoon flour

1 egg yolk

1 teaspoon ground coriander seed

1 tablespoon puréed rehydrated ancho chiles (optional)

¼ cup thinly sliced white onion

4 cloves garlic, minced

2 tablespoons olive oil

1 pound Roma tomatoes, chopped

3 canned chipotle chiles in adobo sauce, julienned

6 cups fish stock (or clam juice)

12 sprigs cilantro

Mince the shrimp and pulse in a blender into a rough paste. Put into a bowl and add the corn, minced onion, minced tomato, canela, oregano, salt, flour, egg yolk, coriander, and ancho purée. Mix together well and set the bowl in a larger bowl half filled with ice and water to keep the mixture cold. Sauté the sliced onion and garlic in the oil for about 15 minutes. Add the Roma tomatoes and chipotles, cover, and cook for a further 25 minutes. Add the stock and bring to a boil. Divide the shrimp mixture into 12 large rounded spoonfuls and poach in the soup for about 5 minutes. Add stock if the soup becomes too thick. Divide equally between the soup bowls and garnish with cilantro.

POSOLE

This is the classic New Mexican soup, made with posole, a special type of corn that is similar to hominy, and pork. It's hard to get authentic Posole except in Hispanic or Mexican homes. The combination of this special corn mixed with sweet pieces of pork, fresh cabbage, crunchy red radish, and Red Chile Sauce is fantastic, and seems to be particularly good for hangovers! When I was in Berkeley, there were many times when I would drive over to Oakland in the pre-dawn hours to track down a bowl of Posole. In Mexico, Posole is often made with menudo, or tripe. The secret of this version lies in the rich stock made from pigs' feet. You can usually buy prepared posole ready for cooking in tortilla shops.

Yield: 6 servings

CLAM SOUP WITH SAUSAGE

6 pounds pigs' feet, cracked or cut

4 tablespoons whole Mexican oregano leaves

2 large white onions, sliced

6 bay leaves

2 large heads garlic, cut in half (across)

3 teaspoons black pepper

10 whole red chiles (mild to medium)

2 teaspoons cumin seed

1 teaspoon dried whole thyme

1 teaspoon salt

5 gallons water

2 pounds prepared posole

2 pounds lean pork meat, diced

¼ head green cabbage, thinly sliced

8 radishes, sliced

½ cup Red Chile Sauce or Ranchero Sauce (see pages 25 and 28)

Simmer pigs' feet, 2 tablespoons oregano, onions, bay leaves, 1 head garlic, pepper, chiles, cumin, thyme, and salt in the water for 6 to 8 hours, skimming often to remove excess fat and scum, especially during the first 2 hours. Strain and reserve stock.

Add the posole, pork, remaining garlic, and 1 tablespoon oregano to the strained stock, cover, and simmer until posole 'buds' open (at least 2 to 3 hours but up to 4 or 5 hours — actually the longer the better). Add more water periodically and skim regularly. Remove garlic and add salt to taste if necessary. Ladle soup into bowls and garnish with shredded cabbage, radish sticks, and Red Chile Sauce or Ranchero Sauce. Garnish with remaining oregano if desired.

The traditional Portuguese combination of clams and sausage can be found in Providence and New Bedford, Rhode Island, where it was introduced by Iberian expatriates generations ago. I have given it a Southwestern touch by substituting the more spicy chorizo sausage which enhances the flavor of the broth without overpowering the clams. If possible, use small clams such as Eastern Littlenecks or Washington Manilas, as these are sweeter and not as tough. Cooking the clams in their shells adds a richness to the broth, and garnishing the soup with a little lime and cilantro will make it come alive.

Yield: 4 servings

½ white onion, chopped

4 large cloves garlic, sliced

2 tablespoons olive oil

1 pound Roma tomatoes

1 large red potato, cut into ½-inch dice

½ pound hot Italian or Andouille sausage cut into ½-inch slices

2 cups fish stock (or clam juice)

20 small Littleneck or Manila clams, washed

¼ bunch cilantro

4 lime wedges

Slowly sauté the onion and garlic in 1 tablespoon of oil for 15 minutes in a covered pan. Broil or sear the tomatoes over a flame for 5 or 6 minutes, chop, add to the pan, and continue to cook slowly for a further 20 minutes. Boil the potato in lightly salted water for 5 minutes. Rinse under cold water and set aside. Sauté the chorizo slowly in the remaining oil for 20 minutes. Reserve the sausage and oil.

Deglaze the pan with a little fish stock, and reserve the juices. Add 1 cup of the stock to the onion, garlic, and tomato mixture, and then add the clams. Cover, and cook over medium heat for 4 minutes. Add the chorizo, the reserved juices, and potato and continue to cook until the clams open. Add the remaining stock. Ladle the soup into bowls and garnish with cilantro and lime wedges.

APPETIZERS
& SALADS

Snack food is very much a part of the Southwestern tradition. When the Spanish settlers came to this region, they introduced the custom of serving appetizers. Antojitos, as they are called, have since become a part of the way of life. Appetizers are also evident in the Indian pueblos today where small plates of food are offered at all times of the day or night.

In Mexico, appetizers like those included in this chapter are also considered street food. The vendors outside the marketplaces offer an incredible array of delights — from plain tortillas to tacos filled with wild venison cooked with a mole sauce. In the Yucatán market of Mérida, for example, you can sample fried fish, raw seafood, skewered tropical fruits, tamales and tacos of all kinds, large hunks of barbecued pork, and just about everything in between. At each stand you get to add as much or as little of their salsas as you like. My favorites are the *cochinita* stands with suckling pig cooked in a black *recuerdo* (a spicy paste made from roasted herbs and ashes), served with a pink pickled radish and onion salad, sprigs of green cilantro, and fresh soft corn tortillas.

Many of the appetizers we serve at Coyote Cafe were inspired by these vendors' treats. These are tidbits to sit over and nibble at for hours while drinking and talking with friends. This is sociable food, party food, fiesta food. These are dishes to spark the conversation and get the evening going. They can also be shared at the table, family-style, where each person puts together their own combinations. (At Coyote Cafe, I prefer this Southwestern style of serving appetizers, where there is a varied assortment of food to choose from, rather than a single item.)

As you travel through the parts of Mexico and Central America that border on the Caribbean, you'll spot the word "mariscos" painted in bright blue, white, or yellow letters on the side of many a building. It can mean anything from little seafood stands selling ceviches in paper cups to elegant restaurants serving elaborate platters of clams, oysters, lobster, shrimp, or crab. In Southwestern cuisine, mariscos are generally served as appetizers or snacks, and go down well with a cold beer on a hot day. They are one of the most popular foods we serve at Coyote Cafe, so I've included a good sampling of mariscos in this chapter.

Seafood appetizers are especially good because they stimulate the appetite without being cloying; there are no creams or heavy sauces; they are neither too rich nor too filling. They carry the essence of the ocean, being a little salty and tangy, and naturally fresh. In general, it is perfectly all right to substitute one seafood for another in these recipes. For example, ceviches can be made with salmon or shark, depending on availability.

In addition to recipes for tasty tidbits, I have included in this chapter some of my favorite salads. I put them here because they make a wonderful light introduction to the more complex flavors that sometimes follow. To my mind a salad can be the perfect appetizer when it is clean-flavored and uses mostly raw ingredients that are not only visually arresting but also stimulating to the palate.

BLACK PEPPER YUCATÁN OYSTERS

This is a very simple dish to prepare, and is popular even with customers who claim they dislike oysters! I made this dish for the PBS television series, "Great Chefs of San Francisco," so it may be familiar. Use large oysters, since small ones tend to be overwhelmed by the sauce.

Yield: 4 to 6 servings

20 to 24 large fresh oysters

2 tablespoons black peppercorns

6 allspice berries

3 large cloves garlic, roasted and peeled

½ teaspoon salt

3 tablespoons olive oil

3 bay leaves

2 tablespoons lime juice

lime wedges

Shuck oysters and reserve shells and liquor. Put oyster liquor in a sauté pan and bring to a boil. Add oysters and poach gently for 2 to 3 minutes, until the edges curl slightly. With a slotted spoon, remove oysters from sauté pan and set aside. Put peppercorns, allspice, garlic, and salt into a mortar and grind to a rough paste. Add ½ cup hot oyster liquor to the mortar and continue to grind. Add olive oil and bay leaves to liquid in pan and bring to a boil. Blend in mixture from mortar, then return oysters to pan and heat very briefly. Remove from heat, cool, and add lime juice. Serve in shells or on deep-fried flour tortilla triangles. Pour sauce over oysters. Garnish with Pico de Gallo Salsa (see page 13) and wedges of lime. Serve cold or at room temperature.

OYSTER EMPANADAS

Empanadas are Spanish/Latin American pastry turnovers. They are made with all manner of fillings, from ground meats to a combination of bananas and cheese. This recipe is sort of a hybrid: I got the idea from a North African dish called brik, which is a turnover-type pastry containing raw tuna. The contrast of hot pastry with fresh seafood is a surprise to the palate both in taste and texture.

Yield: 6 empanadas

1 cup masa harina (or fresh masa)

2 cups high-gluten flour

4 eggs

2 tablespoons water

2 teaspoons kosher salt

2 egg yolks

1 tablespoon achiote paste

4 tablespoons softened butter

1 tablespoon minced serrano chiles

1 tablespoon minced cilantro

2 tablespoons cooked fresh corn kernels

6 Wellfleet or Portuguaise oysters, patted dry

¼ cup coarse cornmeal (polenta)

1 quart peanut oil

Mix masa harina, flour, eggs, 1 tablespoon water, and 1 teaspoon salt in a mixer until a coarse dough is formed. Knead by hand until the dough holds together.

To make an egg wash, beat the two egg yolks, achiote paste, and remaining water with a fork until smooth. Set aside. Combine butter, chiles, cilantro, and corn. Set aside.

To make and assemble the empanadas, roll dough with a rolling pin until a very thin sheet is formed. Cut pasta dough into six 3½-inch circles. Brush each circle of pasta dough with egg wash. Place one oyster off center in each circle. Add 1½ teaspoons chile butter to each one and fold the dough over, sealing carefully to form the empanadas. Brush empanadas with egg wash. Mix polenta with remaining salt, and roll empanadas in the meal. Deep fry in peanut oil for 2 minutes at 350°. Serve as is or with Melon Salsa (see page 18) or with guacamole. This dish can be made ahead of time, and reheated at the last minute (put them on a cookie sheet in a 350° oven for 5 minutes).

SALPICÓN OF TEXAS BLUE CRAB

A salpicón is a salad-like dish made with meat or fish and vegetables and a dressing. If you see it on the menu in a good restaurant, order it. There is such a variation in recipes that they are invariably interesting. This one is a terrific, light version of the usual heavy crab salads that are smothered with mayonnaise or similar creamy sauces. It can also be made with shredded cooked lobster or with shrimp.

Yield: 6 to 8 servings

1 teaspoon minced fresh epazote

1 tablespoon unseasoned rice vinegar

1 teaspoon sugar

1 tablespoon lime juice

2 tablespoons minced shallots (or sweet onions) rinsed under hot water

2 tablespoons extra virgin peanut oil (or extra virgin olive oil)

¼ cup sweet red peppers cut into ¼-inch dice

¼ cup sweet yellow peppers cut into ¼-inch dice

2 tablespoons minced serrano chiles

1 pound fresh cooked Texas blue crab or other crab meat

avocado slices

Combine all the ingredients except for the crab and avocado. Mix well, then add and toss the crab. Serve garnished with avocado slices.

CRAB CUSHIONS

These crunchy little rolls are very popular at Coyote Cafe. If you make them for a party, make plenty, as they just seem to disappear into thin air. Allow four to six per person and serve in baskets lined with colored cloths to keep the Crab Cushions warm. This recipe can also be made with diced shrimp or lobster.

Yield: 4 servings

½ pound fresh crab meat (Dungeness, Maine, or Gulf)

2 tablespoons chopped fresh epazote (or fresh marjoram)

1 to 2 tablespoons heavy cream or Mexican Crema (see page 35)

2 egg yolks

salt and pepper to taste

1 dozen high-quality thin flour tortillas

1 quart peanut oil

Mix together crab meat, epazote, cream, 1 egg yolk, and seasoning. (Keep the mixture in the refrigerator if you are not going to make the crab cushions immediately. It will keep several hours.) Cut the flour tortillas into 2½ x 3-inch rectangles. Place 1 heaped teaspoon of the crab mixture on each tortilla piece. Roll up the pieces to form cushions; there should be about 16 rolls. On the last inch of the strip on the inside, brush the tortilla with some of the remaining egg yolk to make the ends stick together. Put in a pan with the seam on the bottom. Heat the peanut oil to 350 to 375° and deep-fry the Crab Cushions until they are lightly browned. Serve with Tomatillo Salsa (see page 13). This dish can be made ahead of time, and reheated at the last minute (at 325° in the oven for 5 to 7 minutes, or in the microwave for 1 minute).

Note: If the tortillas can be purchased freshly made rather than refrigerated, they will roll much better. Refrigerated tortillas will certainly do the job; but are less pliable and harder to work with. Be sure to use fresh thin tortillas, or you'll have trouble rolling them up.

SWORDFISH EN ESCABECHE

Escabeche is a pickling solution; en escabeche means to be pickled or soused, in which case it refers to food rather than to consumers of several margaritas! Vegetables en escabeche are commonly found in the pickle section of Southwest food stores. Roadside stops and bars (especially in Texas) have large glass jars full of pickled foods, such as jalapeños, hard-boiled eggs, and pigs' feet. This recipe is one of the most unusual and interesting examples of pickled food. It is a version of a pre-Columbian recipe, and its derivation from another time and world is part of the reason for my fascination with it. It can also be made with shark or some other firm, meaty fish; a lighter fish will fall apart too easily. This dish keeps reasonably well for up to 12 hours, but it is best served the same day.

Yield: 4 to 6 servings

1 medium carrot, julienned

1 medium white onion, julienned

2 cloves garlic, sliced

1 poblano chile, roasted, peeled, and julienned

⅓ cup extra virgin olive oil

1½ cups water

4 tablespoons sherry vinegar

⅓ teaspoon cumin seed

4 cloves

½ teaspoon black pepper

2 allspice berries

2 sticks canela (cinnamon sticks may be substituted)

2 bay leaves

2 teaspoons roughly chopped fresh marjoram

1 small bunch cilantro, tied

salt to taste

1 pound 1-inch thick swordfish fillets

juice of 1 lime

Sauté carrot, onion, garlic, and poblano briefly in 2 tablespoons of the olive oil. Set aside. Boil the water, vinegar, spices, herbs, and salt together slowly for 20 minutes. Cool slightly, strain out spices and herbs, and add the sautéed vegetables to the strained liquid. Bring to a boil again. Meanwhile, sear the swordfish in 2 tablespoons of the olive oil until well browned on the outside, but still rare on the inside. Pour hot vegetable souse (marinade) and vegetables over swordfish and let cool to room temperature. Add lime juice and whisk in remaining olive oil. Serve chunks of the swordfish with portions of the vegetables and the souse. This dish can also be served warm as an entrée.

SCALLOP CEVICHE

A wonderful ceviche is a great dish; an ordinary ceviche is something to definitely avoid. For many restaurants, it is an excuse to use fish trimmings or semi-fresh seafood. To make a great ceviche, you must use absolutely fresh seafood. When I make a ceviche at Coyote Cafe, I always try a bit of the raw unmarinated seafood to ensure it is fresh enough.

In a ceviche, the lime juice "cooks" the seafood chemically, preserving it. This technique of pickling fish in the acidic juice of citrus fruit originated in Latin America, but it is not unusual to find it in many other regions, including the American Southwest. This recipe can also be made with halibut, salmon, shark, shrimp, lobster, or oysters — so there's no excuse for not making it!

Yield: 4 servings

½ pound fresh cold-water sea scallops, thinly sliced

¼ cup fresh lime juice

⅓ cup mixed finely diced sweet red and yellow peppers

1 tablespoon pickling juice from canned jalapeños *en escabeche*

1 avocado, peeled and cut into ½-inch cubes

4 red cherry tomatoes, cut in half

4 yellow cherry tomatoes, cut in half

1 serrano chile, minced

2 tablespoons minced cilantro leaves

1 tablespoon extra virgin olive oil

½ teaspoon kosher salt

Put the scallops in a glass, ceramic, or stainless steel bowl. Pour lime juice over scallops and marinate in the refrigerator 30 minutes. Drain. Gently toss the remaining ingredients with the scallops. Serve as is, or with warm tortilla chips.

Note: If using other kinds of fish for this recipe, bear in mind that varieties that are denser, such as salmon, shark, or halibut, require a longer time to marinate. Allow an 1 hour or more for the lime juice to penetrate the fish.

MANILA CLAMS
in Red Chile Broth

I love steamed clams, or "steamers," and whenever I return to New England, I always try to track some down. I can eat almost half a bushel by myself! This recipe satisfies my fondness for clams and my fondness for seafood stews in rich, spicy broths. For this recipe, use good quality dried chiles rather than powder, which is likely to be too dried out and missing the essential oils and flavors. This dish can be used as an appetizer or as a main course in itself.

Yield: 4 servings

48 baby Manila clams

2 cups fresh clam broth (or 1 cup bottled clam juice and 1 cup water)

2 dried New Mexico red chiles, stemmed and seeded

4 tablespoons extra virgin olive oil

4 cloves garlic, roasted and peeled

6 Roma tomatoes, roasted and coarsely chopped

Scrub the clams and set aside. To make the Red Chile Broth, heat clam broth and soak red chiles in broth until limp. Purée in blender. Set aside. In 1 tablespoon of the olive oil, briefly sauté the garlic and tomatoes. Add clams, toss, and add the Red Chile Broth. Cover and let steam until clams open (about 3 minutes). Remove clams and boil up the broth with remaining olive oil for 30 seconds. Serve clams in the broth with Poblano Pesto (see page 15) drizzled over the top, if desired.

SOUTHWEST SPICY STEAK TARTARE

Steak Tartare is a perennial favorite of restaurant people, who often seem to prefer raw, uncooked food as it not only gives their saturated palates a rest, but also gives them respite from cooking smells that serve as a reminder of hot kitchens. At Chez Panisse, we made Steak Tartare from beef that we chopped by hand, capers, and the classic anchovies. This version, which is not hand chopped, is a little bit zingier, and goes particularly well with cold margaritas! For best results, prepare this dish at the last minute. If you must make it ahead, add the lime juice and cilantro just before serving. This dish can also be made with fresh tuna or salmon.

Yield: 4 servings

1 pound very fresh top sirloin

2 to 4 large shallots, very finely chopped

4 to 6 serrano chiles, finely diced

1 bunch cilantro, leaves only, finely chopped

2 to 3 egg yolks

1 tablespoon extra virgin olive oil

kosher salt to taste

freshly ground Tellicherry pepper, to taste

1 teaspoon lime juice, or to taste

lime wedges

blue and yellow tortilla chips

Trim beef of all fat and sinew. Cut the beef into 1-inch cubes and place in the bowl of a food processor. Pulse until meat is finely chopped (be careful not to process so long that the meat becomes like a paste; small chunks of meat should remain). Remove from food processor. Add the shallots, chiles, cilantro, and egg yolks, folding gently to incorporate. Season to taste. Serve with lime wedges and hot tortilla chips. This dish is best prepared at the last minute.

CARPACCIO OF VENISON

Good quality venison, as supplied to Coyote Cafe by the Texas Wild Game Co-operative, does not have an unpleasant over-gamey flavor that many people associate with frozen venison or venison that has not been harvested properly. It has, instead, a satisfactory subtle flavor that includes tones of the wild herbs and bushes that the deer graze on in the open Southwest ranges. Venison is particularly healthy to eat because the animals range in their natural habitat and are not fed additives; the meat is very lean and very low in cholesterol. A carpaccio is thinly sliced raw meat served with a sauce or garnish. This recipe can be made with filet mignon or bottom round of beef if venison is unavailable.

Yield: 4 servings

½ pound venison, inside round

2 to 3 tablespoons light olive oil

16 sheets parchment paper

1 teaspoon medium-hot Chimayo chile powder

1 small fresh ancho chile, seeded, deveined, and finely julienned

kosher salt or sea salt to taste

1 lime cut into 8 wedges (4 for garnish and 4 for squeezing)

thin strips of deep-fried tortilla (¼ x 3 inches)

1 teaspoon roasted pine nuts (optional)

Trim venison of all fat and sinew, and cut into 16 very thin slices across the grain. Oil one side of a piece of parchment and lay a slice of venison on one half. Fold the paper over and gently pound the meat with a flat, heavy veal pounder or rubber mallet. Lay the slice on one of four plates and repeat with remaining venison. When all four plates are covered, sprinkle the carpaccios with the chile powder, ancho strips, and a tiny amount of salt. Sprinkle with freshly squeezed lime juice and garnish with strips of deep-fried tortilla and serve with lime wedges and pine nuts, if desired.

BARBECUED DUCK CAKES

My good friend Larry Forgione is one of the godfathers of American cuisine. He has done much research into our culinary heritage with the purpose of reviving some of the classic American recipes. Larry, whose New York City restaurant is called An American Place, firmly believes — and has proved — that not all good food has to come from Europe, which he refers to as "that other place"! If you're ever in New York, visit An American Place for a great meal. Larry's recipe calls for wild game. In my adaptation, I use roasted domestic duck. The cilantro in the crêpes and the barbecue sauce give it a definite Southwestern orientation.

Yield: Two cakes (8 servings)

2 large eggs

2 tablespoons melted butter

½ cup corn flour (or extra finely ground cornmeal)

1 scant cup milk

1 cup cilantro leaves (no stems)

3 to 4 cups duck meat, roasted medium and finely shredded

2 cups hot, spicy barbecue sauce (use your favorite)

Hot Corn Relish (see page 20)

To make crêpes, combine eggs, butter, corn flour, and milk, whisking until smooth. Let sit for 2 hours. Add half of the cilantro leaves to the batter. Heat crêpe pan and make 10 crêpes, dividing remaining cilantro leaves evenly between crêpes, sprinkling over surface before turning.

You will be making two cakes, so it may help to divide the duck meat in half before you begin. For each cake, place a crêpe dark-side down into a buttered 9-inch cake pan and add some duck meat and barbecue sauce. Top with second crêpe. Repeat for remaining crêpes, making four layers. Cover with foil, parchment, or buttered waxed paper. Make the second cake. Bake at 350° for 20 to 25 minutes. Invert on plates, and cut each cake into four wedges. Garnish perimeter with Hot Corn Relish.

WILD CHANTERELLE SOPES

Masa, the cornmeal dough made from posole, plays a great part in the Southwestern and Tex-Mex culinary tradition. American chefs should work more with this adaptable medium, which can be used so many different ways beyond the tortilla/tamale/quesadilla frontier. Sopes are little boat-shaped shells made of masa. Typically they are filled with salsas, cheeses, refried beans, or shredded chicken or meat and served as appetizers. This recipe combines a flavored masa with a filling of wild mushrooms and a complex chile sauce. I use duck fat because it is so flavorful, but other shortening can be substituted. The garlic, mushroom filling, and sauce can be served without the sopes. The sauce can also be served with roasted chicken.

Yield: 10 servings

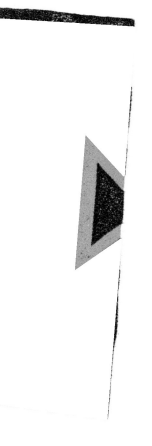

Confit of Garlic

¼ cup duck fat (or lard or cooking oil)

¼ cup hot molido chile powder (or chile caribe)

12 cloves garlic

Guajillo Sauce

8 guajillo chiles soaked, seeded, and stemmed

¼ cup duck fat (or lard or cooking oil)

1 teaspoon Mexican oregano

1 teaspoon cumin seed

1 teaspoon coriander seed

4 tomatoes, roasted

2 tomatillos, roasted

1 white onion, roasted

4 cloves garlic, roasted

2 quarts brown pork stock

salt and sugar, to taste

2 tablespoons peanut oil (or lard)

Filling

½ cup dried cepe mushrooms

2 pounds wild chanterelle mushrooms

2 tablespoons olive oil

6 tablespoons butter

2 cloves garlic, minced

8 guajillo chiles soaked, seeded, and julienned

salt to taste

2 tablespoons minced fresh marjoram

To make the garlic comfit, heat the duck fat and season it with the chile powder, add the garlic and cook over low heat for 1½ to 2 hours. (You can put the garlic and oil in an ovenproof dish and bake it in a 225° oven.) Remove garlic from oil and purée. Set aside.

To make the Guajillo Sauce, fry chiles in duck fat. Roast the oregano, cumin seed, and coriander seed and grind in a spice mill. Simmer chiles and ground spices in stock for 30 minutes or until thickened. Purée and adjust seasoning with salt and sugar. Add oil or lard to a high-sided pan, and heat until almost smoking. Refry sauce at a sizzle for 3 to 5 minutes, stirring continuously.

To make the filling, soak the cepes in 2 cups water for 30 minutes. Remove cepes and set aside. Carefully strain soaking water, measuring out and reserving 1 cup. Skewer chanterelles, brush with olive oil and grill over mesquite until well browned then sauté briefly in butter together with the cepes. Alternatively, skip the grilling step and just sauté mushrooms until browned. Add 2 cloves minced garlic and toss. Sauté 3 more minutes, add Guajillo Sauce, guajillos, and reserved mushroom water. Continue cooking over high heat until sauce thickens. Add salt and marjoram. Spread sopes with puréed garlic and top with mushrooms and Guajillo Sauce.

SOPES

1¼ pounds fresh masa (can be purchased at Latin markets)

½ cup duck fat (or lard or cooking oil)

⅓ cup flour

¾ teaspoon salt

1 teaspoon baking powder

1½ quarts peanut oil

Mix all ingredients except oil and beat until fluffy. Form masa into ¼-cup balls. Using your hands, form each ball into a diamond on waxed paper (diamond should be about 4 x 3 x ⅜-inch thick). Cook diamonds on a hot comal or griddle until lightly browned on each side but still pliable and soft in the middle. Split diamonds in two and pinch up edges of each piece to form a boat. (You may find it easier to roll out thinner diamonds and leave them in one piece.) Just before serving, deep-fry at 350° until brown and crispy, and fill.

HOW THE COYOTE GOT HIS CUNNING

In the beginning, the Sky God called all the animals together, telling them that there was to be a great contest. He asked each animal to make a gift, and declared that whoever made the most worthy gift would win a marvelous prize. Well, the animals were very excited by this, and each set about to make the most worthy gift.

Bear began to weave a blanket of many colors, deciding that the gift of warmth would be the most appreciated. Rabbit chose to work a necklace of semiprecious beads, thinking that surely a gift of beauty was the greatest gift of all. Coyote, however, had another type of gift in mind. He wanted to give the gift of light.

First, however, Coyote needed something in which to catch the light, so he began to make a pot. As the pot spun and then dried in the sun, Coyote danced around it, beside himself with the thought of his foolproof scheme. Next, Coyote painted the pot in shimmering tones of blue. The rim was painted a silvery blue, and gradually the colors deepened, until the base of the pot was exactly the color of midnight. When the pot was ready Coyote looked up to the sky and, seeing that Moon had already risen, began to sing and call to her.

Hearing the faint music of the Coyote's song, Moon bent down a little bit so that she could hear him better. Pretending not to notice Moon, Coyote continued to sing from his heart to woo her. Now Moon was close enough to touch, and before she knew what had happened, Coyote captured her inside his pot, sealing the lid tightly. Moon's radiance shone through the many rings of blue, and Coyote knew that he could not possibly lose the contest.

Smugly now, Coyote waited for dawn and the day of the contest, but the longer he waited, the more he thought morning would never come. Then Coyote heard the silken tones of Moon's voice. She said, "Coyote, Sun cannot come up until she sees me sinking into the sky. If you want tomorrow to come, you must release me." Coyote certainly could see her point, but still he was reluctant to let Moon go, because then he could not possibly win the contest.

Finally, Moon made Coyote a deal. "If you let me go," she coaxed in her silvery voice, "I will give you a prize much better than winning the contest." Intrigued, Coyote asked what this great prize could be. "I will make you the most clever of all the animals. I will give you the gift of cunning." Now Coyote liked the idea of besting the other animals in any way, and in his pleasure at this thought, he quickly unlocked the lid of his pot unleashing Moon's white light into the sky.

The next day, on his way to the contest, Coyote used his new cunning when he passed through a small village. When the village people asked him where he was going, he told them all about the contest. "There will be great gifts to buy and trade there," Coyote said. And all the people agreed that they could not let this opportunity slip by them, so they followed Coyote to what was to become a great market place.

Every year since that first market, the Indians have returned to buy and sell what they believe to be their most worthy treasures. Of course, Coyote takes all the credit, calling this gathering of tribes the market of his cunning. You and I just call it Indian Market.*

*Indian Market is the most festive week of the year in Santa Fe, with visitors coming from far and wide to collect treasures and to enjoy the week's activities. For this occasion, Coyote always cooks up very special meals at the Cafe, featuring the favorite dishes from the year's menus.

CARNITAS RAVIOLIS

Carnitas, small pieces of seasoned cooked pork, are a delicious Mexican snack. The technique of making carnitas gives the pork a texture and taste that cannot be duplicated by any other means. As a filling for ravioli, it keeps its personality, yet is not so heavy as to overwhelm. One of the many good things about Southwestern foods is that it is flavor-intense so you can use small amounts and still make a satisfying dish. The carnitas can also be used in tacos, tamales, empanadas, and poultry stuffings. Believe it or not, I use carnitas to make a Mexican-style pizza. If you prefer, this dish can be served with Poblano Pesto or Pipián Verde (see page 15 and 31), and can be served as an entrée.

Yield: 40 raviolis

Ravioli Dough

1 cup masa harina (or fresh masa)

2 cups high-gluten flour

4 eggs

1 tablespoon water

1 teaspoon kosher salt

Egg Wash

1 egg yolk

1 tablespoon water

Sauce

1½ cups reduced pork stock (or light meat stock)

¼ cup fresh corn kernels

¼ cup mixed diced sweet red and yellow peppers

¼ cup diced roasted and peeled poblano chiles

2 teaspoons minced fresh marjoram

2 teaspoons minced cilantro

3 tablespoons softened butter

Prepare the Carnitas first (see recipe below). Pulse the meat with its fat in a food processor until shredded. (For most other uses, carnitas should be shredded by hand.) Divide into 40 balls and set aside.

Mix all ravioli dough ingredients together in a mixer until a coarse dough is formed. Knead by hand until the dough holds together. Roll dough in a pasta machine until a very thin sheet is formed. Divide into 8 pieces, each about 4 x 10 inches.

To assemble the ravioli, lay out 4 sheets of pasta and lay the balls of carnitas out in a 2 x 5 grid on the pasta sheets. Mix the egg yolk with the water and brush the other four sheets with the egg wash. Lay these sheets over the carnitas, press down between the balls of carnitas, dividing each sheet into 10 raviolis, and cut with a wheel.

To make the sauce, bring pork stock to a boil in a sauté pan. Add corn and cook until stock is reduced by half. Add remaining sauce ingredients and continue to boil briskly until the butter is emulsified. Boil raviolis in 6 quarts of boiling salted water for 3 minutes until al dente. Serve raviolis on the sauce.

CARNITAS

2 pounds pork butt with fat, cut into 1½-inch cubes

2 cups water

3 tablespoons chile caribe

1½ teaspoons kosher salt

4 cloves garlic, roasted, peeled, and chopped

⅓ cup chopped onion

2 cloves

1 teaspoon anise seed

2 teaspoons cumin seed

1 stick canela (or cinnamon)

1 tablespoon Mexican oregano leaves

Put pork, water, chile caribe, salt, garlic, and onion in a heavy saucepan and bring to a slow simmer. Roast spices and oregano in a dry sauté pan over medium heat until fragrant. In a spice mill, grind spices and oregano together to a powder. Add to the pork, and continue to simmer, uncovered, for 1½ hours until tender, adding more water as needed. Increase the heat and cook until all of the liquid evaporates. Reduce heat slightly and continue to cook, stirring until the cubes of meat are a mahogany brown. Let cool.

QUESO FUNDIDO

Queso Fundido is a sort of Mexican cheese fondue. Eating it usually results in long strings of hot cheese that stretch all the way from the dish to wherever your fork happens to be at the time. It's fun to play with, but not to eat. To avoid this stringy mess, use fresh farmer's cheese or goat cheese rather than a stringy mozzarella-type cheese. Goat cheese is especially flavorful. The pumpkin seed pesto adds a crunch and nuttiness to this dish.

Yield: 4 servings

¼ cup green unroasted pumpkin seeds

1 to 2 leaves fresh epazote

1 clove garlic, roasted and peeled

4 tomatillos

1 leaf Romaine lettuce

8 sprigs cilantro

1 small poblano chile roasted, peeled, and seeded

1 tablespoon extra virgin olive oil

¼ cup light brown poultry or veal stock

salt to taste

12 ounces fresh goat cheese (or farmer's cheese or *queso fresco*)

2 tablespoons olive oil

Dry-roast pumpkin seeds in a sauté pan for about 5 minutes until they have finished popping. Combine with epazote, garlic, tomatillos, Romaine, cilantro, poblano, 1 tablespoon extra virgin olive oil, stock, and salt and purée in a blender.

Cut cheese into 4 slices and put a slice in each of four gratin dishes. Brush tops lightly with 2 tablespoons olive oil. Broil until the top is brown and bubbly. Pour pumpkin seed pesto around the cheese and serve with freshly made tortillas or hot tortilla chips. (To make it really colorful, offer a mixture of yellow and blue tortilla chips.)

SQUASH BLOSSOMS

In the summer months, we try to use all local produce, especially indigenous items such as beans, squash, and chiles. We use organic fruits and vegetables grown on nearby Indian reservations such as the Nambé and Tesuque, which are maintaining the agricultural traditions of the Southwest. The best produce we get (and some of it is the best I've seen anywhere) comes from the 450-acre ranch of a good friend of mine, Elizabeth Berry. She lives at the end of a 15-mile ungraded dirt road, and is surrounded by spectacular 1,000-foot red cliffs and meandering streams. One of her specialties is large squash blossoms. Squash blossoms were used extensively in Indian cuisine. In season we use them in soups, quesadillas, and raviolis. One of our favorite dishes is fried squash blossoms. We stuff up to 1,000 a week at Coyote Cafe, and always sell out when they're on the menu.

Yield: 4 servings

1 pound imported Fontina cheese, grated

1 cup sour cream

4 tablespoons minced fresh marjoram

20 squash blossoms with stems and pistils removed

2 eggs

¼ cup water

½ cup all-purpose flour

½ cup cornstarch

1 tablespoon ground cumin seed

1 tablespoon ground coriander seed

1 teaspoon kosher salt

2 tablespoons mild Chimayo chile powder

1 tablespoon ground canela (or 1½ teaspoons cinnamon)

1 quart peanut oil

In a mixer, blend together cheese, sour cream, and marjoram. Put the mixture in a pastry bag with a wide open tip and chill for a few minutes. Stuff the squash blossoms loosely with the cheese mixture. Mix eggs and water until smooth to form an egg wash. Set aside. Sift together flour, cornstarch, cumin, coriander, salt, chile powder, and canela. Individually dip each blossom in the egg wash and then the flour mixture. Deep-fry in peanut oil at 340° until light brown (about 2 minutes). Arrange the blossoms on four plates and serve with Roasted Tomato and Mint Salsa or Pico de Gallo Salsa (see page 13).

MÉRIDA-STYLE OCTOPUS SALAD

One of the ingredients in this salad is coconut milk, which I've seen used this way both in the South Pacific and in Mexico. Coconut milk is available in Thai and Vietnamese markets. (For directions on preparing it yourself, see the glossary.) You can get fresh octopus in Japanese fish markets. Frozen octopus, which works just as well, can be ordered from your local fish market. The mild flesh of the octopus goes really well with the hot chiles and the sweet coconut milk.

Yield: 6 to 8 servings

1½ pounds baby octopus

3 quarts water

3 canned chiles güeros *en escabeche* (or 1 jalapeño *en escabeche*)

1 bunch cilantro, chopped

1 teaspoon roasted anise seed

1 onion, sliced

6 tablespoons coconut milk (or 2 tablespoons coconut cream)

2 tablespoons fresh orange juice

2 tablespoons pickling juice from canned jalapeños *en escabeche*

10 yellow pear tomatoes, halved

10 red pear tomatoes, halved

3 tablespoons minced red onion rinsed under hot water

¼ cup loosely packed cilantro leaves

1 cup peeled orange sections

1 or 2 (or to taste) canned jalapeños *en escabeche*, chopped

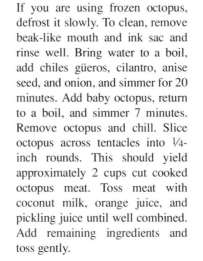

If you are using frozen octopus, defrost it slowly. To clean, remove beak-like mouth and ink sac and rinse well. Bring water to a boil, add chiles güeros, cilantro, anise seed, and onion, and simmer for 20 minutes. Add baby octopus, return to a boil, and simmer 7 minutes. Remove octopus and chill. Slice octopus across tentacles into ¼-inch rounds. This should yield approximately 2 cups cut cooked octopus meat. Toss meat with coconut milk, orange juice, and pickling juice until well combined. Add remaining ingredients and toss gently.

PICKLED SHRIMP AND CORN SALAD

This recipe comes the Gulf Coast of Texas, where the combination of seafood and chiles has a long tradition, as the New Orleans and Cajun cuisines demonstrate so successfully. For best results, marinate the shrimp overnight. If you can't get fresh baby corn, use corn cut off the cob. Canned baby corn is not a good substitute.

Yield: 4 servings

Pickling Liquid

4 cups water

2 cups unseasoned rice vinegar

6 serrano chiles, cut lengthwise

1 bunch cilantro, tied

1 bunch marjoram, tied

2 tablespoons coriander seed

12 allspice berries

5 large cloves garlic, sliced

4 tablespoons sugar

2 teaspoons salt

Salad

2 jalapeño chiles, cut in rings

1 serrano chile, cut in rings

1 sweet red pepper, diced

1 sweet yellow pepper, diced

½ large white onion, diced

18 whole baby corn (or 2 cups fresh corn kernels)

1 pound small shrimp (25 to 30), unpeeled

1 bunch cilantro, tied

1 bunch marjoram, loose sprigs

3 tablespoons extra virgin olive oil

2 heads Bibb lettuce, shredded

To make pickling liquid, place ingredients in a stainless steel or enamel saucepan, and bring to a boil. Lower the heat, cover, and cook for 1 hour. Remove from heat and let cool. Strain through a fine sieve, pressing down on contents to extract liquids. Reserve the liquid and discard the remainder.

To prepare the salad, place chiles, peppers, chiles, onion, and baby corn in a stainless steel or enamel saucepan (if using corn kernels, do not add at this stage as they take less time to cook). Add the pickling liquid and simmer for 10 minutes, until soft. Strain vegetables: reserve liquid and set vegetables aside. Add shrimp to liquid and cook for approximately 4 to 6 minutes; do not overcook. Remove shrimp, reserve liquid and cool in refrigerator. If you are using corn kernels, steam them in ¼ cup water for 1 minute and allow to cool. Mix together vegetables and shrimp (and corn kernels if these are used instead of baby corn), and add cilantro and marjoram. Add the reserved liquid when cool, pushing the herbs well down. Let marinate for 6 to 24 hours. Remove and peel shrimp. Whisk olive oil into liquid mixture. Arrange lettuce on plates; with a slotted spoon, remove vegetables from liquid and arrange on lettuce. Top with shrimp, a little liquid, and cilantro sprigs. Serve with tortilla chips.

SONORA SALAD

This is a salad I invented to refresh the palate on a hot summer day. The citrus, mixed with anise, hot chiles, and garden greens has a miraculous cooling effect. The presentation of the salad is very rustic and country-style, and also very colorful. The Sonora Salad goes well with grilled meats.

Yield: 4 servings

1 teaspoon minced serrano chiles, with seeds

½ cup orange juice

3 tablespoons virgin olive oil

½ teaspoon orange zest

½ teaspoon anise seed, roasted and chopped

1 head Romaine lettuce, inner leaves only

½ head iceberg lettuce, outer leaves discarded, cut into chiffonade

4 poblano chiles, roasted, peeled, and seeded

4 Anaheim chiles, roasted, peeled, and seeded

6 radishes, sliced

1 small red onion, sliced

1 to 2 blood oranges, peeled and sliced

6 red cherry tomatoes, cut in half

6 yellow cherry tomatoes, cut in half

½ cup crumbled fresh goat cheese

½ teaspoon whole anise seed

To make the dressing, combine serrano chiles, orange juice, olive oil, zest, and chopped anise seed. Let stand at least 30 minutes. Toss dressing with remaining salad ingredients except for cheese and whole anise seeds. Arrange salad on plates with greens on bottom, poblano and Anaheim chiles next, then remaining tossed ingredients. Sprinkle the goat cheese and whole anise seed over the top.

LOBSTER AND CORN SALAD

When I was growing up in New England, I used to spend my summers with a lobster fisherman's family in Kennebunkport, Maine. Lobster was everywhere there — for breakfast, lunch, and dinner — but New England clambakes, which included lobster, steamers, and corn on the cob cooked in seaweed at the beach, were a special treat. In Maine I acquired a taste for the combination of fresh lobster and corn. This main course salad gives a Southwestern accent to an old standby.

Yield: 4 servings

2 lobsters, 1¼ to 1½ pounds each

1 teaspoon sugar

1 quart water

12 ears fresh baby corn

¾ cup extra virgin olive oil

juice of 1 lime

1 bunch fresh marjoram, finely chopped

1 head radicchio

3 heads baby oak leaf lettuce

3 to 4 heads Bibb, greenleaf, or baby red lettuce

3 to 4 large poblano chiles, roasted, peeled, seeded, and julienned

2 sweet red peppers, roasted, peeled, seeded, and julienned

2 sweet yellow peppers, roasted, peeled, seeded, and julienned

12 small red and yellow miniature "teardrop" tomatoes, cut in half

8 lime wedges

Steam lobsters, 8 minutes per pound. Cool slightly; remove tail meat but leave claws intact. Add 1 teaspoon sugar to a quart of water and bring to a boil. Blanch baby corn 2 minutes, drain, and cool. To make a dressing, mix olive oil, lime juice, and marjoram together and set aside. Wash the salad greens, dry carefully, and toss lightly in dressing. Arrange on large plate, alternating salad greens for colorful display. Toss corn in dressing very lightly, and arrange on top of greens in spoke fashion around the plate. Arrange chiles and peppers in spokes between the corn. Place lobster claws and lobster slices in center. Garnish with tomatoes and lime wedges, in spokes. Pour extra dressing on top of lobster.

MARK'S CAESAR SALAD

The Caesar Salad was invented in 1926 by Alex-Caesar Cardini in Tijuana, which qualifies it as a legitimate Southwestern recipe. Mark's Caesar Salad was invented in 1979 at the Fourth Street Grill in Berkeley. That Caesar far surpassed all the other salads in popularity. It was definitely a runaway success — customers would run away if they found out it wasn't on the menu that night! We made hundreds and hundreds a week; in fact, in my five years there, I estimate that we produced about 300,000 of my Caesar salads! At Coyote Cafe, we still serve hundreds a week, and each one is made to order. Be sure to use a large bowl: to allow proper tossing it should be less than half full.

Yield: 6 large servings

6 cloves garlic

½ pound butter

1 cup light olive oil

6 cups day-old French bread cut in ¾-inch cubes

6 heads Romaine lettuce, inner leaves only

8 egg yolks

¾ cup shredded dry Parmesan cheese

To make croûtons, purée garlic with butter and olive oil. Heat together until 200° or until just below a simmer. Toss with bread and bake in a 350° oven until lightly browned.

Separate lettuce leaves. In a large bowl, lightly combine egg yolks with the dressing (see below). Toss together with lettuce, half the Parmesan, and croûtons, making sure leaves are thoroughly coated. Arrange leaves on oval plates, sprinkle with remaining cheese and more cracked Lampong pepper.

CAESAR DRESSING

1½ cups light extra virgin olive oil

6 cloves garlic

¼ cup premium anchovies

1 tablespoon Dijon mustard

2 tablespoons fresh lemon juice

2 tablespoons sherry vinegar

cracked Lampong pepper to taste

To make the dressing, blend together the oil and garlic in a food processor. Sieve to press out remaining juice from garlic, and discard the garlic. Cut the anchovies finely, and mix together with the oil and garlic, and the remaining ingredients.

TAMALES

 I remember the first tamales I ever ate. It was some fifteen years ago; I was traveling by bus in Chiapas, in the south of Mexico, and we were waiting at a stop. A woman with a basket of tamales balanced on her head was selling her wares to passengers through the bus window, but, because she was speaking in an Indian dialect, I couldn't understand her. I offered her some money (way too much), but before I could get change, the bus was moving on, so I ended up with the whole basket of tamales. I passed them out among my fellow travelers, and we all ate them among the pigs, goats, and chickens that were also passengers on the bus. I still vividly recall the flavor of those tamales: sweet corn mixed with a strong goat cheese and almost medicinal herbs. Now I always look for these baskets covered with clean colored napkins at bus stations and in the marketplaces. They were true tamales, not the gluey, heavy concoctions that are served in most local Mexican restaurants.

Since then, I've learned a lot about tamales. One of the wonderful things about them is their seemingly infinite variety. In New Mexico we have blue corn tamales stuffed with green chiles or served with a green chile sauce, while in Texas, they're usually made out of yellow corn, and stuffed with beef or pork with red chiles. In Ensenada, in Baja California, tamales are made with fresh corn (grown just for this purpose), red chiles, and olives. In San Miguel, in northern Mexico, I learned to make pastel-colored tamales for dessert. Further south, in the Yucatán, the tamales are wrapped in banana leaves instead of corn husks, giving them quite a different flavor. Another variation is an anise-flavored leaf wrapping, *yerba santa*, which I have seen used for fish tamales.

Tamales are fun food because each one is like a mini-present — you never know what wonderful surprise is waiting for you inside the wrapping. They're great at parties, and are an excellent, inexpensive way to entertain a large number of people — just multiply the recipes, and use your imagination as to fillings. They hold well, so they can be made ahead of time, refrigerated or frozen, thawed, and then steamed as needed. They can also be held in a warmer for hours at a time, if necessary, without compromising their quality. On New Year's Eve, in traditional Santa Fe style, we have a huge bonfire out in the yard, and line the walls with glimmering *farolitos* (paper bags containing candles held in sand). We sit around the fire on the cold clear night and eat delicious warm tamales from a huge pot that never seems to empty as guests come and go.

Forming tamales can be a little time-consuming when done in large numbers (ask the people who helped us make over 1,000 of them in Los Angeles last September at the Meals-on-Wheels Benefit organized by Wolfgang Puck)! But it is a quick enough process to make eight or twelve for a few friends. If you're making them for a crowd, you might want to follow the Mexican custom. There, making tamales is a social event, often a time for family gatherings, where many hands and much conversation turn what could be a tedious task into a brief and lively interlude.

Most of the recipes that follow are designed as main dishes. At Coyote Cafe, we also use tamales as appetizers and desserts, and prepare them with interesting sauces. The demand for them is so great that we have a special tamale on the menu each weekend.

GENERAL INSTRUCTIONS

Traditional recipes for making tamales call for large amounts of lard and very long cooking times — up to two hours or more. I have modified the basic techniques to create lighter, fresher, more flavorful tamales. The most crucial part of the whole process is getting the proper texture of masa, or dough. It should be very moist, fluffy, and light. Although you can do it by hand, the process is much simplified if you have a small mixer with a flat paddle attachment such as a KitchenAid.

Preparing Masa

Some confusion may arise regarding the word "masa," so a word of clarification is in order. Masa harina refers to dried corn that has been ground and treated. It is the basic ingredient used in making the tamale dough, which is also called masa. There is also "fresh masa," an unflavored masa dough that you may be able to get from tortilla factories. Masa harina and fresh masa are both used to make "masa," the tamale dough.

If you are able to get fresh masa, you would mix it with some kind of fat, baking powder, salt, and sometimes stock or sauces, to make a flavored tamale dough. However, since fresh masa is not widely available, most of the recipes in this chapter follow the alternative method, in which dry masa harina is moistened with water, flavored stocks, milk, or sauces and mixed with a spoon or whisk until the masa doesn't stick when pressed with the fingers. Meanwhile, softened room-temperature butter or fat is whisked or beaten at high speed in a mixer, usually together with baking powder and salt, until it becomes light and fluffy. Then the masa mixture is added piece by piece to the butter mixture and beaten until well incorporated, and then the whole is whisked or mixed at high speed for a further 5 to 10 minutes.

The basic proportion is two parts masa harina to one part fat — ounce for ounce, not cup for cup. We give rough volume equivalents for those who do not have kitchen scales, but remember, weight and volume are not always equal. The masa should be tasted and the seasonings adjusted if necessary (keep in mind that the steaming process leaches out some of the flavor intensity). The masa is now ready to use. At Coyote Cafe, we always make one test tamale with the filling, to check the balance of spices. I recommend this procedure as it is difficult to taste raw masa and conceptualize the finished product.

Forming Tamales

Soak corn husks in hot water to cover until they are soft and pliable, about 15 minutes. Separate the larger husks, discarding small or torn ones. Lay out one husk with the top (narrow part) of the husk pointed away from you. Take approximately 2 ounces (or 4 tablespoons) of flavored masa dough with a spatula and spread it in the middle of the corn husk to form a 4-inch square, leaving a border at the edges of the tamale of at least 1 inch. In those recipes that use a filling, place a 1-ounce (or 2-tablespoon) cylinder of filling in the middle of the square. Place fingers under the edges of the tamale and fold one side over the other so the masa dough covers the filling. Roll the husk up completely, but loosely. Fold the top of the husk over and tie it with a thin strip of husk (about 6 inches by ¼ inch) torn from one of your discarded husks. You can create your own style of tying, and use different materials for ties. For example, colored ribbons make an attractive and festive means of securing the tamale, but make sure whatever you use is not soluble. Your Adidas shoelaces will probably not be well received, but a little imagination can make your tamales fun and as high-tech (or low-tech) as you like.

Cooking Tamales

Lay the tamale seam-side down in a steamer. As an alternative to the traditional Mexican tamale steamer you can use a Chinese steamer, obtainable at Oriental grocery stores, a couscous pot, or a collapsible vegetable steamer set in a large saucepan. Steam 30 minutes.

Remember: making the next tamale will be easier! Besides which, forming a tamale takes less time than it does to read this.

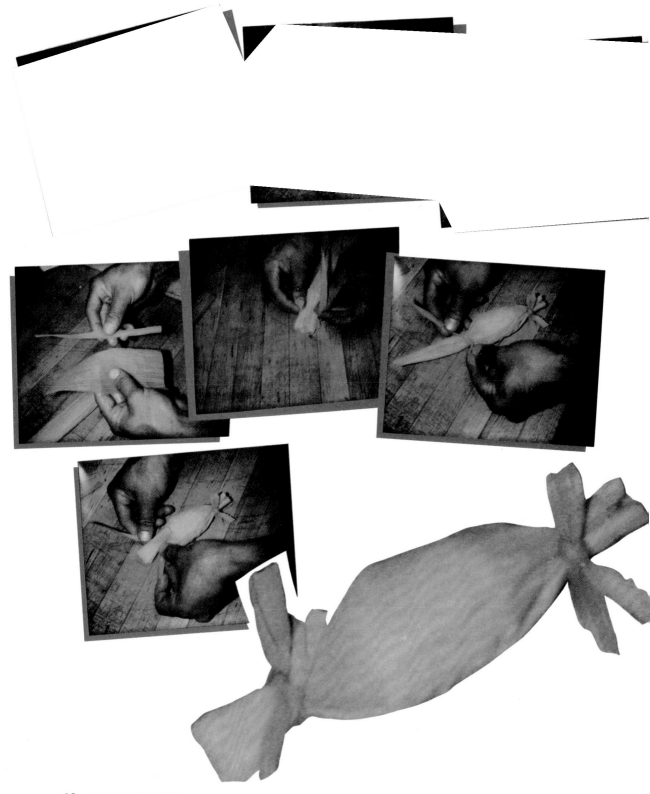

TAMALE DE ELOTE

The tamale de elote, or fresh corn tamale, is the most common tamale of all, and each region has its own particular variation. There is a certain purity about the tamale de elote which exemplifies two underlying philosophies of Southwestern cuisine: that the original flavors should never be hidden, and that the food should not be tinkered with (not too much, anyway!). The corn used in making the tamale should be roasted, while the finished tamale can be steamed and then grilled to give a subtle taste. The tamales can be eaten plain or accompanied by any sauce. You can use this recipe as the basis for your own inventions — fill the tamales with any of a variety of ingredients, such as fresh herbs or sundried tomatoes. In the pages that follow, I give you some of my own variations of this basic tamale.

Yield: 8 tamales

½ cup milk

1¼ cups plus 2 tablespoons roasted fresh corn kernels (1 or 2 ears)

1 cup masa harina

¾ cup plus 2 tablespoons butter, softened

1 teaspoon baking powder

½ teaspoon salt

½ cup (2 to 3) finely diced roasted fresh New Mexico green chiles or poblano chiles

½ cup jack cheese

8 large dried corn husks, soaked in hot water until pliable

In a sauté pan, simmer the milk and corn together over medium heat until the corn becomes soft (about 10 minutes). Strain the corn, reserve 1 cup, and purée the remainder with the milk. Add the purée to the masa harina, and mix with a spoon or whisk. In a large bowl, whip the butter, baking powder, and salt together until light

and fluffy. Incorporate the masa in 2-ounce (4-tablespoon) increments, whisking until light and fluffy (about 10 to 15 minutes total). Fold in the green chile, remaining corn, and cheese.

Divide masa evenly between the corn husks; roll and tie tamales, and steam for 30 minutes (see General Instructions). Let cool slightly and serve.

CHICKEN TAMALE

This is a cantina favorite that comes in handy as there are always pieces of chicken around that need to be used up. The Chicken Tamale is as versatile as the Tamale de Elote, and goes well with just about any flavoring, and almost any sauce. You can create Chicken Tamales with hot Pipián Rojo, or a mole, or wrap it in fresh yerba santa or giant basil leaves to give it a more delicate taste. For a more unusual flavor, use a banana leaf wrapping instead of the corn husk (see next recipe). Unlike other tamales, Chicken Tamales should not be reheated after they have been cooked as the meat gets dry and tough. This recipe goes particularly well with Pico de Gallo Salsa or Tomatillo Salsa (see page 13). Try it also as a mini-tamale (a tamalita), and serve it with salsa as an appetizer at cocktail parties.

Yield: 8 tamales

masa dough as prepared for Tamale de Elote (see preceding recipe)

½ pound boneless chicken meat, skin on

pinch salt

pinch pepper

¼ cup rich chicken stock

2 teaspoons balsamic vinegar

¼ cup chopped green onions

2 heaped tablespoons (about 5 leaves) basil, cut into chiffonade

2 teaspoons minced fresh marjoram

pinch ground Mexican oregano

8 large dried corn husks, soaked in hot water until pliable

Prepare masa dough. Season the chicken meat with salt and pepper, and cook skin-side down in a skillet over medium heat. When skin is brown and crisp, turn chicken over and cook other side. Allow to cool, and then remove and discard skin. Shred chicken (with the grain). Mix chicken, stock, and vinegar together and cook in a sauté pan over low heat until the liquid has been absorbed but the chicken is still moist (about 5 minutes). Fold in green onions and herbs. Let cool slightly. Divide masa and filling evenly between the corn husks; roll and tie tamales, and steam for 30 minutes (see General Instructions). Let cool slightly and serve.

YUCATÁN CHICKEN TAMALE
in Banana Leaves

Banana leaves are commonly used throughout the tropical parts of Mexico. I have spent a lot of time in the Yucatán and have come to enjoy its regional cuisine. Achiote, which is the principal seasoning, is used in many Yucatán specialties. It has a strong iodine-like flavor that may take some getting used to, as it imparts a somewhat bitter note, not unlike Campari. When accompanied by citrus and other fruits, achiote helps create some memorable dishes. In this case, the bright red achiote inside the dark green banana leaf is visually striking. In addition, the leaf wrapping imparts a different flavor to the corn masa than do corn husks. Banana leaves are available in most Thai food stores, and can be kept indefinitely in the freezer. Pass them through a gas flame for a few seconds before use to bring out their aroma.

Yield: 8 tamales

masa dough as prepared for Tamale de Elote (see page 61)

2½ cups chicken stock

5 cloves garlic, roasted, peeled, and puréed

½ teaspoon salt

6 allspice berries, ground

2 teaspoons achiote paste

1 teaspoon medium molido chile powder

1 tablespoon balsamic or sherry vinegar

½ pound boneless chicken breasts, skin on

1 tablespoon olive oil

8 large banana leaves

Prepare masa dough. Mix together the stock, garlic, salt, spices, chile powder, and vinegar. Poach the chicken in the stock mixture over very low heat until half-cooked (about 7 to 8 minutes). Remove chicken. Reduce stock to ⅔ cup and purée. Transfer chicken to a sauté pan and cook in the oil until skin is brown and crisp. Cook on one side only. Allow to cool, and then shred skin and meat (with the grain). Toss the chicken with the reduced puréed stock, return to pan, and cook over low heat until the liquid has been absorbed but the chicken is still moist (about 10 minutes). Let cool slightly. Divide masa and filling evenly between the banana leaves; roll and tie tamales, and steam for 30 minutes. (See General Instructions.) Let cool slightly and serve.

BLACK BEAN TAMALE

Refried black beans, when prepared correctly, are exquisite. They should be glossy and light, and have a wonderful flavor and texture. You can serve them as a side dish with just about anything, and they also make a great tamale stuffing. Once you've tried them this way, you'll never again settle for the dull, cold paste they are served as too often. The combination of beans and corn is one of the oldest in Southwestern cuisine, and is hard to beat. This tamale should be served with simple grilled meats, and can be garnished with different flavored cremas, such as Red Chile Crema or Chipotle Crema (pages 34 or 83).

Yield: 8 tamales

masa dough as prepared for Tamale de Elote (see page 61)

4 ounces bacon (about 4 slices)

3 cloves garlic, roasted, peeled, and chopped

¼ cup coarsely chopped yellow onion

1 cup cooked black beans (see Black Bean Soup, page 32)

1 teaspoon sherry vinegar

½ cup Monterey jack cheese

8 large dried corn husks, soaked in hot water until pliable

Prepare masa dough. Cook bacon in a skillet until crispy. Add garlic and onion and cook over low heat for 5 minutes. Remove bacon, garlic, and onion with a slotted spoon, and purée together with beans and vinegar. Refry purée in the hot bacon fat. Cook over low heat, stirring constantly, until the edge of the purée becomes crusty and easily forms a ball when rolled with a spatula in the pan (about 15 to 20 minutes). Fold in cheese; and allow to cool. Divide masa and filling evenly between the corn husks; roll and tie tamales, and steam for 30 minutes (see General Instructions). Cool slightly. Serve.

MINCEMEAT TAMALE

The idea of a sweet, spicy, meaty dish accompanying the main course is a little foreign to American palates, but it represents the Spanish influence on Southwestern food. At Coyote Cafe, we serve this tamale with grilled free-range chicken, and we've had more than one diner proclaim it as the best tamale they've ever tasted!

Yield: 8 tamales

masa dough as prepared for Tamale de Elote (see page 61)

½ pound Christine's Venison Mincemeat (see page 132)

8 large dried corn husks, soaked in hot water until pliable

Prepare masa dough. Divide masa and mincemeat filling evenly between the corn husks; roll and tie tamales, and steam for 30 minutes (see General Instructions). Let cool slightly and serve.

CARNITAS TAMALE

Pork is the most traditional filling for tamales in central Mexico (beef is more common in northern states such as Sonora and Chihuahua). Pork has more natural moisture than beef, and so makes a good filling for tamales. This recipe provides a useful means of using up ends of loins or other cuts of pork not used for entrées. The flavors of tropical fruit and pork go particularly well together, which is why the Manchamantel Sauce is the perfect accompaniment for this tamale.

Yield: 6 to 8 tamales

½ pound Carnitas (see page 51)

1 cup masa harina

¾ cup plus 1½ tablespoons warm chicken stock

¾ cup softened butter

1 teaspoon baking powder

¾ teaspoon salt

1 teaspoon roasted anise seed

2 teaspoons cayenne pepper

2 teaspoons paprika

6 to 8 large dried corn husks, soaked in hot water until pliable

2 cups Manchamantel Sauce (see page 28)

Prepare the Carnitas and shred the cooked meat by hand. Mix the masa harina and stock together with a spoon or whisk. In a large bowl, whisk together the butter, baking powder, salt, anise, cayenne, and paprika until light and fluffy. Incorporate the masa in 2-ounce (4-tablespoon) increments, whisking until light and fluffy (about 10 to 15 minutes total). Divide masa and carnitas filling evenly between the corn husks; roll and tie tamales, and steam for 30 minutes (see General Instructions). Let cool slightly and serve over Manchamantel Sauce.

CONFIT OF DUCK TAMALE

There tends to be a lot of misunderstanding about exactly what modern Southwestern cuisine is. At Coyote Cafe we employ time-honored methods and ingredients to create new recipes which have a respect for original traditions. In this way, these traditions remain a live art form, rather than existing only in old cookbooks or museums. This recipe is a good example of how traditional European techniques can be applied to Southwestern flavors to create modern Southwestern cuisine.

Duck confit has a rich and hearty flavor and a unique texture. The term "confit" refers to the French technique of cooking and preserving more fatty meats such as duck, goose, or pork. Interestingly, some recipes in old Pueblo Indian cookbooks also refer to preserving game and meat in fats or oils as a means of maintaining a steady supply through the winter. While this recipe may seem a little daunting, it exemplifies the complexity of Southwestern cuisine, and is well worth the effort. The confit must be prepared at least a week in advance. The duck can also be used in soups or pastas, and can also be sautéed or grilled.

Yield: 8 tamales

Confit of Duck (recipe follows)

1¼ cups Mole Rojo (see page 29)

1 cup masa harina

½ cup plus 2 tablespoons duck fat from confit

½ teaspoon salt

8 leaves blanched mustard greens

8 large dried corn husks, soaked in hot water until pliable

Prepare the Confit of Duck. Slowly heat the confit and drain off and reserve the fat. Remove and discard skin from duck legs and cut meat into ½-inch cubes. Mix meat with ½ cup of Mole Rojo. Heat 2 tablespoons reserved confit fat in a skillet and sauté duck meat and mole for 5 minutes, stirring occasionally.

To make the masa, mix the masa harina and the remaining ¾ cup Mole Rojo with a spoon or whisk until consistency is like putty. Beat the remaining seasoned room temperature duck fat with the salt and incorporate the masa in 2-ounce (4-tablespoon) increments, whisking until light and fluffy (about 10 to 15 minutes total).

Divide masa evenly between the corn husks. Place 1 leaf of mustard greens on the masa and the evenly divided duck meat filling on top; roll and tie tamales, and steam for 30 minutes (see General Instructions). Let cool slightly and serve with more Mole Rojo sauce.

CONFIT OF DUCK

4 duck legs

½ teaspoon ground sage

½ teaspoon ground lavender

½ teaspoon ground allspice

½ teaspoon ground canela (or ¼ teaspoon cinnamon)

½ teaspoon ground juniper berries

½ teaspoon ground coriander seed

1 teaspoon kosher salt

2 teaspoons cracked black pepper

¼ cup mild chimayo chile powder

8 cloves garlic

2 cups duck fat

Put the duck legs in a suitable container and distribute the spices, salt, and pepper over them. Let cure uncovered in the refrigerator for 36 hours.

Place duck in a close-fitting crock, add chile powder and garlic, and toss. Melt duck fat and pour it over duck to cover. Place crock uncovered in oven at 250° for 2 to 3 hours, or until duck is pierced without resistance by a wooden skewer. Remove from oven and let cool to room temperature. Cover tightly and refrigerate for 7 to 10 days.

BLUE CORN TAMALE

Since tamales have corn as their base, they marry well with other summer ingredients. This means that one can be very adventurous in adding all kinds of fresh minced herbs to flavor the masa, and can stuff tamales with various kinds of cheeses, vegetables, and sauces to create interesting appetizers or entrées. The speckled appearance of this tamale is particularly attractive, and the herbs exude a wonderful perfume when the tamales are steamed.

Yield: 4 tamales

1 cup blue corn masa harina

½ cup plus 1 tablespoon milk

1 cup plus 1 tablespoon butter, room temperature

½ teaspoon baking powder

¾ teaspoon salt

1 cup cooked white corn kernels

1 tablespoon minced basil

3 tablespoons minced chives

2 tablespoons minced parsley

1 tablespoon minced mint

⅓ cup chopped arugula (or watercress)

4 large dried corn husks, soaked in hot water until pliable

Mix the masa harina and milk together with a spoon or whisk. In a large bowl, whisk together the butter, baking powder, and salt until light and fluffy. Incorporate the masa in 2-ounce (4-tablespoon) increments, whisking until light and fluffy (about 10 to 15 minutes total). Fold in the corn, herbs, and arugula. Divide masa evenly between the corn husks; roll and tie tamales, and steam for 30 minutes. (See General Instructions.) Let cool slightly and serve.

BLUE CORN SHRIMP TAMALE

The subtle flavor of blue corn goes very well with the delicate taste of seafood. This combination may seem unusual, as Santa Fe is so far away from the sea, but the delightful mixture of earthiness and sweet tones is wonderful, surpassed only by the striking appearance of this dish. The yellow wrapper containing the blue corn, and the fresh pink shrimp peeking out through the green sauce is a visual treat.

Dried shrimp in the markets of Mexico City are large and meaty, but they are difficult if not impossible to obtain in Hispanic markets in this country. They can usually be purchased in the refrigerated section of Chinese food stores.

Yield: 8 tamales

Shrimp Butter

¾ cup butter

4 ounces dried Mexican shrimp

3 cloves garlic, roasted and peeled

2 teaspoons roasted ground Mexican oregano

Shrimp Stock

1¼ pounds large fresh shrimp (about 24)

3 to 4 ounces dried Mexican shrimp

⅔ cup shellfish or fish stock

⅔ cup water

1 bunch cilantro

1 white onion, diced

1 stalk celery, diced

1 carrot, peeled and diced

1 cup blue corn masa harina

½ teaspoon sea salt

2 teaspoons medium chile powder

½ teaspoon baking powder

8 large dried corn husks, soaked in hot water until pliable

4 tablespoons Mole Verde (see page 30)

2 tablespoons red radish cut in ⅛-inch dice

2 tablespoons tomatillo cut into ⅛-inch dice

To make Shrimp Butter, melt butter and add remaining ingredients. Simmer over very low heat for 30 minutes. Do not let mixture brown. Purée in a blender and strain through a fine sieve. Allow to cool and solidify.

To make Shrimp Stock, remove shells from fresh shrimp. Reserve the shrimp, and place shells and other stock ingredients in a pan and simmer for 30 minutes. Strain through a fine sieve, pushing hard on ingredients. Reserve broth and discard dried shrimp and shells.

To make masa, whip 4 ounces cool shrimp butter until light and fluffy and set aside. Add 1½ cups hot shrimp stock to masa harina. Stir with a wooden spoon until smooth and slightly fluffy. Cool masa to room temperature. Incorporate the masa into the shrimp butter in 2-ounce (4-tablespoon) increments, whisking until light and fluffy. Whisk in salt, chile powder and baking powder. Set mixture aside.

Divide masa evenly between the corn husks. Place ½ tablespoon of Mole Verde on the masa in each tamale and lay three fresh shrimp on top of the mole. Roll and tie tamales, and steam for 15 minutes. (Don't steam any longer or the shrimp will be hard and dry.) Turn heat off and let tamales sit, covered, for an additional 15 minutes. Mix together the radish and tomatillo and serve with the tamales.

LOBSTER AND SALMON TAMALE

This recipe is a great way to use up the fattier parts of salmon or pieces that are not thick enough to grill. The salmon can be combined as chunks or a puréed mixture. This tamale contains no masa, but the husk imparts a subtle flavor during the steaming process that I find very attractive.

Yield: 8 to 10 tamales

3 ounces lobster meat

9 ounces salmon scraps or belly meat

12 ounces fresh salmon

¾ teaspoon salt

1 egg, beaten

4 tablespoons butter, finely cubed

⅓ cup coarsely chopped cilantro

1 tablespoon finely chopped serrano chile

2 tablespoons heavy cream

8 to 10 large dried corn husks, soaked in hot water until pliable

Parboil the lobster for about 3 minutes, or a little less than half-cooked, and cool. Cut lobster and salmon scraps into ½-inch dice and set aside. Purée 12 ounces salmon with salt and egg in a food processor. In a bowl set over ice and water, mix purée with diced lobster and salmon, butter, cilantro, serrano, and cream. Divide mixture evenly between the corn husks; roll and tie tamales, and steam for 8 minutes (see General Instructions). Let cool slightly and serve with Smoked Tomato and Jalapeño Sauce (page 27) or Green Chile Sauce (page 26).

WHITE TRUFFLE TAMALE

The combination of Parmesan-like cheese mixed with sweet white corn and earthy truffles results in a tamale which commands attention. We presented these tamales at the Robert Mondavi Master Chef Classes in Napa Valley a few years ago, served with roasted Texas black buck antelope and an ancho-cherry sauce, accompanied by a fantastic 1978 Mondavi Reserve Cabernet Sauvignon; they made a big impression! This is not a tamale that you'll find two-for-a-dollar at a roadside stop in Texas! It can be served as an accompaniment to game, roast fowl, or veal.

Yield: 4 tamales

2 ears white corn in the husk

½ cup milk

½ cup chicken stock

4 tablespoons butter

1 teaspoon kosher salt

½ cup white cornmeal

½ cup grated dry jack cheese

4 large dried corn husks, soaked in hot water until pliable

1 white truffle (or more if pocketbook allows!)

Place the unshucked ears of corn directly on the oven rack in a 450° oven and roast for 15 minutes. Let cool, shuck, and cut the corn from the cobs. Meanwhile bring the milk, stock, butter, and salt to a boil. Whisk in the cornmeal and continue stirring with a wooden spoon over low heat for 15 minutes. Remove from heat and stir in cheese and then corn. Adjust seasoning and divide the mixture evenly between the corn husks; roll and tie the tamales, and steam for 10 minutes (see General Instructions). Let cool slightly and open up. Grate white truffle over the tamales and serve.

WILD MOREL
TAMALE

*This tamale has a very intense
wild mushroom flavor. Even
though it may not seem like a traditional dish, it does in fact date
back to pre-Columbian times. My
collection of original recipes from
this era informs me that this one
was used by the Aztec royal court.
While the smoked chile may seem
at first to be too strong compared
to the other ingredients, it successfully complements the earthiness
and sweetness of the morels. These
tamales go very well with roast
beef or grilled saddle of lamb.
Mushroom powder is available in
specialty food shops, or you can
make your own by grinding dried
mushrooms in a spice mill.*

Yield: 4 tamales

1 ear corn in the husk

½ ounce dried morel mushrooms
   (or other wild mushrooms)

¾ cup hot water

3 tablespoons softened butter

1½ tablespoons minced cilantro

3 cloves garlic, roasted, peeled, and
   chopped

6 ounces lard

2 teaspoons kosher salt

¾ teaspoon baking powder

3 teaspoons minced chipotle chiles in
   adobo sauce

1½ tablespoons powdered wild
   mushrooms

12 ounces fresh masa
   (or 6 ounces masa harina mixed
   with ¾ cup chicken stock)

1½ tablespoons olive oil

4 large dried corn husks, soaked in
   hot water until pliable

Place the unshucked ear of corn
directly on the oven rack in a 450°
oven and roast for 15 minutes. Let
cool, shuck, and cut the corn from
the cob. You need 6 tablespoons
kernels. Soak the dried morels in
the hot water. Meanwhile mix the
butter with the cilantro and 2
cloves of the garlic, and set aside.
Whip the lard with 1 teaspoon of
the salt, baking powder, chipotles,
and mushroom powder. Incorporate the masa in 2-ounce (4-table-
spoon) increments, whisking until
light and fluffy (about 10 to 15
minutes total). Fold in the corn.

Drain the morels, carefully straining the liquid, and reserving both
mushrooms and liquid. Pick stems
off mushrooms, clean off any grit,
and chop roughly. Sauté the morels
in the olive oil over medium heat
for 5 minutes. Add the strained
soaking liquid, and the remaining
salt and garlic. Cook over
medium-high heat until all of the
liquid evaporates. Let cool slightly
and mix with the butter mixture.

Divide masa and filling evenly
between the corn husks; roll and
tie tamales, and steam for 30 minutes (see General Instructions). Let
cool slightly and serve.

GOAT CHEESE AND MINT TAMALE

Gary Paul Nabhan in his excellent book, Gathering the Desert, proves that Indians in this region used over 200 wild herbs and spices in their cooking. Wild mint, which grows all over the Southwest, was commonly used by the Pueblo Indians. I am particularly interested in recreating this wide repertoire of older flavors and complex tastes. Mint will add a zing to refried black beans, while mint and goat cheese are a great combination at any time.

Yield: 8 to 10 tamales

8 ounces fresh goat cheese

4 tablespoons mint cut into chiffonade

1 cup masa harina

¾ cup plus 2 tablespoons milk

2 tablespoons extra virgin olive oil

6 tablespoons softened butter

1 teaspoon kosher salt

8 to 10 large dried corn husks, soaked in hot water until pliable

Mix the goat cheese with 2 tablespoons of the mint and set aside. Mix the masa harina and milk together with a spoon or whisk. Combine the olive oil, butter, salt, and the remaining mint and incorporate the masa in 2-ounce (4-tablespoon) increments, whisking until light and fluffy (about 10 or 15 minutes total). Divide the masa evenly between the corn husks; roll and tie the tamales, and steam for 10 minutes (see General Instructions). Let cool slightly and serve.

CURRANT AND CANELA TAMALE

Sweet tamales are a New Mexico tradition. They are prepared for major saints' days and holidays, especially All Souls' Day, on November 2nd — the Day of the Dead — when they are used as offerings for departed spirits. I like sweet tamales not only as a dessert item, but to accompany very spicy dishes, rather like serving chutney with curry. At Coyote Cafe, we serve this tamale with our Red Chile Quail.

Yield: 4 tamales

4 tablespoons butter

4 tablespoons lard

⅓ cup red chile honey (or another spicy honey)

⅛ teaspoon salt

1 teaspoon baking powder

2 tablespoons ground canela (or 1 tablespoon cinnamon)

pinch cayenne pepper

1 cup masa harina

½ cup currants

4 large dried corn husks, soaked in hot water until pliable

Whip butter and lard together until fluffy. Continue whipping while adding the honey, salt, baking powder, canela, and cayenne. While beating, gradually add the masa, and continue to beat until light and fluffy. Fold in the currants. Divide masa evenly between the corn husks; roll and tie the tamales, and steam for 15 minutes or longer (see General Instructions). Let cool slightly and serve.

SWEET BLACKBERRY BLUE CORN TAMALE

Sweet tamales are usually served for dessert. The combination of the corn with fruit and other sweet flavors is a natural and satisfying one. The sweetness of the corn means that less sugar is necessary, a technique also found in Italy, where corn is used as the base for Polenta Cake. This recipe results in a rustic, colorful tamale that will make an unusual and interesting finale to any dinner party. The praline paste is available at French bakeries.

Yield: 8 tamales

¾ cups strained blackberry purée

¼ cup water

½ cup sugar plus 2 tablespoons sugar

½ tablespoon molasses

1 cup blue corn masa harina

2 tablespoons butter

½ teaspoon fresh lemon juice

2 tablespoons praline paste

4 tablespoons chopped roasted pecans

¾ cup sour cream

¼ cup heavy cream

1 teaspoon vanilla extract

1 tablespoon cognac

2 cups fresh blackberries

8 large dried corn husks, soaked in hot water until pliable

Bring the purée, water, ½ cup sugar, and molasses to a boil. Whisk in the masa harina and stir over low heat for 10 minutes. Stir in the butter and the lemon juice. Divide masa evenly between the corn husks. Mix the praline paste and the pecans together and place ¾ tablespoon on top of the masa in each tamale. Roll and tie the tamales, and steam for 10 minutes (see General Instructions). Meanwhile, whip sour cream, heavy cream, remaining sugar, vanilla, and cognac together until it forms very soft peaks. Let tamales cool slightly, open them up, garnish with blackberries and the cream mixture, and serve.

SEAFOOD & FISH

Seafood in the high desert? Or where around Santa Fe did you catch that salmon? Modern times have made it very easy for us to use seafood. Air transportation and expert packing mean that the same fish I would have received in my Bay Area restaurants is only three or four hours older when it arrives in Santa Fe, and sometimes my Gulf Coast seafood is even fresher. In fact, many people say that our oysters are the best they've ever eaten.

Still, I am often asked why we do so many dishes with seafood when it is obviously not a native product. Well, aside from the fact that the seafood dishes at Coyote Cafe are very popular, there are also a number of personal reasons why we feature them at the restaurant. First of all, I grew up in New England and in the summers lived on the Maine coast with a lobster fisherman's family in Kennebunkport, and then later spent time in Wellfleet on Cape Cod. I enjoyed seafood as a youngster, and love it still, though now, I'd spice up those steamers with some chiles.

My travels have had a great effect on me. I've spent a lot of time in the coastal areas of Latin America — particularly the Yucatán peninsula in Mexico, where the mixture of seafood with chiles and spices has been taken to new heights. I have also traveled in Thailand and other parts of Southeast

Asia where chiles and seafood always go together. And in Morocco I've enjoyed grilled sardines and crab with fresh-cut chiles and onions. So, now that we have the means, it seems only natural to bring seafood to a region where chiles form such an integral part of the culinary tradition.

For me, Southwestern spices and chiles go particularly well with seafood because they act as a foil against the richness. On the other hand, very delicate seafood, or varieties of fish that have a rather bland taste, can be livened up by spices and chiles. Occasionally, people ask, "Doesn't the flavor of the lobster or sole get lost in the heat of all those chiles and spices?" This is where the skill of the chef comes in. You must try to create a balance of flavors that enhance rather than detract from the starring role of the main ingredient. You have to find that point where the spices do not overwhelm but instead create accents to form more interesting combinations. You should strive to use very fresh spices with a light (but not *too* light) hand.

Fresh raw (or cooked) fish and shellfish are complemented perfectly by freshly-made salsas. Salsas made with chiles, cilantro, or ripe tropical fruit heighten the fresh, simple, clean flavors yielded by perfect seafood. These salsas do not mask the seafood or make it "heavier" at all.

RED CHILE PESTO CLAMS

The flavor of red chiles goes well with fresh clams, and highlights their clean taste. You can use double the number of ancho chiles if New Mexico chiles are unavailable. The pine nuts that go into the pesto are indigenous to the Southwest, and are an important part of the cuisine. This dish can also be served as a thick soup or as a sauce over pasta.

Yield: 4 servings

5 dozen clams

12 dried ancho chiles

12 dried New Mexico red chiles

½ cup pine nuts

10 large cloves garlic, roasted and peeled

2 tablespoons fresh oregano (or 2 teaspoons roasted Mexican oregano)

¼ cup extra virgin olive oil

zest of 2 lemons

juice of 2 limes

5 cups fish stock (or clam juice)

12 sprigs coriander

Scrub clams and discard any open ones. Clams that have a strong odor or are heavy (indicating that shells contain sand) are likely to be dead and should also be discarded. Preheat oven to 350°. Roast the dried chiles in a large skillet over medium-high heat for 4 to 5 minutes, turning frequently to avoid burning. Remove stems and seeds and place chiles in a large bowl. Pour boiling water over them, cover, and let sit until they are very soft, about 40 minutes. Roast the pine nuts in the oven for about 8 minutes until golden, stirring occasionally. Place chiles, roasted garlic, lemon zest, and oregano in food processor or blender and purée until smooth. Add olive oil and blend thoroughly. Add pine nuts and process until coarsely chopped. Season to taste with the fresh lime juice.

Place clams in a large pan over medium-high heat with the fish stock. When the clams open, remove from cooking liquid. Reduce liquid by half, then whisk in the chile pesto. To serve, divide clams evenly between four soup bowls, pour the pesto mixture over them, and garnish with coriander leaves. Serve immediately.

RED CHILE RISOTTO CLAMS

I had many inspirations for the creation of this dish — the great seafood paellas of Spain, fragrant saffron rices, Italian risotto, and New Mexican Red Chile Rice, which is often served with "combination plates." Accompanied by a salad, this makes a wonderful, easy-to-prepare dinner. The quality of the chiles is particularly important in this recipe, and only very fresh chile powder should be used: old or stale chile powder will give a dull and dusty flavor (see glossary for notes on buying chile powder). The smallest hardshell clams, such as Manilas or Eastern Littlenecks, work best as there is more clam meat per pound with these varieties. Use Italian arborio rice; it is generally available from specialty grocery stores. The technique of adding the liquid in gradual increments prevents the rice from becoming too mushy. As you cook the risotto, you must keep stirring it all the while.

Yield: 4 servings

5 dozen small clams (about 4 pounds)

6 large cloves garlic, sliced

6 stems fresh parsley

4 cups water

1 cup white wine

6 to 7 cups clam juice (or fish stock)

½ cup finely diced white onion

7 tablespoons butter

2½ cups arborio rice

4 teaspoons very finely minced garlic

4 tablespoons chopped Roma tomatoes

2 tablespoons hot New Mexico chile powder (or medium molido and cayenne mixed)

4 tablespoons diced sweet red pepper

4 tablespoons diced sweet yellow pepper

6 tablespoons finely ground fresh imported Parmesan cheese

2 teaspoons finely chopped fresh parsley

Scrub clams and discard any dead ones (see recipe above). In a wide-bottomed stainless steel or enamel pan, place the sliced garlic, parsley, 4 cups of water, wine, and the clams in a single layer. Cover, bring to a boil, and then simmer over low heat until the clams open up, no more than 4 to 5 minutes. Turn heat off and let sit for a further 5 to 10 minutes. Remove clams from broth and extract meat from shells. Open any clam shells that remain closed with a knife over a separate bowl, in case any are bad. Allow broth to cool, remove garlic and parsley, and strain if necessary to remove sand or other foreign particles. Combine the broth with enough clam juice to equal 11 cups liquid, and keep warm.

Sauté onion with 3 tablespoons butter over medium heat in a large pan until soft, about 15 minutes. Add rice and cook for 5 minutes over medium-low heat, stirring constantly (cooking any longer will make the rice tough). Add half the hot broth in ½-cup increments, stirring continuously. This should be absorbed after about 10 minutes or so. At this stage, the rice should be about half-cooked. (If preparing this dish ahead of time, stop at this point and lay out the rice on a long, flat sheet pan to prevent it gumming together.)

Add the minced garlic, tomatoes, and chile powder, and continue stirring and cooking over medium heat for 10 minutes. Then add a further 2-½ cups hot broth in ½-cup increments. Add the peppers, and incorporate the remaining broth in ¼- cup increments and allow to absorb for about 8 to 10 minutes. Add the clams just long enough to warm them through. Remove pan from heat, stir in the remaining butter and cheese, and garnish with parsley sprinkled on top.

CURRIED OYSTERS
with Banana Salsa

I once tried a dish similar to this one in Martinique, a French territory in the Caribbean. The people of the island speak French, and the style of cooking there has a decided French flair mixed with Creole cuisine. Here a classic sauce is spiced with curry and combined with a tropical salsa to give the oysters an unusual and exciting twist. The fish fumet produces a flavorful stock that provides the base for the sauce. It can be used to prepare other sauces for seafood.

Yield: 4 servings

4 tablespoons good-quality curry powder

4 tablespoons melted butter

2 tablespoons minced shallots

2 cloves garlic, blanched and puréed

2 cups Fish Fumet (recipe follows)

2 cups heavy cream

juice of 1 lime

salt to taste

20 large Wellfleet oysters

Banana Salsa (recipe follows)

In a heavy skillet, sauté the curry powder in the butter until fragrant. Stir in the shallots and garlic, and add the fumet. Reduce the mixture until ¼ cup remains. Whisk in the cream and continue reducing until slightly thick. Whisk in lime juice and salt.

Broil or grill the oysters over pecan or mesquite until they open. Remove top shell, pour curry sauce over them and top with Banana Salsa.

FISH FUMET

2 pounds whitefish trimmings

1 cup sliced mushrooms

1 small carrot, chopped

1 medium white onion, sliced thin

1 cup oyster liquor

1 cup white wine

4 cups water

1 bay leaf

1 teaspoon peppercorns

½ teaspoon fennel seed

2 sprigs parsley

1 teaspoon minced fresh thyme

Combine all the fumet ingredients together in a large pan and bring to a boil. Lower heat and simmer for 40 minutes. Remove from heat and let sit a further 30 minutes. Strain and reserve liquid.

BANANA SALSA

4 ripe red bananas cut into ¼-inch dice

2 teaspoons minced serrano chiles

2 teaspoons palm oil (or corn oil)

2 tablespoons fresh lime juice

2 tablespoons minced cilantro

2 teaspoons minced mint

2 tablespoons tamarind paste

½ cup sweet red pepper cut into ¼-inch dice

Mix all the salsa ingredients together and chill.

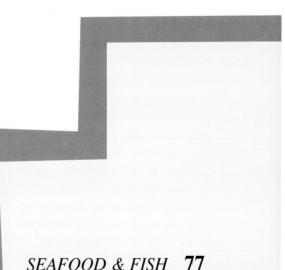

CHIPOTLE MUSSELS
with Orange Mayonnaise

I am very fond of this combination of ingredients; the flavor of chipotle is a perennial favorite and goes particularly well with orange. My friend, Dean Fearing, the Executive Chef at The Mansion on Turtle Creek in Dallas, was especially partial to this dish when we served it at the opening party for Coyote Cafe in March 1987. Mussels should be carefully washed and cleaned; one bad mussel will spoil the lot. You can test for dead ones by placing your thumb and forefinger on each side of the shell and pushing in opposite directions; if the mussel is dead, the shell will give and come apart. Remove the beard with a paring knife, and if you are storing the mussels on ice, allow them to drain, otherwise the fresh water will kill them.

Yield: 4 servings

4 pounds fresh mussels, washed (about 50)

3 tablespoons thinly sliced garlic

zest of 2 oranges, cut into long strips

4 tablespoons canned chipotle chiles, puréed

4 cups water (or light fish broth)

3 tablespoons olive oil

4 tablespoons fresh orange juice

12 sprigs cilantro

Orange Mayonnaise (recipe follows)

To prepare the mussels, place in a large pot together with the garlic, orange zest, chipotle, and water. Cover, bring to a boil, and steam for 4 minutes. Remove pan from heat and let sit for 5 minutes; mussels should then be open. Remove mussels and keep covered in a warm place. Reduce liquid by half and add oil and orange juice. Divide mussels on the half-shell evenly between soup plates, and add the broth. Garnish each bowl with 1 tablespoon of Orange Mayonnaise and 3 sprigs of cilantro.

ORANGE MAYONNAISE

1 extra large egg yolk, room temperature

1 cup virgin olive oil

1 tablespoon orange zest, very finely chopped

4 tablespoons fresh orange juice

1 tablespoon fresh lime juice

2 tablespoons finely chopped cilantro

Beat the egg yolk in a glass or stainless steel bowl until a light lemon color. Transfer to a blender, and add the oil, drop by drop for the first 1/4 cup, and the remainder in a slow steady stream, mixing at high speed until emulsified. Add the remaining ingredients and blend together. Let sit for at least 1 hour to allow the orange flavor to develop.

LOBSTER ENCHILADAS

This is one of the trademark dishes of Coyote Cafe. We usually serve it on special occasions such as New Year's Eve or during Indian Market Week. This dish may seem a little contradictory: lobster is usually thought of as rare and refined, while enchiladas have the opposite reputation. However, this recipe shows just how elegant an enchilada can be! This is a very rich dish, which goes perfectly with an older, fuller Chardonnay. The crêpe batter makes eight crêpes; only four are needed for the enchiladas, so use the remaining four with scrambled eggs the next morning. You can make the various components of this dish ahead of time: final assembly will just take 5 or 10 minutes.

Yield: 4 servings

Lobster Sauce

2 lobsters, 1¼ pounds each

4 cups lightly salted water

1 onion, chopped

1 carrot, chopped

4 sticks celery, chopped

6 peppercorns

3 allspice berries

1 teaspoon coriander seed

6 sprigs parsley

¼ pound mushrooms, chopped

4 tomatoes, diced

½ cup tomato purée

Filling

6 tablespoons fresh corn kernels

reserved lobster meat

3 tablespoons butter

1 cup reserved lobster sauce

6 tablespoons tomatoes, peeled, seeded, and diced

1 tablespoon finely minced cilantro

3 drops habanero sauce (or Louisiana hot sauce)

salt to taste

1 cup combined poblano chiles and sweet red and yellow peppers, roasted, peeled, and julienned

6 tablespoons cooked black beans, drained (see Black Bean Soup, page 32)

8 sprigs cilantro

4 lime wedges

1 sweet red pepper, julienned

4 Guajillo Crêpes (recipe follows)

Red Chile Mayonnaise (recipe follows)

To make the sauce, boil lobsters in the water for 4 minutes. Remove lobsters and reserve the water. When cool, remove lobster meat. Slice tail meat, but keep the claw meat whole, and set aside, saving shells. Add to the water the onion, carrot, 1 stick of celery, peppercorns, allspice, coriander, and parsley. Simmer for 30 minutes and strain; reserve liquid and vegetables. Add to the liquid the lobster shells, mushrooms, tomatoes, tomato purée, and remaining celery, and simmer for 20 minutes. Remove and discard lobster shells. Purée liquid and reserved vegetables in blender and pass through a strainer. Return to pan and reduce over high heat until thickened. Set aside.

To prepare the filling, smoke the corn lightly, 20 to 25 minutes. Sauté the reserved lobster meat in butter until barely warm. Add the lobster sauce, tomatoes, poblanos, peppers, beans, corn, cilantro, habenero, and salt. Divide lobster meat, and about half of the sauce, evenly between the crêpes. Fold crêpes over to form a cone. Arrange the remaining half of the sauce and vegetables around the crêpes. Using a plastic ketchup squirt bottle or small pastry tube, pipe 2 tablespoons of the Red Chile Mayonnaise in a Southwestern zig-zag pattern on each crêpe. Garnish with cilantro, lime wedges, and red pepper strips.

GUAJILLO CRÊPES

⅓ cup flour

1 tablespoon ground roasted guajillo chiles (or ½ tablespoon each paprika and cayenne)

3 eggs

1 cup beer

3 tablespoons oil

To make the crêpes, mix all the ingredients until smooth, then allow to set for 1 hour. Heat a small frying pan and grease it with a few drops of oil. Pour in just enough batter to cover the pan with a very thin layer, tilting pan so that the mixture spreads evenly. When cooked on one side, toss or turn with a spatula and cook on other side. Repeat process, stacking the cooked crêpes between sheets of waxed paper to keep them from sticking together.

RED CHILE MAYONNAISE

2 egg yolks

½ cup peanut oil

½ cup virgin olive oil

1 tablespoon sherry vinegar

1 tablespoon fresh lime juice

4 tablespoons dried New Mexico red chiles, soaked, puréed, and strained

In a blender or food processor pulse the yolks until light and frothy, then add the oil drop by drop until the mixture becomes very, very thick. After all the oil has emulsified, blend in remaining ingredients.

LOBSTER AND SCALLOPS
with Vanilla in Corn Husks

This recipe, which is one of the most requested dishes at Coyote Cafe, originates from the Gulf Coast area where seafood is cooked in corn husks to impart a complementary flavor. The vanilla perfectly balances the natural sweetness of the lobster and scallops. Grilling the corn husks adds an interesting, slightly smoky taste. This dish should be served with a semi-spicy rice, and goes well with a fruity, high-acid white wine such as a good Gewürztraminer.

Yield: 4 servings

1 cup butter

1 teaspoon ground vanilla bean

1 teaspoon vanilla extract

5 cups lightly salted water

2 lobsters, 1½ pounds each

¾ pound scallops

½ cup cooked corn kernels

8 large corn husks soaked in hot water until pliable

16 leaves basil cut into chiffonade

Cream together the butter and vanilla bean and extract. Parboil the lobster in the water until three-quarters done (allow about 5 to 6 minutes per pound of lobster meat). Cool, remove meat, and slice it. Divide scallops lobster, and corn evenly between corn husks and top with 2 tablespoons of the creamed butter. Roll and tie the corn husks (see page 59 for instructions). Grill over pecan or fruit wood until cooked (about 6 to 8 minutes), being careful not to let butter leak out. Garnish with basil leaves, if desired.

TEXAS BLUE CRAB CAKES

The best crab cakes are those that are made almost entirely of crab and have very little filler. This dish, which is very light, is a favorite at special events and during the Gulf crab season, between May and September. At Coyote Cafe, we get the crab flown in fresh from the fishing boats in Galveston, and we use 100 pounds of crab meat over a weekend. If you can't get Texas blue crab, substitute other types of crab meat.

Yield: 4 servings

⅓ cup thinly sliced green onions (green part only)

1 cup plus 2 tablespoons clarified butter

1 pound fresh Texas blue crab lump meat

2 tablespoons diced sweet red pepper

2 tablespoons diced sweet yellow pepper

1 large egg

1 pound fresh white bread (high-quality country loaf)

2 tablespoons heavy cream

1½ teaspoons chopped fresh marjoram

Wilt the green onions in 2 tablespoons of the butter, about 1 minute. Place crab meat in a bowl, breaking up any lumps and removing any bits of shell or cartilage. Add the cooled green onions and the peppers. Beat the egg. Remove bread crust and make bread crumbs of the bread. Add the egg, ½ cup bread crumbs, cream, and marjoram to the bowl, and mix together by hand. Form into 8 patties, about ¾-inch thick and 2½-inches across. Lightly press more bread crumbs onto each side of the patties, and refrigerate if not cooking immediately. To cook, heat remaining butter in a large, heavy sauté pan, so that crab cakes sizzle when put in pan. Cook at lowest setting for 4 minutes on one side and 3 minutes on the other. Crab cakes should be golden but not brown. Serve with Green Chile Chutney (see page 20), or Smoked Tomato and Jalapeño Sauce (see page 27).

SPICY SOFT-SHELL CRAB
with Minted Tamarind Chipotle Sauce

Soft-shell crab is native to Louisiana and Maryland. It is now being raised on the Texas Gulf Coast, so it's a delicacy that's available here in season, which runs from May through early August. When buying the crabs, make sure they look lively. Feel the shell; if it seems at all hard, try another one. Clean the crab carefully and remove the gills, preferably with scissors, as this minimizes the amount of liquid given off. The richness of the crab is foiled very well by spicy sauces and flavors.

Yield: 8 servings

1 cup butter

2 bunches fresh mint, julienned

3 cups Tamarind Chipotle Sauce (see page 27)

3 eggs

1 ½ cups milk

½ cup all-purpose flour

2 tablespoons ground cumin

2 tablespoons ground coriander

2 teaspoons powdered dried jalapeño chile

8 jumbo soft-shell crabs (4 to 5 ounces each)

1 cup clarified butter

8 lime wedges

Melt 1 cup butter in small saucepan. Reserve 8 sprigs mint for garnish, and roughly chop the rest.

Add mint to butter and cook covered over very low heat for 30 minutes. Strain out and discard mint. Whisk flavored butter into Tamarind Chipotle Sauce.

Beat together the eggs and milk. Combine the flour, cumin, coriander, and chile. Dip the crabs in the egg wash, then in seasoned flour. Heat half the clarified butter in a large sauté pan. Cook 4 crabs at a time over low heat, 5 minutes each side (less if the crabs are small). Strain butter off and repeat. Place about 6 tablespoons of sauce on each plate, topped by the crab. Serve with a lime wedge and a sprig of mint.

SCALLOP HASH

The idea for this recipe came to me on the weekend of my 35th birthday (it seems like an awfully long time ago now!). I had enjoyed my friend Larry Forgione's scallop hash at his former restaurant, The River Cafe, and I vividly recall looking out over the New York skyline on that bright, blustery February morning and later, walking back across the Brooklyn Bridge, mulling over this dish. My version uses fresh scallops instead of the traditional corned beef: shrimp or lobster could be used as an alternative. Serve it as an entrée, or as an appetizer.

Yield: 4 servings

1 pound fresh sea scallops

2 eggs

2½ tablespoons heavy cream

1 teaspoon salt

⅓ cup finely diced sweet red pepper

2 tablespoons plus ½ cup clarified butter

⅓ cup finely chopped green onion (green and white parts)

2 teaspoons minced serrano chile

2 teaspoons chopped fresh marjoram (optional)

1 teaspoon fresh lime juice

1 cup parboiled, peeled, and grated red potato

2 cups Smoked Tomato and Jalapeño Sauce (see page 27)

1 cup Pico de Gallo Salsa (see page 13)

Purée ¾ pound scallops with the eggs, cream, and salt. Dice the remaining scallops and set aside. Sauté the pepper with 2 tablespoons butter for 2 minutes over medium heat. Add the green onion and sauté for a further minute. Remove from heat, cool, and add to the puréed scallops. Then add serranos, marjoram, lime juice, and the remaining diced scallops. Rinse the potatoes, which should be soft but not mushy, under cold water, and squeeze out excess water. Add to the scallops, and mix well. Form into 8 patties about 3 inches by ½ inch thick, and brush with butter. Brush a heavy-bottomed pan or griddle with butter and cook the scallop cakes over low heat 5 to 6 minutes per side plus an additional 5 minutes; check that the center is cooked. Place Smoked Tomato and Jalapeño Sauce on top of scallop cakes and garnish with Pico de Gallo Salsa.

SHRIMP BROCHETTE
with Wild Boar Bacon

Smoked meat, especially pork, complements seafood particularly well. The combination of the two is a standard feature of the cuisines of Southern Europe (the paellas of Spain are a prime example). Wild boar bacon is a native Southwestern specialty. This dish is rounded out nicely with Red Chile Rice and grilled vegetables.

Yield: 6 to 8 servings

2 pounds medium or large shrimp, peeled and deveined

¼ pound wild boar bacon (or Amador, Smithfield, or Harrington's corn cob smoked bacon), cut paper thin

1 sweet red pepper, cut into 1 x ½-inch strips

1 sweet yellow pepper, cut into 1 x ½-inch strips

1 cup Tamarind Chipotle Sauce (see page 27)

Wrap each shrimp in a very thin piece of bacon. Skewer the shrimp and peppers, alternating colors. Brush the brochettes with the sauce and grill or barbecue over a hot flame, basting frequently until the shrimp are cooked, about 4 to 5 minutes. Pour 1 tablespoon sauce over each brochette and serve.

PAILLARD OF SALMON
with Squash Salsa and Chipotle Crema

The idea of using smoked chiles first occurred to me at around the time I was opening the Santa Fe Bar and Grill in Berkeley in 1980. I had been traveling in the Yucatán, especially around Isla Mujeres north of Cancún, and the combinations of seafood and smoked chiles (especially the turtle meat with smoked chile sauce at the Casablanca Bar) were enough to convince me! I first used this crema at a wine-tasting dinner held at the Fourth Street Grill, and used it to accompany poached scallops, fresh lobster, and other seafood. Later, we tried the leftover crema with salmon in the kitchen, and, lo and behold, a no-fail combination was born! Make sure the Chipotle Crema is not too spicy, or else it might overwhelm the salmon. A great accompaniment for this dish is the Blue Corn Black Bean Relleno (see page 154). A paillard is a very thin piece of meat or fish.

Yield: 4 servings

4 salmon paillards (preferably Pacific salmon), about 7 ounces each, 4 x 6 x ½ inch thick

1 teaspoon fine sea salt

1 cup Squash Salsa (see page 19)

2 cups Chipotle Crema (recipe follows)

2 tablespoons canned chipotle chiles in adobo sauce, puréed

In a large nonstick sauté pan, lightly salt salmon and cook until brown and crispy, but still moist, about 2 to 3 minutes per side. Salmon should be rare to medium rare inside.

Spread ½ cup Chipotle Crema on each plate, and place the salmon in the middle. Draw a zig-zag design in the crema with the puréed chipotle. Put ¼ cup of Squash Salsa on top of each paillard of salmon, and serve immediately.

CHIPOTLE CREMA

2 cups Mexican Crema (see page 35)

1 clove garlic, roasted and peeled

2 tablespoons canned chipotle chiles in adobo sauce

Purée crema with garlic and chipotle (for a milder sauce, use less chipotle). Leave at room temperature

SALMON FILLET
with Black Bean Corn Salsa

Pacific king salmon is the variety we use at Coyote Cafe for this recipe; it has a darker color and stronger flavor than other types. Otherwise, domestic Northwestern farmed salmon is the best alternative. Red chile honey is a specialty of the Taos area in northern New Mexico; it is made with the honey of wild flowers mixed with New Mexican chile. See Glossary for notes on making your own.

Yield: 4 servings

4 salmon fillets, 8 ounces each
sea salt to taste
8 tablespoons red chile honey
Black Bean Corn Salsa (see page 16)

Preheat oven to 450°. Lightly salt both sides of each fillet. In a large sauté pan or oven pan placed in the oven, sear the fillet for 2 minutes on one side. Before turning over, brush each fillet with 1 tablespoon of honey on the uppermost side. Then cook the other side for 5 minutes, and brush the tops with another tablespoon of honey. Place a serving of Black Bean Corn Salsa on each plate, top with the salmon, and serve immediately.

BROOK TROUT
with Blue Cornmeal, Raisins, and Pine Nuts

Ideally, you would get up before sunrise and head out to the Pecos Wilderness or the Jemez Mountains, and watch the morning light over the lakes and streams. You'd cast out, and the bubbles from the rising trout would ripple out over the peaceful water. As you wait for that ever so slight pull on the line, you look forward to frying up a breakfast of cutthroat, German brown, or rainbow trout and a day's relaxation. . . . The next best method is to head on down to the nearest fishmonger that sells live farm trout. This may be less exhilarating, but the best results are gained from cooking fish just hours out of the water. The Indians of the Southwest have been fishing for trout for thousands of years, and enjoying the flavor of this native food. In fact, the trout appears as a symbol on Mimbres pottery and in ancient petroglyphs, confirming its historical significance.

Yield: 4 servings

BLUE CORN TROUT
with Crab and Green Chiles

4 tablespoons pine nuts

1 cup blue cornmeal

1 teaspoon kosher salt

¼ cup Chimayo chile powder

1 egg

1 cup milk

4 fresh trout, about ¾ pound each

¼ cup clarified butter

¼ cup corn oil

1 small sweet onion, finely diced

3 slices wild boar bacon (or Amador, Smithfield, or Harrington's corn cob smoked bacon), cut into ½-inch dice

4 tablespoons raisins

3 tablespoons balsamic vinegar

Roast the pine nuts for 5 to 7 minutes in a 350° oven and set aside. Combine the cornmeal, salt, and chile powder. Beat together the egg and milk. Dip trout in the egg wash, then in seasoned cornmeal. In a large sauté pan, heat the butter and oil, cook the trout over medium heat for about 4 minutes each side, and set aside. Sauté the onion with the bacon until the bacon colors slightly. Remove from heat and add the raisins and then the vinegar. Return to the heat and boil until the vinegar is reduced by half. Pour the mixture over the trout, sprinkle the roasted pine nuts on top, and serve.

Many anglers — and chefs — have trout stories, and I'm no exception! I was taking a week's horseback riding trip through the Gila Wilderness in southern New Mexico, led by a couple of tough old wranglers. We only came across two other people the whole time. One evening, I fixed a meal of freshly caught trout stuffed with wild porcini mushrooms, which I had picked in the woods. I'll never forget those leathery cowboys who told tales of rustling cattle on the White Sands missile ranges, but were afraid to eat wild mushrooms! This Southwestern trout dish has no mushrooms, but it does feature two more common native foods, blue corn and green chiles. Even tough old cowboys will enjoy this one!

Yield: 4 servings

12 roasted green chiles, peeled, seeded, and chopped (about 1 cup)

1 pound fresh crab meat

4 fresh trout, about ¾ pound each

salt and pepper to taste

1½ cups milk

4 large eggs

2 cups blue cornmeal

1 teaspoon kosher salt

2 tablespoons medium chimayo chile powder

1 cup clarified butter

2 cups Red Chile Sauce (see page 25)

4 lemon wedges

Toss the green chiles together with the crab meat. Salt and pepper the insides of the trout and stuff with the crab mixture. Beat together the egg and milk. Combine the cornmeal, kosher salt, and chile powder. Dip trout in the egg wash and then in the seasoned cornmeal. Heat the butter in a large sauté pan, and cook the trout over medium heat for 8 to 10 minutes each side, until cooked. Serve on a base of Red Chile Sauce and garnish with a lemon wedge.

GRILLED TUNA
with Black Beans and Goat Cheese

This may at first seem an unusual combination, but it works very well — once you've tried it, you'll be converted! The freshness of tuna is perfectly balanced by the earthiness of black beans and the acidity of goat cheese. The tuna should be very fresh and moist. Cook it halfway at most, otherwise it becomes too dry and tough.

Yield: 4 servings

4 high-quality center-cut bluefin tuna steaks, about 8 ounces each

8 tablespoons olive oil

zest of ½ lime

6 sprigs cilantro

4 corn tortillas

2 tablespoons peanut oil

2 cups cooked black beans (see Black Bean Soup, page 32)

½ teaspoon ground cumin

½ teaspoon salt

1 teaspoon diced serrano chile

2 pounds Roma tomatoes, diced

4 ounces strong dry goat cheese, room temperature

½ cup Pico de Gallo Salsa (see page 13)

8 lime wedges

Marinate the tuna in 6 tablespoons olive oil, lime zest, and cilantro for about 20 to 30 minutes. Fry the tortillas briefly in the peanut oil until softened. Purée the black beans, and add the cumin, salt, and serrano. Heat the remaining 2 tablespoons olive oil in a sauté pan and cook the bean purée mixture and tomatoes over low heat for 3 to 4 minutes, stirring constantly. Do not let beans dry out or become pasty. Put one tortilla on each serving plate, portion out the beans equally on top of the tortillas, and crumble the cheese over the beans. Grill the tuna for 2 to 3 minutes per side — the center should be rare. Place tuna on top of the cheese and put 2 tablespoons Pico de Gallo Salsa on each serving. Garnish with lime wedges.

TUNA TARTARE RELLENOS
with Cilantro Mayonnaise and Avocado Crema

This is a very versatile dish which can be served as a light lunch entrée or as an appetizer. Try to use small poblanos, or cut large ones in half, stuff, and serve cut-side down. The tuna must be very fresh; the meat should be oily and dark. My favorite way of serving this dish is with an Oaxacan Relleno (see page 114). I really like the combination of cold raw food with hot and spicy cooked food.

Yield: 4 servings

1 pound very fresh sashimi-quality tuna, center cut only

2 Roma tomatoes, diced

6 tablespoons diced sweet red pepper

2 poblano chiles, roasted, stemmed, peeled, and seeded

Cilantro Mayonnaise (recipe follows)

Avocado Crema (recipe follows)

Chop tuna in small dice, and mix with tomato, pepper, and ½-cup Cilantro Mayonnaise. (Finely minced serrano chile can also be added if a hotter tartare is preferred.) Cut the poblanos in half and stuff with the tuna mixture. Place Avocado Crema on the plates and top with stuffed poblanos cutside down.

CILANTRO MAYONNAISE

1 bunch cilantro plus 2 tablespoons chopped cilantro

1 tablespoon water

2 eggs, at room temperature

1 cup light olive oil

juice of 1 lime

2 serrano chiles, minced

In a blender, purée the bunch of cilantro with the water and push through a strainer, reserving the liquid. Pulse the eggs until light and frothy, then add the oil drop by drop until the mixture becomes very, very thick. Add the strained liquid, lime juice, chiles, and chopped cilantro and mix together well.

AVOCADO CREMA

1 fresh avocado

1 cup Mexican Crema (see page 35)

juice of 1 lime

To prepare the crema, pulse the avocado, crema, and lime juice together until combined.

CUMIN SWORDFISH
with Sweet Red Pepper Sauce

The swordfish in this recipe is marinated and then grilled. The mustard greens give this dish a hot taste, while the sauce made with sweet red peppers provides a balancing sweetness and a wonderful color contrast.

Yield: 4 servings

¼ cup virgin olive oil

zest of 1 lemon

2 cloves garlic, crushed

1 tablespoon crushed black pepper

1 tablespoon roasted cumin seed

1 tablespoon fresh lemon juice

6 sprigs cilantro

4 swordfish fillets, center cut, about 8 ounces each

2 bunches mustard greens, washed and stems removed

2 tablespoons olive oil

2 pequin red chiles

4 tablespoons cooked black beans (see Black Bean Soup, page 32)

Sweet Red Pepper Sauce (recipe follows)

Combine virgin olive oil, lemon zest, garlic, pepper, cumin seed, lemon juice, and cilantro, and marinate swordfish in this mixture in refrigerator for 4 to 5 hours. Blanch mustard greens, and lightly sauté in 2 tablespoons oil with whole red chiles and black beans. Set aside. Remove fish from marinade and grill 4 minutes on one side, 3 on the other — less, if the grill is very hot. To serve, place swordfish on top of mustard greens and beans, and pour Sweet Red Pepper Sauce over swordfish.

SWEET RED PEPPER SAUCE

½ white onion, sliced

2 tablespoons olive oil

2 cloves garlic, roasted and peeled

2 large sweet red peppers, roasted and peeled

1 tablespoon balsamic vinegar

3 tablespoons butter

salt to taste

Lightly sauté the onion in the oil. In a blender, purée onions, garlic, and peppers until smooth, and then add the vinegar. Heat sauce in a pan and add butter and salt.

HUACHINANGO

True huachinango, or red snapper, is distinguished by its large head and red flesh, and is one of the great fishes of the world. Most fish that is sold as snapper is actually rock cod or some other rock fish and does not have the subtlety of the genuine article. At Coyote Cafe, we use snapper that is flown fresh and whole off day boats from Galveston on the Gulf of Mexico. If you can't get snapper, striped sea bass will work.

This is an adaptation of one of the oriental seafood dishes I like the most — fried whole fish with spicy chiles and colorful peppers. I always order this when I go to the Ocean Restaurant, my favorite Chinese seafood restaurant in San Francisco. Further inspiration came from another favorite restaurant, Wolfgang Puck's Chinois on Main, in Santa Monica. His deep-fried catfish with ginger and sweet peppers is out of this world.

Yield: 4 servings

2 whole Gulf red snapper, about 2½ to 3 pounds each, with heads, cleaned and scaled

2 quarts peanut oil

2 tablespoons olive oil

2 poblano chiles, seeded and julienned

4 serrano chiles, cut into rings

2 large sweet red peppers, seeded and julienned

2 large sweet yellow peppers, seeded and julienned

4 cloves garlic, minced

3 tablespoons fresh ginger, peeled and julienned

2 cups fish stock

1 bunch cilantro

zest of 1 orange

zest of 1 lime

zest of 1 lemon

½ teaspoon sugar

salt to taste

1 tablespoon fresh lemon juice

1 tablespoon fresh lime juice

Cut 2 or 3 slashes on each side of the snapper down to the bone, about 3 inches apart (this allows the snapper to cook more evenly). Heat peanut oil to 350° and deep-fry snapper for about 12 minutes.

Meanwhile, to prepare sauce, heat olive oil in a skillet and sauté chiles, peppers, garlic, and ginger over medium heat for 5 minutes. Add stock, ½ bunch of cilantro, tied, and citrus zest. Cook for a further 5 minutes, and then remove cilantro. Add sugar and salt, bring sauce to a boil and add citrus juice. Remove from heat, allow to cool slightly and pour over fish. Garnish with cilantro sprigs taken from the remainder of the bunch, and serve snapper whole (each serves at least 2 people).

SANTA FE SEAFOOD STEW

The combination of shellfish and fresh fish in a delicious sauce makes one of the world's truly finest dishes, whether it be a French bouillabaisse, an Italian cioppino, or some other version. When you're in the mood for a seafood stew, head for a restaurant that specializes in it, because otherwise it might be made up of leftovers. I prefer seafood stews that are spicy rather than those that are creamy or rich. This recipe is made with dried red chile, and the earthy flavor perfectly complements the seafood.

Yield: 4 servings

4 Roma tomatoes

6 cloves garlic, roasted and peeled

4 cups fish stock

2 tablespoons olive oil

1 large red onion, diced

2 lobsters, about 1½ pounds each

1 cup Mark's Red Chile Sauce (see page 25)

½ cup dark beer

1 bunch cilantro

pinch roasted Mexican oregano

2 pounds Manila clams (about 20)

1 pound large shrimp, peeled

1 pound sea bass, monkfish, or other firm white fish, cut into 1-inch chunks

½ pound (about 8) large sea scallops

12 sprigs fresh cilantro

8 corn tortillas

With a comal or black iron skillet over medium-high heat, cook the tomatoes until blackened all over. Cool slightly and chop. Purée the garlic and 1 cup of the fish stock together. Heat the oil in a large, deep sauté pan and cook the onion over low heat for 15 minutes. Add chopped tomatoes, puréed garlic, lobsters, chile sauce, beer, cilantro, and oregano to the pan. Cover and simmer for 6 minutes. Meanwhile, heat the remaining 3 cups fish stock. Remove lid, add clams and shrimp, and cook for a further 5 minutes. Then add the fish, scallops, and hot stock, and cook for another 2 minutes. Remove cilantro and bring to a boil. Cut lobsters in half lengthwise. Serve stew in large flat bowls. Garnish with cilantro sprigs and serve with warm tortillas.

CARIBBEAN SEAFOOD STEW

This variation on seafood stews uses ingredients from the region of Mexico that borders on the Caribbean. The flavors of ginger, pineapple, banana, and citrus fruit go surprisingly well with fresh chiles. For a really colorful presentation, serve this with Spicy Green Rice (see page 146) on the side.

Yield: 4 servings

2 pounds Manila clams (about 20)

8 large shrimp

5 cups lightly salted water

2 lobsters, about 1½ pounds each

2 tablespoons olive oil

6 tablespoons diced white onion

½ sweet red pepper, cut into large dice

½ sweet yellow pepper, cut into large dice

1 clove garlic, sliced

4 Roma tomatoes, peeled, seeded, and diced

4 tablespoons fresh ginger, peeled and julienned

6 serrano chiles, cut in rings

1 bunch cilantro

zest of 1 lime

3 cups fish stock

1 pound red snapper, cut into 1-inch chunks

¼ pound fresh squid, cut in rings

1 pineapple, peeled, cored, and cut into ½-inch dice

4 tablespoons coconut milk

pinch sugar

pinch salt

juice of 1 lime

juice of ½ orange

Scrub clams, peel shrimp, and set both aside. Parboil lobsters in salted water for 8 minutes. Cool slightly and remove meat. Heat the oil in a large, deep sauté pan and cook onion, peppers, garlic, tomatoes, ginger, serranos, ½ bunch cilantro, tied, and lime zest over low heat for 10 minutes. Add clams, shrimp, lobster tail meat, and ½ cup stock, cover, and cook over medium heat for 5 minutes. When clams open, add snapper and the remaining 2½ cups stock. Cook for a further 2 minutes but do not allow to boil. Add squid, pineapple, coconut milk, sugar, and salt, and cook for a further minute over medium heat. Add citrus juice and serve. Garnish with cilantro sprigs taken from the remainder of the bunch.

GAME & FOWL

Black buck antelope steaks, roasted shoulder of Axis venison, and wild turkey are some of the dishes we prepare at Coyote Cafe. These may seem exotic now, but at one time, they were quite usual fare. In pre-industrial days, the Western ranges were full of wild game and fowl. In fact, these animals were one of the magic sources of protein for the Southwestern Indians. The Indians lived mainly in large, unified adobe towns or pueblos that were centered along the Rio Grande and other rivers of the Southwest. These groups developed very ingenious and sophisticated irrigation systems that allowed them to grow corn, beans, and squashes. They supplemented their diets by fishing and hunting native game which included elk, deer, duck, wild birds, and small animals such as rabbit and squirrels. They would travel from the pueblos over a forty-mile radius for up to two days at a time to gather wild plants, herbs, and game.

Game is a relatively new food item for me because we were a family of fishermen, not hunters. My first contact with game was cooking at Chez Panisse with Jean Pierre Moullé, who was an excellent hunter and particularly liked working with wild birds, especially duck and quail. After tasting some of Jean Pierre's dishes, wild fowl became one of my favorite foods and to this day I can think of nothing better than grilled fowl accompanied by a fine Burgundy. In the last few years I have developed many game and fowl dishes in my restaurants. At Coyote Cafe, the robust flavors of wild game are particularly appropriate during the long fall and winter months in Santa Fe. When the nights are cold and the smell of piñon burning in the fireplace fills the restaurant, our menu features many game and fowl dishes that are enjoyed by our guests.

The flavor of game is rich and wonderful — it has all the tones of fragrant forests, and wild herbs and berries. Best of all, it is very healthy, being low in fat and cholesterol, and high in protein. Many people are reluctant to cook game because they feel the flavor is too "gamey." This quality is usually associated with animals that were not well dressed, or else were overcooked. Since game contains very little internal fat, it must be cooked no more than medium rare or it becomes dried out. Game must be harvested during the right season or it can be too lean and tough. When properly harvested, cleaned, and cooked, game has a very subtle, rich taste and a delicious array of natural nuances that cannot be duplicated with commercial meats.

Luckily for us, game is now being raised on "open" ranches where it is allowed to range freely in its natural habitat. The animals forage on native bushes and grasses which give the meat its distinctive flavor. At Coyote Cafe, we are fortunate in having an especially good source of wild game — Mike Hughes's Broken Arrow ranch in Ingram, Texas, one of the best-managed game ranches in the world.

Both domestic and wild fowl have the same wonderful flavor spectrum that the larger game animals have. The dark richness of squab and the herbaceous, light and gamey taste of quail are two of my favorites. There is also something almost primordial about whole birds; you can pick up the bones and gnaw on them just as man has been doing for millions of years.

I think game will once again become a much more important part of our diets because the taste of most commercial meats is not what it used to be. Flavorless chickens and supermarket meats cannot be the proper base for a strong chile or stew. One of the more esoteric attractions of game is that it provides us with a connection to our natural environment. It links us to our food in a way that meat wrapped in plastic and styrofoam never can. In this chapter, we come closest to the earthy tradition of the campfire and romantic images of man as hunter-gatherer.

TIPS ON COOKING GAME AND FOWL

Always ensure game and fowl is at or near room temperature (between 60° and 75°) before you cook it. This allows for a shorter cooking time, which is particularly important because game has little or no internal fat with which to baste itself. The shorter the cooking time, the less dry the meat will be.

Marinate game for up to 24 hours; this also ensures a shorter cooking time and adds moisture to the meat.

For the marinade, use wild herbs and spices that are similar to what would be found in the animal's natural habitat. Desert tastes such as juniper, sage, wild thyme, and prickly pear also complement game and fowl particularly well both in marinades and sauces.

Check for the small pin feathers that surround the wing tips of wild fowl, and pull out by hand.

When serving roasted or grilled game, cut ½-inch thick slices across the grain. This makes for a better presentation and keeps the meat juicier and warmer. Thin slices dry out and become tough.

VENISON CHILE

*Nothing is as satisfying as a
hearty bowl of well-made chile,
especially on a cold, crisp winter's
day, and we get plenty of those in
Santa Fe. I use black beans to
make this chile rather than the traditional pinto beans. Black beans
have greater depth of flavor and a
richness that pinto beans do not
provide. They are a better complement to the more complex tones of
the venison. At Coyote Cafe, we
serve this chile with grilled spicy
sausages made with venison, currants, and dried cherries.*

Yield: 6 to 8 servings

¼ cup rendered bacon fat (or olive oil)

2 large onions, coarsely chopped

8 cloves garlic, minced

8 jalapeño chiles, stemmed and
minced

3 pounds shoulder of venison, diced
(or venison chile-stew meat)

2 teaspoons salt

4 ounces canned chipotle chiles in
adobo sauce

½ pound hot New Mexico chile
powder

2 tablespoons roasted ground cumin

2 tablespoons roasted ground
Mexican oregano

1 pound Roma tomatoes

4 cups beef stock

1 bottle Mexican beer (preferably
Bohemia or Dos Equis)

8 cups cooked black beans (see Black
Bean Soup, page 32)

1 cup Mexican Crema (see page 35),
or sour cream

½ cup finely chopped onion

Warm bacon fat in a large skillet
over medium heat. Add onions,
garlic, and jalapeños, lower heat
slightly and sauté for about 20
minutes, stirring once or twice
until very tender. Meanwhile, add
the meat and salt to a heavy 5-
quart ovenproof casserole or Dutch
oven and brown over medium
heat, stirring often until the meat
has lost all pink color, about 20
minutes. Add the sautéed onion
mixture to the casserole, and stir in
the chipotle, chile powder, cumin,
and oregano. Cook, stirring often,
for 5 minutes. Then stir in the
tomatoes, beef stock, and beer, and
bring to a boil. Lower the heat and
simmer, uncovered, for 1½ hours,
stirring occasionally.

Taste, correct the seasoning, and
continue to simmer, stirring often,
for another 30 minutes, or until the
meat is tender and the chile is
reduced to your liking. Stir in the
black beans and simmer for another
5 minutes. Garnish with crema or
sour cream, and chopped onion.

GRILLED VENISON
with Ancho and Prickly Pear Sauce

*The flavors of fruit complement
game very well, especially desert
fruit such as prickly pears (this is
the colorful fruit of the cactus, not
the flat paddles). In this recipe,
the prickly pears enhance the
mild, plum-like flavor of the ancho
chiles. Venison chops are very
expensive; roasted saddles of venison were traditionally used for
royal banquets, and you almost
need to be nobility to afford it! But
for that extra special occasion,
nothing compares with these cuts
of venison.*

Yield: 4 servings

4 venison loin-end chops, about 8
ounces each

4 slices bacon

4 large porcini mushroom caps

Ancho and Prickly Pear Sauce (recipe
follows)

To prepare venison, grill chops,
preferably over a hot pecan grill,
or broil, 6 to 8 minutes per side.
Fry bacon until just done. Grill
porcini caps for 1 to 2 minutes.
Serve porcini on top of bacon next
to the venison chop, which should
be placed over the sauce.

ANCHO AND PRICKLY PEAR SAUCE

2 cups brown venison or beef stock

2 cups venison trimmings, browned

4 ancho chiles, seeded

5 prickly pears, peeled

GRILLED TEXAS AXIS VENISON
with Wild Herb Marinade

Using a stainless steel or enamel saucepan, bring ½ cup of the stock to a simmer and add venison trimmings and ancho chile. Continue to simmer gently, replacing evaporated stock with reserved stock until it has all been used. Remove and reserve the ancho chiles and strain the stock, pushing down hard on trimmings to release all the liquid. Purée stock with the reserved ancho chiles. Sieve, return to pan and reduce further, skimming occasionally, until 1 cup stock remains. Cut half of one of the prickly pears into 1-inch dice. Purée venison sauce with the remaining prickly pears and push through a sieve. Add diced prickly pear to sauce and heat through.

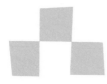

The marinade in this recipe works really well to intensify the delicious, subtle flavors of game meat. It tenderizes the venison and raises its level of complexity. When I prepared this dish for the First International Game Conference in Las Cruces, New Mexico, many of the participants told me it was one of the best meals they had ever had. Begin preparations a day ahead to allow time for the meat to marinate (make the sauce first, because you need it for the marinade). If prickly pear juice is unavailable, use bottled pomegranate juice, which can be bought at Middle Eastern stores. You can make prickly pear juice by puréeing prickly pears and straining out the liquid.

Yield: 8 servings

6 juniper berries

1 sprig rosemary

10 fresh sage leaves

4 tablespoons tellicherry pepper

6 allspice berries

2 tablespoons kosher salt

2 wild leeks (or domestic), green and white parts, sliced in rings

4 whole bulbs wild garlic, cut in rings, tops included (or 6 large cloves domestic garlic, sliced)

½ cup Desert Prickly Pear Sauce (recipe follows)

1 leg Texas Axis venison, trimmed and butterflied

¼ cup olive oil

Purée the herbs, spices, salt, leek, and garlic together in a food processor or blender. Combine with ½ cup Desert Prickly Pear Sauce in a large stainless steel or enamel roasting pan or tray. Rub venison leg with mixture and then with olive oil. Marinate in pan at room temperature for 4 hours and then overnight in the refrigerator. Bring venison to room temperature, and then grill over pecan wood with periodic additions of sage and rosemary bundles to the fire. Alternatively, roast at 425° to an internal temperature of 120° (about 30 minutes). Let sit for 5 to 8 minutes. Then cut in ½-inch slices across the grain. Serve on top of remaining Desert Prickly Pear Sauce.

DESERT PRICKLY PEAR SAUCE

½ gallon reduced venison stock

2 ounces dried wild mushrooms

1 bunch fresh thyme

2 bay leaves

6 fresh sage leaves

1 teaspoon crushed juniper berries

4 cloves garlic, smashed

5 dried ancho chiles, seeded

1 tablespoon freshly cracked black pepper

8 to 10 prickly pears, peeled

2 tablespoons unseasoned rice vinegar

1 cup prickly pear juice (or pomegranate juice)

Place stock, mushrooms, herbs, spices, garlic, chiles, and pepper in a stainless steel or enamel pan and gradually reduce over very low heat, skimming often. Cook until reduced by half, about 1 hour. Add whole prickly pears and continue to reduce slowly, breaking up fruits until mixture becomes syrupy and lightly coats the back of a wooden spoon, about 45 minutes. Purée sauce in a blender. Pass it through a food mill, then through a very fine strainer. Stir in rice vinegar and prickly pear juice.

ROASTED VENISON

with Green Chiles and Wild Boar Bacon

This recipe can be made with either a boned-out shoulder or leg of venison. The shoulder is less expensive and a little tougher, but it is more flavorful. At Coyote Cafe we use a leg, which makes a better roast and allows a more interesting presentation. This recipe adapts the classic European technique for cooking chicken, pork, and beef where the meat is stuffed, rolled, tied, and braised. In this case, though, the meat is seared and oven-roasted. Wild boar bacon does not have as smoky a taste as regular bacon, but is sweeter and does not fall apart as easily. Italian pancetta bacon can be substituted, or a good quality country ham cut thick and julienned (if using Smithfield ham, blanch first to remove excess salt). With these substitutes, use a milder variety of green chile, like an Anaheim, fresh roasted.

Yield: 4 to 6 servings

¾ pound wild boar bacon (or pancetta or country ham), diced

1 white onion, julienned

3 or 4 poblano chiles, roasted and julienned

½ teaspoon fresh marjoram

7 cloves garlic, roasted and peeled

½ teaspoon salt

¼ teaspoon freshly ground black pepper

1 leg venison, (4 to 5 pounds) boned or a 3-pound shoulder, butterflied

2 tablespoons olive oil

2 tablespoons corn oil

Preheat oven to 400°. In a skillet, sauté bacon until just cooked. Strain fat from bacon, reserve both, and set aside. In 2 tablespoons of the fat, sauté onion over medium heat until tender, about 5 to 7 minutes, and remove from heat. In a large bowl, combine bacon, onion, poblanos, marjoram, garlic, salt, and pepper. Spread this mixture evenly over the cut side of the meat, then roll the meat back up into its original shape and tie tightly with string. Sear venison in the combined oil, until uniformly brown. Place in oven and roast at 400° to an internal temperature of 125° (about 20 to 25 minutes). Let sit for 5 to 8 minutes. Then cut in ½-inch thick slices across the grain. Serve with black beans (see Black Bean Soup recipe, page 32) and Tamale de Elote (see page 61)

PAN-FRIED QUAIL

in Red Chile Cider Sauce

The quail for this recipe and the three that follow should be wild quail, preferably from Texas or California. The most common variety is bobwhite quail. I never use boned-out quail as this process is done mechanically, which I think sours the meat. In any event, I feel that using one's fingers and chewing on the bones is altogether more satisfying. Quail has little internal fat, and so does not freeze well. If it is frozen, be sure not to keep it too long or it will become too dry. We serve this dish with Pecan and Wild Boar Bacon Waffles. The sauce can be made first and held.

Yield: 4 servings

8 quail, room temperature

salt and pepper to taste

4 tablespoons clarified butter

4 ounces wild boar bacon (or Amador, Smithfield, or Harrington's corn cob smoked bacon), diced

4 Pecan and Wild Boar Bacon Waffles (see page 147)

8 tablespoons softened butter

4 tablespoons red chile honey

Red Chile Cider Sauce (recipe follows)

RED CHILE QUAIL

Remove backbone of quail with scissors. Flatten out, pushing on the breast with the palm of your hand. Season with salt and pepper. Heat clarified butter in a skillet until almost smoking, then reduce to medium heat. Add bacon and quail to pan and sauté until quail are golden brown, about 10 minutes (7 minutes for the first side, 3 minutes for the second), keeping butter bubbling but not smoking. Meanwhile, prepare waffles and mix together the butter and honey to make a flavored butter. Remove quail and bacon from pan, and serve quail on top of Red Chile Cider Sauce. Place waffles next to quail, and top with flavored butter.

RED CHILE CIDER SAUCE

2½ cups brown or regular chicken stock

½ cup dried wild mushrooms

1 cup unfiltered cider

1 teaspoon chile caribe

Bring the stock and mushrooms to a boil. Reduce heat and simmer until reduced to 1 cup, about 40 minutes. Finely strain the reduced stock, and add cider and chile caribe. Cook over medium heat until reduced by half, about 20 minutes.

This recipe is an adaptation of a dish created by Chris Chung, who worked with me at the Fourth Street Grill. One of his specialties there was a great Chinese-style deep-fried quail. (Chris now owns his own restaurant, Christopher's, in Berkeley.) We have served this version at Coyote Cafe since we opened, and it's a particular favorite of Robert del Grande, another restaurant-owner friend of mine (he owns Cafe Annie in Houston). It is important to marinate the quail long enough, preferably overnight, so the flavors penetrate to the bone. Bringing the quail to room temperature before deep-frying ensures that it cooks evenly.

Yield: 4 servings

Marinade

½ cup mild Chimayo chile powder

2 tablespoons medium Chimayo chile powder

½ cup dark brown sugar

1 ounce dried cèpes

½ bunch cilantro

½ tablespoon coriander seed, roasted and ground

3 allspice berries, ground

1 tablespoon roasted ground Mexican oregano

1 sprig mint

1 bunch wild spring onions (or 1 large bunch green onions), chopped

3 star anise

1 tablespoon sassafras

4 cups water

8 quail, room temperature

peanut oil for deep-frying (at least 4 inches deep)

1 tablespoon red wine vinegar

⅓ cup virgin olive oil

salt to taste

6 cups assorted medium-sized greens, such as frisée, red oak, or red Boston

Combine all marinade ingredients in a saucepan, mix together, and bring to a boil. Cool to room temperature, pour over quail and marinate overnight in refrigerator, or for at least 6 hours.

Remove quail from marinade, pat dry, and bring to room temperature. Heat peanut oil to 330° to 350° and deep-fry quail for about 6 minutes (if oil is too hot, quail will burn before they are fully cooked). While quail are frying prepare salad by beating vinegar into the oil and adding salt. Toss with the greens, place quail on top, and serve with Currant and Canela Tamale (see page 70).

COYOTE AND HIS FLUTE

One night, not too long ago, Coyote was sitting around the Cafe just talking to Rabbit who was tending bar. He realized that he hadn't seen Mountain Lion or Raccoon or even Bear lately. He started to worry that maybe he had done something to upset his friends. "Rabbit," he said, "where is everyone? Is there something I've done to keep them away?"

"No, no," Rabbit assured him. "It's just that everyone is so down lately. Bear spends his whole day growling because he can't get to sleep. Raccoon is just as miserable. Every night he prowls around looking for something good to steal, but he turns up empty every time. 'What good is a bandit', he says, 'if he can't find anything to steal'. And Fox — Fox has it worst of all. Suddenly there's not a chicken coop within 100 miles."

"This is awful," Coyote thought. "All my friends are so depressed. I have to do something about it." Then he remembered Ancient Medicine Man who was supposed to know everything. "What about Ancient Medicine Man, Rabbit? Do you think he can help?" Rabbit nodded, saying it couldn't hurt to try. "That's it," Coyote decided. "He's got to help, he's just got to, Rabbit."

After traveling across the desert for two days and worrying that he would never find the great man, Coyote spotted a small fire atop a high mesa. He climbed to the summit and there sat the medicine man, obviously deep in thought. "I'm sorry to disturb you, Sir," Coyote started. "But I have a terrible problem and I thought that you might be able to help me."

The old man sat very still and listened to Coyote's story. Then at last he spoke. "Long ago, we had a way of ridding ourselves of all our troubles. We would make the image of a great towering man. He had a big round head and arms which moved wildly about him. On one night each year we gave all our troubles to him and then set him on fire. When he burned, all our problems disappeared. We called him Zozobra.*"

"And it really worked?" asked Coyote.

"If we believed, then it worked," replied the ancient one. "The trouble is that sometimes it's difficult to get people to trust. For some reason they want to hang on to their troubles. But if you and your friends are willing, I don't see how you can fail. Here, take this with you. Its magic will help." Ancient Medicine Man handed Coyote a simple flute of silver with little gold stars scattered across it. Coyote thanked the old man effusively and off he went, back across the desert, determined to make a Zozobra and help his friends.

After a week's time, all was ready. As night fell, Coyote grabbed his flute and ran to call everyone. Just like the old man had predicted, Bear, Raccoon, Fox, Squirrel, and even Rabbit were reluctant to go with him. Then he remembered his flute and he began to play. A wonderful melody filled the canyons. One by one, all the animals started to follow along behind Coyote. As he continued to play, he led them to where his Zozobra stood. When everyone had gathered around, Coyote told them what they must do. "Life is too short to be so troubled, my friends. Be rid of your problems and let's enjoy all that we have." Then Coyote set Zozobra on fire and one by one, Bear and Fox and Squirrel and all the others let go of all their worries. Coyote picked up the flute and once again the beautiful melody was all around them. The animals danced with Coyote, first lightly, and then with everything they had. All of them were so happy, especially Coyote, because he had been able to help his friends feel good again. Then Coyote led his dancing procession back to Coyote Cafe where they laughed and talked and had more fun than they had had in years.

*The burning of Zozobra takes place in Santa Fe during Fiesta Week, which is always in mid September. Zozobra represents Old Man Gloom who is burned in effigy to signify the end of the old year and the birth of the new one.

PAN-ROASTED QUAIL

with Artichoke / OysterTimbales

The idea for this recipe comes from Cajun and Creole cuisines and the Louisiana bayous where seafood and woodland fowl or game are an important resource. The combination of oysters and artichokes is, in fact, a Creole classic. I love to serve this dish — the oyster hidden in the center of the timbale is always a delightful surprise for the diner. Make the corn bread first — you'll need half of it for the timbales — and make the timbales next.

Yield: 4 servings

8 quail

8 cloves garlic, minced

4 bay leaves, halved

16 sprigs fresh thyme, about 2 inches long

8 sprigs fresh rosemary, about 1 inch long

1 cup clarified butter

1 quart brown poultry stock

2 ounces dried wild mushrooms

4 Artichoke/Oyster Timbales (recipe follows)

Preheat oven to 500°. Stuff the quail with garlic, bay leaves, thyme, and rosemary. In a large ovenproof pan or skillet, heat clarified butter over medium-high heat until almost smoking. Quickly sear quail until golden brown on all sides, about 5 minutes. Remove butter from pan and roast quail in oven for 12 to 15 minutes. Meanwhile, cook the stock and mushrooms together and reduce down to 1 cup. Strain, and pour over quail. Serve unmolded timbales next to quail.

CORN BREAD BASE

¾ cup melted butter

2 cups fine yellow cornmeal

½ teaspoon salt

½ cup boiling water

1½ cups milk

2 eggs

1 teaspoon baking powder

Preheat oven to 425°. Grease an 8-inch square pan. Blend butter, cornmeal, and salt in a food processor for a few seconds. Pour in boiling water and blend again for a few seconds to form a smooth batter. Scrape down the sides of the bowl, add the remaining ingredients and blend for a further 5 seconds. Place mixture in prepared cake pan and bake for 30 minutes, or until center is firm and the edges draw away from sides of pan. Do not overcook and dry out. Turn onto rack to cool. Use right away or cover fully with plastic wrap to preserve moisture.

ARTICHOKE/OYSTER TIMBALES

1 large or 2 medium artichokes

1 cup plus 3 tablespoons green onion (green and white parts), sliced in rings

3 tablespoons butter

½ cup diced sweet red pepper

1½ teaspoons minced garlic

1 teaspoon olive oil

2 slices bacon

½ teaspoon salt

⅛ teaspoon pepper

⅛ teaspoon cayenne

1 teaspoon dried sage, rubbed, or powdered dried sage

½ teaspoon dried thyme

8 ounces corn bread, crumbled

1 egg, beaten

1 tablespoon Tabasco sauce

½ cup cream

1 tablespoon softened butter

4 large freshly shucked oysters

To prepare timbales, cook artichokes in boiling salted water for about 40 minutes. Allow to cool, remove and clean hearts, and dice; yield should be about ¾ cup. In a large skillet over medium heat, wilt green onion in 2 tablespoons of butter until soft and translucent (but not brown), about 2 minutes, and set aside. Sauté red pepper in 1 tablespoon butter for 2 minutes. Remove from pan and set aside. Sauté garlic in oil for 2 minutes and set aside. Dice bacon and fry until just done, but not crisp.

Preheat oven to 350°. In a large bowl, mix salt, pepper, cayenne, herbs, corn bread, artichoke, green onion, red pepper, garlic, bacon, egg, Tabasco, and cream, and mix well. Rub the inside of four 3-inch ramekins with the softened butter. Fill each ramekin halfway with the mixture, and pat down. Add one oyster to each ramekin and then fill with the remaining mixture, to just below the top of the ramekin, and pat down again. Cover the ramekins with buttered parchment paper and set them in a bain-marie or pan with at least 2-inch sides filled with hot water reaching halfway up the sides of the ramekins. Bake for 30 to 40 minutes until firm and set. Let sit for 3 to 4 minutes and then loosen around inside edge with a small paring knife. Keep warm. When ready to serve, turn upside down, knock sharply on bottom and unmold.

HIBISCUS QUAIL

In the markets of Mexico, the large jars containing purple-colored iced water are liquados made from dried hibiscus or jamaica blossoms. Hibiscus blossoms have a wonderful taste, something like sour cherries. It occurred to me that using them in a light fruit marinade would be ideal for fowl or game. This marinade turns the quail a rich, purple color, and the flavor permeates the whole bird. The pineapple and jalapeño glaze gives it an extra crustiness and flavor contrast. This dish is visually striking, especially if fresh hibiscus blossoms are available as garnish. A single Hibiscus Quail makes a great appetizer.

Yield: 4 servings

Marinade
1 bottle dry Sauvignon Blanc
1 cup dried hibiscus blossoms
2 cloves garlic
1 bunch cilantro, tied
1 slice lime

8 quail
1 cup water
1 cup reserved marinade
2 tablespoons brown sugar
1 ripe pineapple, diced
4 jalapeño chiles, seeded
juice of 1 lime
¼ teaspoon salt
¼ teaspoon pepper

Salad
½ cup fresh orange juice
⅓ cup olive oil
2 tablespoons fresh lime juice
1 tablespoon unseasoned rice vinegar
2 bunches mâche or arugula
2 bunches baby red leaf lettuce or oak leaf lettuce
12 fresh hibiscus flower petals (optional)

To prepare the marinade, bring the wine and the hibiscus blossoms to a boil in a stainless steel pan, cover, and simmer for 30 minutes, or until about 3 cups remain. Allow to cool, strain, and discard blossoms. Add the garlic, cilantro, and lime slice.

Remove backbone of quail with scissors. Flatten out, pushing on the breast with the palm of your hand, and fold wings underneath. Add the quail to marinade and refrigerate for 2 to 3 hours. Turn over every hour. Remove and bring to room temperature. Measure out 1 cup of the marinade and reserve.

To make the glaze, combine water, 1 cup marinade, brown sugar, pineapple, and jalapeños in a saucepan. Bring to a boil, lower the heat, and simmer for 15 minutes until the water evaporates and the liquid is reduced to a light glaze. Purée in a food processor or blender and add lime juice.

Season quail and grill over a medium fire for about 6 minutes or broil for about 5 minutes per side. Baste with the glaze at the very end, cooking for a further 30 seconds per side at most. Combine orange juice, olive oil, lime juice, and vinegar to make a light dressing and toss with salad greens and hibiscus. Serve quail on the salad.

CUMIN SQUAB

The idea for this recipe comes from the Middle East, where cumin and chiles are commonly used. The rich, dark flavor of squab takes very strong marinades and sauces, and in this case, the marinade acts to create interesting flavor notes that give the dish a greater complexity without obscuring the taste of the bird itself. The Pipián Rojo echoes harissa, the North African chile sauce made with cumin, red chile, and garlic. This recipe calls for overnight marinating.

Yield: 4 servings

Marinade
zest of 3 oranges
zest of 2 lemons
juice of 3 oranges
juice of 1 lemon
¼ cup medium molido chile powder
1 cup Zinfandel wine
⅓ cup ground cumin
2 cups coarsely chopped cilantro
½ tablespoon roasted anise seed
½ tablespoon cinnamon
2 teaspoons salt
4 tablespoons brown sugar
2 cups olive oil

4 squab
1 cup Pipián Rojo (see page 30)

Combine all marinade ingredients except the oil in a large bowl. Whisk in oil. Add squab and marinate in refrigerator overnight. Preheat oven to 425°. Remove squab, clean with a damp cloth, and bring to room temperature. Strain marinade, and gently heat liquid in pan. Place squab in an oven pan and roast for about 25 minutes, until moist and tender, with a crisp, dark color. Do not overcook. Baste every 5 to 10 minutes with heated marinade. Serve squab on top of Pipián Rojo.

BRAISED DUCK
with Posole

It's too bad that more restaurants do not offer "homey" stews and braised dishes. Instead, most restaurants specialize in pasta dishes or "nouvelle California cuisine" so that, unfortunately, culinary students all too often are not pressed to learn the traditional techniques of preparing meat that require a long cooking time. This dish is unusual — it is both hot and sweet, giving it an almost Mediterranean taste, though of course the chiles give greater depth and flavor! Prepare the posole ahead of time.

Yield: 4 servings

2 cups chicken stock

5 cups water

1 cup fresh posole

2 tablespoons medium New Mexican chile powder

2 ducks, room temperature

½ cup salt

6 cloves garlic, puréed

⅔ ounce dried ancho chiles

⅔ ounce dried pasilla chiles

⅔ ounce dried mulato chiles

3 cups water

½ cup clarified butter

½ cup diced carrot

1½ cups diced onion

2 cups diced chayote

1 cup diced zucchini

2 cups chicken stock

1½ cups red chile honey

2 bay leaves

2 sticks canela (or cinnamon)

To prepare posole, put stock, water, posole, and chile powder in a pan. Bring to a boil, lower heat, cover, and simmer 3 hours.

Quarter the duck, rub with salt and garlic, and let sit for 30 minutes. Meanwhile, remove stems and seeds from chiles and roast in a 250° oven for 3 to 4 minutes. Shake once or twice and do not allow to blacken. Add to the water in a covered pan and simmer very low for 20 minutes to rehydrate. Allow to cool. Taste the chile water, and if not bitter, add about 2 cups and the chiles to a blender (use plain water if bitter). Purée and strain, reserving both liquid and purée.

Wash off duck and dry thoroughly. In a skillet, sear the duck breasts with the butter over medium heat for about 10 minutes. Then add the remaining quarters and cook for a further 10 minutes. Remove from pan and drain off excess fat. Sauté vegetables over medium heat until lightly browned, about 10 minutes.

Preheat oven to 225°. Place reserved chile liquid, duck, vegetables, and posole in a casserole with a lid. Deglaze sauté pan with ½ cup stock and add to casserole. Then add remaining stock, red chile honey, chile purée, bay leaves, and canela. Cover and bake for 2 hours. Remove duck and keep warm. Transfer vegetables, posole, and sauce to a pan. Discard bay leaves and canela, skim off fat, and reduce sauce to medium thickness. Place duck on plate with posole, vegetables, and sauce, and serve.

SAUTÉED DUCK
with Wild Mushrooms and Corn Cakes

Wild mushrooms are at their best after the rains in late spring and early fall, when varieties such as morels, chanterelles, and porcini can be found in the mountains around Santa Fe and Taos, as well as in the Gila Wilderness in southern New Mexico. At Coyote Cafe, we try to use as many fresh wild mushrooms as possible when they are available. A mixture of dried wild mushrooms can be used as an alternative if you can't get fresh mushrooms. For the mushroom stock, use inexpensive dried mushrooms such as Argentine black wild mushrooms. The duck breasts should be sautéed slowly to render off excess fat, and are best served rare to medium rare or they lose their juiciness.

Yield: 4 servings

Mushroom Stock

2½ cups duck stock (or brown poultry stock)

½ cup dried mushrooms

⅓ cup red wine

1 clove garlic, finely minced

½ teaspoon fresh marjoram

4 cups fresh wild mushrooms (mixture of morels, chanterelles, cèpes and porcini), thinly sliced

salt and freshly ground black pepper to taste

Corn Cakes (see page 149)

4 large duck breasts

salt and freshly ground black pepper to taste

¼ cup clarified butter

To prepare mushroom stock, put duck stock and dried mushrooms in a saucepan, bring to a boil, reduce heat, and simmer until reduced to 1 cup, about 40 minutes. Strain finely. Add to the stock the wine, garlic, and marjoram, and reduce again over medium heat to 1 cup, about 20 minutes. Add fresh mushrooms, salt, and pepper, and simmer for 10 minutes. Set aside.

Prepare the Corn Cakes. With a knife, score fat-side of duck breasts in cross-hatches (if less fat is desired on the duck, trim some of it out before scoring). Season with salt and pepper. Heat butter in a skillet, and sauté duck over medium-high heat, skin-side down first for 7 minutes, then the other side for 3 minutes. Remove, and allow to cool for 2 to 3 minutes. Slice each breast into 8 to 10 pieces on a diagonal and arrange in a fan. Serve on top of sauce, with Corn Cakes on the side.

DUCK CARNITAS RELLENOS
with Wild Mushrooms

In many people's minds, a relleno is synonymous with a canned chile stuffed with processed cheese. This is unfortunate, because rellenos are a great concept. It's just that the dish is usually poorly executed. In this recipe, we use roasted fresh poblano chiles stuffed with Duck Carnitas and wild mushrooms. This dish also makes a great appetizer if small chiles are used. The relleno can alternatively be served with Mark's Red Chile Sauce, or the Tomatillo Chipotle Sauce (see page 25 or 26). The Duck Carnitas need to be prepared ahead of time.

Yield: 6 servings

1 pound very ripe Roma tomatoes

½ onion, chopped

2 cloves garlic

4 tablespoons duck fat

3 cups duck stock (or brown poultry stock)

1 clove

6 roasted poblano chiles, stems on, peeled and seeded

Duck Carnitas (recipe follows)

To prepare the sauce, purée tomatoes, onion, and garlic. Melt fat in a skillet and fry purée over high heat for 3 minutes. Add duck stock and clove, and simmer for 15 minutes until slightly thick.

Preheat oven to 350°. Stuff poblanos with the Duck Carnitas. Arrange on a ceramic dish, pour sauce around, and bake in oven until hot, about 10 minutes.

DUCK CARNITAS

4 duck legs, skin and bone removed

½ pound wild chanterelle mushrooms, quartered if large

2 cloves garlic

6 tablespoons duck fat

1 teaspoon canela

½ teaspoon cumin seed, roasted and ground

½ teaspoon coriander seed, roasted and ground

1 teaspoon roasted ground Mexican oregano

3 tablespoons medium Chimayo chile powder

2 cups duck stock (or brown poultry stock)

1 cup mushroom stock (see preceding recipe)

water to cover

salt and pepper to taste

Combine all the ingredients in a large saucepan. Bring to a simmer and let cook until duck meat is tender, about 1 hour. Increase heat and boil until all the liquid evaporates. Continue cooking, stirring constantly, until duck is well browned and crispy. Adjust seasoning and set aside to cool. Shred meat by hand.

PHEASANT
with Chorizo and Blue Corn Bread Stuffing

This is a great holiday dish adapted from a recipe created by my friend Stephen Pyles, who owns Routh Street, a wonderful restaurant in Dallas. It is important to buy pheasant that is large enough — at least 2½ to 3 pounds — to have plenty of internal body fat, otherwise it tends to be tough and will dry out while cooking. In this recipe, the richness of the pheasant meat is not overwhelmed by the spicy Chorizo stuffing. When serving, cut pheasant in half or take the breast meat off the bone and serve with the thighs; the drumsticks tend to be stringy and hard to chew. Make the corn bread first.

Yield: 4 to 6 servings

1½ pounds Chorizo (see page 152), or spicy pork or Italian sausage

¼ cup butter

1½ cups chopped onion

¼ cup diced celery

10 serrano chiles, stemmed, seeded, and minced

2 cloves garlic, minced

8 cups coarsely crumbled Blue Corn Bread (recipe follows)

4 teaspoons chopped fresh thyme leaves

1 teaspoon dried sage

1 cup chopped cilantro

⅓ cup half-and-half

1 egg, beaten

½ teaspoon freshly ground black pepper

1 cup clarified butter

2 pheasants, at least 2½ to 3 pounds each, at room temperature

6 slices bacon

To prepare stuffing, crumble and sauté Chorizo in a skillet until brown, about 5 minutes. Drain, and set aside. Melt butter in the same skillet, and add onion, celery, serranos, and garlic, and sauté over medium-high heat for 2 to 3 minutes. Transfer to a large bowl and add Chorizo, corn bread, thyme, sage, and cilantro. Toss well, and moisten with half-and-half and the egg. Add pepper and mix well.

Preheat oven to 400°. In a large ovenproof pan or skillet heat clarified butter over medium-high heat until almost smoking. Quickly sear each pheasant until golden brown, about 1 to 2 minutes per side. Remove pheasants from pan and allow to cool. Stuff, and truss with string. Place 2 bacon slices under the string, crossed, over the breast. Then place a bacon slice across the back, also under the string. Place pheasants on baking sheet or in ovenproof pan and roast 30 to 40 minutes until crispy but moist, and no blood runs when pierced with a skewer. Do not overcook.

BLUE CORN BREAD

½ cup melted butter

1 cup blue cornmeal

¼ cup whole wheat flour

¾ cup unbleached white flour

2 teaspoons baking powder

½ teaspoon baking soda

1 egg

¾ teaspoon salt

1½ cups buttermilk

Preheat oven to 425°. Grease an 8-inch square pan. Combine all the ingredients except buttermilk in the bowl of a food processor and blend for about 3 seconds. Scrape down the sides of the bowl, add the buttermilk, and blend for a further 5 seconds, again scraping down the sides of the bowl. Place mixture in prepared pan and bake for 30 minutes, or until center is firm and the edges draw away from sides of pan. Do not overcook and dry out, or corn bread will be tough. Turn onto rack to cool. Use right away or cover fully with plastic wrap to preserve moisture.

CHICKEN ROULADE

At Coyote Cafe, we seem to have four times as many chicken legs as we do chickens. This is not because we use a special four-legged variety, but because we use the breasts more than other parts of the bird. This recipe is one way of using the darker, more flavorful boned-out thigh meat of free-range chickens. This is a great dish, warm or cold, and is a favorite of mine for picnics.

Yield: 4 servings

1½ pounds wild boar bacon (or Amador, Smithfield, or Harrington's corn cob smoked bacon), diced

1 cup julienned white onion

3 sweet red peppers, roasted, peeled, and julienned

9 poblano chiles, roasted, peeled, and julienned

¾ teaspoon fresh marjoram

3 cloves garlic, roasted, peeled, and sliced

½ teaspoon salt

½ teaspoon pepper

8 free-range chicken legs, boned with skin on

2 tablespoons clarified butter

1 cup Green Chile Sauce (see page 26)

Preheat oven to 375°. To prepare stuffing, sauté bacon in a skillet until crisp. Strain, and reserve both bacon and rendered fat. In 2 tablespoons of the bacon fat, sauté onion until tender. In a large bowl, combine the bacon, onion, peppers, poblanos, marjoram, garlic, salt, and pepper, and mix well. Spread the stuffing mixture evenly over the cut side of the chicken legs, roll them up, and secure with toothpicks or wooden skewers. In a skillet, heat butter until almost smoking, reduce to medium, and sear chicken until golden, about 2 minutes per side. Bake for 12 minutes. Check that meat is cooked and no blood runs when pierced with a skewer. Remove and serve on top of Green Chile Sauce.

GRILLED BREAST OF CHICKEN
with Wild Boar Ham and Herbed Goat Cheese

Chicken has made something of a comeback over the last few years, and with greater public awareness of nutritional issues, the demand for free-range chicken has burgeoned. The more varied diet, lack of hormones and antibiotics, and the greater freedom of movement of free-range chickens contribute to a superior flavor and texture compared to other chickens. Free-range chickens usually weigh up to 5 pounds, and while they may be more expensive, I feel they are worth it. Most types of cheese can substitute for the goat cheese in this recipe. Flavored jack cheese is a good alternative.

Yield: 4 servings

4 large boneless free-range chicken breasts, skin on

salt and pepper to taste

¼ cup olive oil

6 ounces fresh mild goat cheese

1 tablespoon minced fresh marjoram

1 clove garlic, roasted, peeled, and mashed

4 slices wild boar ham (or prosciutto or Smithfield Ham)

1½ cups Green Chile Sauce (see page 26)

Make a horizontal slit in each of the chicken breasts for the ham and cheese. Season lightly with salt and pepper, and marinate in the olive oil for 30 minutes. Meanwhile, combine the cheese, marjoram, and garlic to make a smooth mixture. Remove the breasts from the oil and stuff with 1 slice of ham and one-fourth of the cheese mixture each. Grill over mesquite or pecan at medium-low heat until the skin is crispy and brown, and the chicken is cooked through. Alternatively, sauté until brown and bake at 450° for about 10 minutes. Serve on top of the Green Chile Sauce, accompanied by a Tamale de Elote, if desired (see page 61).

YUCATÁN STUFFED WILD TURKEY

This is a fiesta dish for special occasions — we served it at the opening party for Coyote Cafe. The recipe may seem complicated, but those who have tried it swear that the effort is well worthwhile. Imagine what it was like to prepare this dish for 1,200 guests at the Meals-on-Wheels benefit organized by Wolfgang Puck in Los Angeles! I can assure you it's easier to cook at home for a few special friends. At the restaurant, we use organically-grown wild turkey. The flavor is gamier and the texture superior to domestic turkeys, but if unavailable, try to buy fresh turkey from an organic food store. The stuffing combines a number of Yucatán flavors I really like, which is appropriate because wild turkey is commonly served in that part of Mexico, often with a black chile sauce. The beans and chile-achiote purée can be prepared a day ahead.

Yield: 8 to 10 servings

1 cup dried black beans, soaked overnight and drained

7½ cups water

3 tablespoons canned chipotle chiles in adobo, puréed

1 bay leaf

⅔ cup long-grain rice

3 dried cascabel chiles (or 2 Chinese red chiles with seeds)

2 tablespoons achiote seeds

1 bunch fresh marjoram, large stems removed

2 cups fresh orange juice

2 tablespoons fresh lime juice

½ teaspoon salt

¼ teaspoon freshly ground black pepper

2 tablespoons olive oil

1 pound medium shrimp, peeled and deveined

1 medium onion, finely diced

1 small carrot, finely diced

1 medium sweet red pepper, finely diced

1 pint freshly shucked oysters with their liquor (about 20)

⅓ cup green unroasted pumpkin seeds

1 large bunch cilantro, coarsely chopped (about ½ cup)

1 teaspoon finely chopped orange zest

1 fresh turkey, about 10 to 12 pounds, room temperature

In a medium saucepan, combine the black beans with 4½ cups of the water, 1 tablespoon of the chipotle purée, and the bay leaf. Bring to a simmer over moderately low heat and cook until tender, about 1½ hours. Drain the beans and let cool; discard the bay leaf. Put the rice and 2 cups of the water in a small saucepan. Bring to a boil, lower heat, and cook, covered, until tender, about 15 minutes. Fluff up the rice and let cool.

In another small saucepan, combine the cascabel chiles with the achiote and the remaining cup of water. Cook over medium-high heat until the achiote seeds are soft and no liquid remains, about 5 to 10 minutes. Transfer the chiles and

seeds to a blender and add the marjoram, orange juice, and lime juice. Purée the mixture for 10 seconds. Strain through a wide-mesh sieve. Season the purée with salt and pepper, and set aside.

In a large skillet heat 1 tablespoon of the olive oil. Add the shrimp and sauté over high heat, tossing, until just pink, about 2 minutes. Transfer shrimp to a plate and allow to cool. Add the remaining tablespoon of olive oil to skillet and reduce heat to low. Add onion, carrot, and sweet red pepper and cook, covered, until tender, about 5 minutes.

In a small skillet, combine the oysters and their liquor with 2 tablespoons of the chipotle purée. Cook over high heat until the edges of the oysters just begin to curl, about 2 minutes. With a slotted spoon, transfer the oysters to a plate. Reduce the cooking liquid to ¼ cup, about 2 minutes; it will be a thick paste. Add any liquid that drains from the oysters.

Dry-roast pumpkin seeds in a sauté pan for about 5 minutes until they have finished popping. In a large bowl, combine the black beans, rice, shrimp, oysters and reduced paste, vegetables, pumpkin seeds, cilantro, and orange zest to make the stuffing.

Preheat the oven to 325°. Stuff the turkey front and back, and sew up or truss. Set the turkey in a large roasting pan and pour over the reserved chile-achiote purée. Roast the turkey, basting every 20 minutes and adding water to the pan if the glaze starts to caramelize. Continue to roast until the temperature measured in the inner thigh near the bone reads 155°, about 3 hours. Cover the turkey with foil if the skin gets too dark.

SMOKED RABBIT ENCHILADAS

Meats tend to dry out during the smoking process unless a humidity box is used in the smoker or unless the meat is marinated in a brine to provide extra moisture. The brine, of course, can also add extra flavor to the meat. Rabbit, which is a very mild meat, easily takes on the flavors of the chiles. Unsmoked rabbit meat can also be used for this recipe. The crêpe used in this recipe makes the dish more delicate and flavorful, and the Red Chile Sauce provides an interesting, decorative presentation. It is best to make the crêpes to order, or reheat in a microwave; they can also be covered with foil in a sauté pan and kept warm, but they should not be kept in the oven where they will quickly become dry, hard, and brittle.

Yield: 4 servings

2 quarts water

¼ cup salt

¼ cup sugar

1 tablespoon dried thyme

3 tablespoons chile caribe

1 whole rabbit

½ cup clarified butter

2 cups brown poultry stock (or chicken stock)

1 carrot, coarsely chopped

2 celery stalks, coarsely chopped

1 bay leaf

1 Roma tomato, coarsely chopped

½ pound mushrooms, sliced

½ teaspoon minced garlic

2 tablespoons butter

8 Guajillo Crêpes (see page 79)

1 cup Mark's Red Chile Sauce (see page 25)

To make a brining solution, combine water, salt, sugar, thyme, and chile caribe in a large pot. Put the rabbit in the brine and soak for 4 hours in the refrigerator. Remove rabbit and bring to room temperature. Smoke rabbit over fruit wood for 2 hours (do not use any wood that burns very hot). Cut in half below ribs to fit into large sauté pan. Sear the rabbit in the clarified butter over medium heat until golden brown, about 4 minutes per side. Remove butter from pan and add stock, vegetables, bay leaf, and tomato. Cover pan and simmer for 25 minutes until meat turns white and no blood runs when pierced with a skewer. Do not overcook. Discard bay leaf and reserve vegetables. Allow rabbit to cool, then remove meat from bones and set aside.

Sauté mushrooms and garlic in butter over medium heat for 2 to 3 minutes. Add the rabbit meat and reserved vegetables and sauté a further 5 minutes.

Prepare crêpes (see page 79). Stuff each crêpe with ½ cup of the rabbit mixture, fold to form a cylinder, and serve 2 crêpes per plate. Top with Mark's Red Chile Sauce.

HORNO-STYLE GOAT LEG
with Mint and Onions

The first time I tried this dish was at a Fourth of July picnic on my friend Elizabeth Berry's ranch at Abiquiu, New Mexico. The goat leg was prepared by José, who works for Elizabeth, and was cooked in an adobe brick horno oven for 3 to 4 hours. It was the best goat I had ever tasted. We do not have a horno oven at Coyote Cafe, so I duplicated the flavor and tenderness of the goat leg by wrapping it in potter's clay and cooking it slowly for a long time. For a great party presentation, try breaking the clay at the table! The best time of year to prepare this dish is around Easter, when Greek communities traditionally cook young goat; Mexican and Spanish food markets also usually carry fresh goat. Alternatively, this recipe can be made with a leg of lamb.

Yield: 6 to 8 servings

10 pounds baking clay

1 goat leg, 4 to 5 pounds, bone in

5 tablespoons olive oil

3 white onions, julienned

24 cloves garlic, thinly sliced

salt and pepper to taste

10 bunches mint, washed, and trimmed of lower stems

On parchment paper, roll out clay into a 12 x 15-inch rectangle approximately ½ inch thick, and cover with a piece of foil the same size. Let clay sit while preparing the goat.

Heat 3 tablespoons of oil in a large skillet over high heat until almost smoking, reduce to medium and sear goat leg for about 4 minutes per side. Allow to cool. Sauté onions in the remaining 2 tablespoons of olive oil until tender. Make 6 cuts of approximately 2 inches across goat leg and against the grain down to the bone on both sides. Stuff cuts with garlic and onions, and salt and pepper the leg.

Preheat oven to 225°. Place half the mint on the foil as a bed for the goat leg. Place the leg on top of the mint, and cover with the remaining mint. Fold foil around the leg, leaving the bone exposed, and crimp the foil to seal. Trim any sinews off the bone. Fold clay over foil in the same manner and pinch well to secure. Decorate the clay or etch patterns if the fancy takes you. Place on a parchment-covered sheet pan and roast in oven for about 4 hours. Remove and let sit for 10 to 15 minutes. Crack open clay with a mallet and serve.

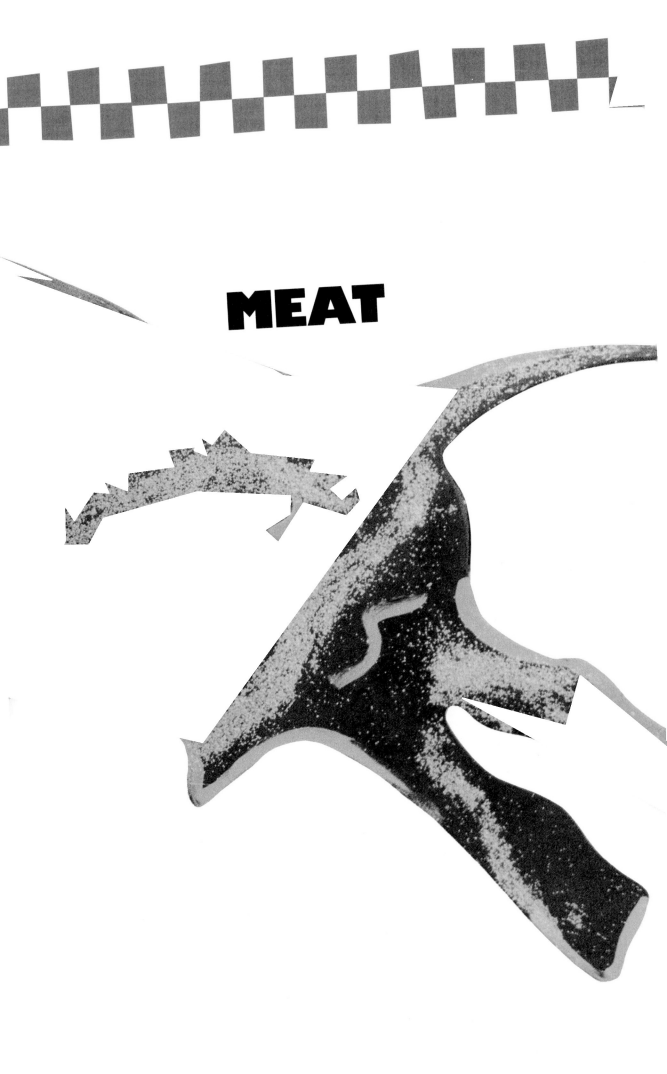

MEAT

At Coyote Cafe we enjoy cooking meats that have a lot of flavor and we go out of our way to get top quality meat. Our beef is dry-aged New Mexican prime Angus and we recently began featuring Churro lamb. Churros are an historic breed of sheep that originated in Spain and were introduced to the New World at the time of Cortés. For over 400 years, Churros were the mainstay of Spanish settlers, particularly in the Southwest, and for Pueblo Indians and Navajos who also used the fleece for traditional weaving. They have recently been reintroduced as commercial livestock in the Southwest. This range-raised lamb which feeds on wild sage and snowberries is low in cholesterol, and high in protein.

In general, I think grilling is the best way to cook meat. We grill over pecan wood which has a light, fruity smoke and burns cool so that it does not char the meat. The smoke is also gentle enough for delicate fish and other meats. Pecan wood is particularly good to use in New Mexico because the state has some of the best pecan orchards in the country. Be sure the wood you use is dry-aged and that you have a good ventilation system. Of course, less tender cuts of meat benefit from slow cooking in stews or braised dishes, and large cuts are best roasted, especially when you wish the flavors of a marinade to predominate.

As with game and fowl, it is critical that the meat be at room temperature (somewhere between 60° and 75°) so that it will cook evenly. If it is cold, it will char on the outside before it is cooked on the inside. The cooking times for meat given in the old cookbooks are often misleading or inaccurate. As a rough guide, rare meat is equivalent to an internal temperature of 120° to 125°; medium rare is at 125° to 135°; and medium is about 140°. After that, feel free to throw the meat out! To eliminate guesswork, invest in a small instant-read meat thermometer. Professional chefs use them all the time, especially with large pieces of meat. But be sure not to leave the thermometer in the oven!

Some of the sauces that go best with meat are dried red chile sauces, and sauces made from earthy ingredients such as roasted garlic, roasted cumin, and blackened tomatoes. All of these wonderful sauces cry out for something substantial — they need a partner of equal strength in order to be balanced.

While a healthy diet should not include large amounts of meat everyday, a well-balanced diet should, from time to time, include great beef dishes or really fresh roasted lamb or barbecued pork. Besides being a good source of protein, it would be a shame to leave these flavors and textures out of one's diet. In my opinion, too many people are dogmatic about red meat. To understand and fully appreciate the style and tradition of Southwestern food, it is necessary to experience the meats and sauces that have been used for hundreds of years. This is food from the ranch that sustained ranch hands and cowboys: food that has traditionally nourished hard-working people living in a harsh environment. It can provide us with a link to an older way of life.

COWBOY STEAK
with Red Chile Onion Rings

This recipe, which recently made the cover of Bon Appetit *magazine, is a trademark item at Coyote Cafe. Our customers never fail to remark on the sight of the 22-ounce, bone-in aged prime rib steak and the huge mountain of onion rings served on an oversized plate. We are talking large steaks here! It can be fun to see who orders it — everyone from burly cowboys in ten-gallon hats to petite elderly English ladies. In fact, we call it Cowboy Steak because it is large enough to satisfy the biggest appetite gained from riding in the open air out on the range. I love the primordial quality of large cuts of meat complete with chunky bones to gnaw on.*

Yield: 4 servings

4 aged prime bone-in rib-eye steaks (or T-bone or porterhouse steaks), 1½-inches thick

4 white onions, cut into ⅟₁₆- to ⅛-inch rings

3 cups milk

3 cups sifted all-purpose flour

½ cup medium molido chile powder

2 tablespoons plus 2 teaspoons corn starch

3 teaspoons salt

3 teaspoons ground cumin

2 teaspoons sugar

2 teaspoons hot Hungarian paprika

vegetable oil (for deep frying)

salt and freshly ground pepper to taste

Pico de Gallo Salsa (see page 13)

Bring the steaks to room temperature. Soak onions in milk in a large bowl for 1 hour. Drain well. Mix flour, chile powder, cornstarch, salt, cumin, sugar, and paprika in another large bowl. Dredge onions in flour mixture; shake off excess. Heat oil in large heavy saucepan to 360°. Add onions in batches and cook until golden brown, about 45 seconds. Transfer to paper towels using a slotted spoon; drain well.

Meanwhile, season steaks with salt and pepper and place in a cast-iron or other heavy skillet over medium-high heat. Cook to desired doneness, about 7 minutes per side for medium rare. Pour off excess fat before turning. Finish on a grill if desired. Transfer to plates. Serve immediately with onion rings and Pico de Gallo Salsa.

FILLET OF BEEF
with Smoked Oysters

I have studied Mexican cuisine for some time now and have collected over 100 cookbooks from different regions of the country. This has been a great source of inspiration for new dishes at Coyote Cafe. This recipe is one example. It is my hope that more Mexican regional cookbooks will become available, especially in translation for the North American market. This is a relatively easy dish to prepare, and the sauce can be prepared ahead of time.

Yield: 4 servings

4 aged center cut beef fillets (about 6 ounces each)

1 quart beef stock

1 tablespoon roasted ground cumin seed

1 tablespoon roasted dried thyme

6 cloves garlic, roasted, peeled, and minced

1 cup Black Pepper Yucatán Oysters, (see page 43), puréed

4 tablespoons softened sweet butter

12 small fresh Pacific oysters (*e.g.*, Hog Island or Crescent Bay), scrubbed

4 slices wild boar bacon (or Amador, Smithfield, or Harrington's corn cob smoked bacon), ¼ inch thick

salt and pepper to taste

2 tablespoons virgin olive oil

4 leeks (both green and white parts), cut into thin julienne

1 cup Pico de Gallo Salsa (see page 13)

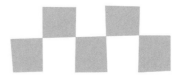

Bring the steaks to room temperature. To prepare sauce, combine stock, cumin, thyme, garlic, and puréed oysters. Cook for 20 minutes over low heat, and then strain. Add 2 tablespoons of the butter and incorporate.

Cold-smoke fresh oysters for 20 to 30 minutes in a smoker (put a tray of ice in the smoker and keep the temperature below 180°), or barbecue over a very low fire with wood chips, covered, for 10 to 15 minutes, until shells open slightly; be sure oysters do not dry out or "boil" in shells. Allow to cool, shuck, and set aside.

Wrap a slice of bacon around each fillet and season with salt and pepper. Over high heat, bring oil in pan to almost smoking, then reduce heat to medium and saute beef fillets 5 minutes each side. Beef should be crusty and browned on the outside, rare to medium rare inside.

To prepare leeks, cook in lightly salted water for about 2 minutes. Drain carefully, toss in remaining 2 tablespoons butter, and salt and pepper to taste.

Place the sauce on a large dinner plate, and the beef in the center, on the sauce. On each plate, divide leeks into three portions around the beef, and place an oyster on top of each leek portion (three per plate). Garnish with Pico de Gallo Salsa.

BEEF FILLET
with Tomatillo Chipotle Sauce

The high acidity and roasted, smoky flavor of the tomatillos perfectly accents the earthy tones of the beef. The sauce does not contain any beef stock, and so seems lighter than a heavy reduced beef sauce, while the cheese provides a contrasting richness. Jack or soft Oaxacan cheese can be used as an alternative to Fontina.

Yield: 4 servings

4 aged center-cut beef fillets (about 6 ounces each)

salt and pepper to taste

3 tablespoons olive oil

4 corn tortillas

3 tablespoons corn oil

4 slices Fontina cheese, about 1 ounce each

3 cups Tomatillo Chipotle Sauce (see page 26)

½ cup coarsely chopped cilantro

Bring the steaks to room temperature. Season with salt and pepper. Over high heat, bring olive oil to almost smoking in a heavy pan, then reduce heat to medium and sauté beef for 5 minutes each side. In a separate pan, soften tortillas in heated corn oil. Remove and dry excess oil with paper towels, and keep warm. Place a warm tortilla on each plate, and the beef on top of the tortilla. Put the cheese on top of the beef and place under the broiler until the cheese melts. Surround the beef with about ¾ cup of sauce per plate, covering the tortilla. Garnish by sprinkling coarsely chopped cilantro over the beef.

SEARED TENDERLOIN
with Green Chile Jerky

Using a spicy dry rubbed marinade is similar to the Cajun technique of seasoning prior to roasting. This method is also used in parts of northern Mexico for making Carne Seca, a very popular jerky-style dried beef, especially around Monterrey.

The tenderloin should be frozen enough so that it can be sliced thinly. In fact, you can adapt the tenderloin part of the recipe, with the spices, to make a wonderful carpaccio, and serve the raw sliced meat with fried tortilla strips, Red Chile Mayonnaise, and fresh lime. Jerky, or cured dried beef, is a traditional Western snack food that is a favorite for riding trips and camping. It is easy to prepare and if stored in a closed container in the refrigerator will keep for months. Prepare at least a day ahead.

Yield: 8 to 12 servings

1 beef tenderloin (about 4 to 5 pounds)

3 tablespoons cumin seed

1 teaspoon anise seed

1 teaspoon coriander seed

2 tablespoons roasted ground Mexican oregano

1 tablespoon dried thyme

2 cloves

1 cup Chimayo chile powder

1 tablespoon kosher salt

4 tablespoons brown sugar

¼ cup olive oil

2 quarts brown beef stock

Green Chile Jerky (recipe follows)

Trim and clean tenderloin of all fell and membranes. Toast cumin, anise, coriander, oregano, and thyme together in a skillet until fragrant. Grind together in a spice mill with the cloves. Add the chile powder, salt, and sugar, and mix well. Oil the tenderloin and coat it thoroughly with the chile powder mixture. Let the meat sit at room temperature for 2 hours (or longer) to season.

To prepare the sauce, shred the Green Chile Jerky by hand. Put the jerky and beef stock in a saucepan and simmer 30 minutes. Cook the tenderloin on a grill or in a cast-iron skillet until rare to medium rare, about 20 to 25 minutes. Let rest for 5 minutes and carve into ¾-inch thick slices. Serve with a little Green Chile Jerky and some sauce.

GREEN CHILE JERKY

2 pounds top round, frozen to firm

1 cup green chile powder

¼ cup kosher salt

¼ cup finely ground black pepper

Preheat oven to 150° or at lowest setting. To prepare the jerky, cut beef with a knife or on a meat slicer across the grain into ⅛ to 1⁄16-inch slices. Place on a rack over a sheet pan. Combine chile powder, salt, and pepper and dredge meat in mixture liberally. Replace on rack, and place in oven overnight, or for 10 to 12 hours, until dry and chewy.

OAXACAN RELLENOS

Oaxaca, in southern Mexico, is the only region where I have seen this particular variation of the traditional relleno, or stuffed chile. The dried red chile, which replaces the usual fresh green chile, comes as a pleasant and colorful surprise. The guajillo chiles should be on the small side — no more than 3 inches long and about an inch wide. Brisket is the best cut of beef for this recipe as it holds its texture and flavor during the long cooking process. Leftover lamb, chicken, or pork carnitas can also be used. In Oaxaca, the sauce is made from coloradito chiles, which are not available here (we use anchos and cascabels). This dish goes well with Tamales de Elote (see page 61).

Yield: 4 servings

1 pound beef brisket

salt and pepper to taste

10 dried ancho chiles

10 dried cascabel chiles

2 tablespoons olive oil

3 quarts water

1 onion, quartered

2 carrots, roughly chopped

2 bay leaves

2 sticks canela (or 1 stick cinnamon)

1 tablespoon ground cumin

4 cloves garlic, smashed

8 dried guajillo chiles

2 teaspoons canned chipotle chiles, puréed

½ cup currants, plumped in warm water for 20 minutes

1 tablespoon capers, well drained

1 Roma tomato, blackened and chopped

2 sweet red peppers, roasted, seeded, and diced

2 cloves garlic, roasted, peeled, and finely chopped

4 eggs, separated

¼ bottle Mexican beer

1½ cups all-purpose flour

1 quart corn oil

2 cups Mark's Red Chile Sauce (see page 25)

Preheat oven to 350°. Trim the beef brisket of fat and season with salt and pepper. Dry-roast ancho and cascabel chiles in oven for 5 minutes. Let cool and remove seeds. In a large ovenproof stewing pot, sear brisket in oil over medium-high heat for about 4 minutes per side.

Reduce oven to 300°. Bring water to a boil and add onion, carrots, bay leaves, and canela. Add to meat. Then add the ancho and cascabel chiles, cumin, smashed garlic, and more salt and pepper to taste. Cover with foil and bake in oven for at least 5 hours or until meat shreds apart. Let brisket sit in cooking stock until cool, or refrigerate overnight. Reserve chiles and 2 cups cooking liquid, and shred meat.

To prepare the rellenos, steam the guajillos in a vegetable steamer until soft, about 1 hour. Carefully cut lengthwise slits in the guajillos, gently remove seeds, keeping stems attached, and set aside. Reduce reserved cooking liquid to 1 cup. Purée 1 cup reserved cooked chiles and strain out seeds and skin. Place meat, chile purée, reduced cooking liquid, chipotle purée, currants, capers, tomato, peppers, roasted garlic, and salt in a bowl and mix well. Stuff the chiles with meat mixture.

To prepare the batter, beat the egg whites with a pinch of salt until stiff, and set aside. Mix together the beer, 1 cup flour, and egg yolks, and fold in the beaten egg whites. Dip the stuffed chiles in remaining flour and in the batter. Heat the oil to 375° and deep-fry the chiles until golden, about 4 to 6 minutes. Place ½ cup Mark's Red Chile Sauce on each plate, and serve two rellenos on top of sauce.

YUCATÁN LAMB
with Smoked Chile Sauce

I prepared this dish for the PBS television series "Great Chefs of the West," and many of the viewers who tried out the recipe have told me they've had great success with it. This dish combines many traditional flavors of the Yucatán, whose regional cuisine is my favorite. The recipe is adapted from a wild deer version. The sweet rice acts as a foil to the spicy, smoky lamb crust, while the optional cactus provides an unusual accent. The lamb is best if allowed to marinate in the refrigerator overnight. It is important to let it come to room temperature before cooking. The lamb can alternatively be boned and butterflied, and slivers of fresh garlic can be inserted in the meat to give extra flavor. Allow six hours to prepare stock

Yield: 6 to 8 servings

1 leg of lamb (about 6 to 7 pounds)

Stock

1½ pounds lamb trimmings (and additional meat if necessary)

2 quarts water

1 small onion, halved

½ carrot, sliced

1 celery stalk, including leaves, sliced

2 sprigs thyme (or ½ teaspoon dried thyme)

2 sprigs parsley

3 peppercorns

2 dried or canned chipotle chiles

Marinade

1½ tablespoons cumin seeds

3 tablespoons black peppercorns

3 tablespoons roasted ground Mexican oregano

3 tablespoons dried thyme

½ teaspoon sea salt

2 dried or canned chipotle chiles, broken

3 tablespoons olive oil

8 to 10 nopales (optional)

1 tablespoon olive oil

salt and pepper to taste

Sweet Cinnamon Rice (see page 147)

Carefully trim all the fat and outside membranes from the leg of lamb with a boning knife, and set aside, covered with plastic wrap.

Preheat oven to 350°. To make the stock, roast the lamb trimmings and meat in a shallow oven pan for 30 minutes, or until brown. Bring water to a boil over high heat, add trimmings, vegetables, herbs, peppercorns, and chiles, and reduce heat to medium. Skim frequently until scum stops rising. Then simmer over low heat, uncovered, for about 6 hours. Add additional water if stock level falls below level of ingredients. Strain and reserve stock.

To prepare marinade, toast the cumin seeds, peppercorns, oregano, and thyme in a small skillet over medium heat. Stir frequently and remove from heat when ingredients smell roasted, and before they start to smoke. Add salt and chiles, and grind the mixture into a fine powder. Rub the lamb with olive oil and then with powdered marinade ingredients. Place in refrigerator, preferably overnight, to marinate.

Bring lamb to room temperature (about 4 to 6 hours before cooking). Preheat oven to 350°. Place lamb on a rack in a shallow roasting pan and roast for about 1 hour, or until meat reaches an internal temperature of 120° (reduce cooking time if the leg has been butterflied). Raise heat to 450° for 5 to 10 minutes to brown the exterior, or until lamb has a temperature of 130°. Remove from oven and let sit for 10 minutes before carving, to allow meat juices to be reabsorbed.

While the lamb is roasting, remove any needles from the cactus pads and wash in cold water. Brush with olive oil and season with salt and pepper. Grill over a low charcoal fire or under a broiler for about 5 minutes per side, or until tender.

To make the sauce, pour off the lamb fat from the roasting pan and add 6 cups reserved lamb stock. Reduce over high heat, stirring occasionally, until the stock is reduced by two-thirds. Adjust seasoning.

Carve the lamb and serve on a platter with the rice. Garnish with cactus leaves and spoon sauce over the meat.

RACK OF LAMB
with Rosemary-Serrano Aïoli

Aïoli is the traditional accompaniment for lamb in the Provençal cuisine of southern France. In this recipe, the unusual combination of rosemary and roasted serranos works well, and gives the aïoli a Southwestern accent. Black olives and orange zest can also be added to the aïoli if desired.

Yield: 4 servings

Aïoli

6 egg yolks

½ cup fresh lime juice

¼ teaspoon salt

2 cloves garlic

4 teaspoons fresh rosemary (or 2 teaspoons dried)

5 small serrano chiles, roasted and seeded

2 cups olive oil

2 tablespoons chopped fresh cilantro

2 half-racks of lamb (each with 4 double rib chops, serving 2 double rib chops per person)

salt and pepper to taste

4 tablespoons olive oil

To make the aïoli, purée the egg yolks, lime juice, salt, garlic, rosemary, and serranos in a blender. With the blender running, slowly add the olive oil and blend until thickened. Remove purée to a small bowl and fold in cilantro. Chill for 30 minutes. Serve cool, but not cold.

Preheat oven to 400°. Season lamb with salt and pepper. In a skillet over high heat, bring olive oil to almost smoking, and reduce heat to medium. Sear lamb in olive oil until browned, about 1 to 2 minutes per side. Remove from pan, place in oven and cook until medium rare, or until internal temperature reaches 130°, about 12 minutes. Adjust seasonings of aïoli to taste and serve on top of the lamb.

PECAN CRUST RACK OF LAMB

Most people associate pecans with Louisiana, Texas, and Georgia, but New Mexico is also a big producer of high-quality pecans. Besides using a lot of pecans at Coyote Cafe, we also grill over pecan wood. In this dish, the crunchy pecan crust acts as a counterpoint to the tender eye of the rack of lamb. It is important to chop the pecans very finely and to toast them conservatively; if they are too dark, they will burn up in the oven later. I developed this recipe with my red-headed sous-chef, Jeff Koscomb, who is a whiz on the grill and entertains our patrons at the exhibition-kitchen counter with his cooking tips, badinage, and occasional samples of grilled goodies and sauces.

Yield: 4 servings

½ cup Dijon mustard

2 tablespoons honey

2 tablespoons molasses

4 cloves garlic, smashed

1 rack of lamb (about 3½ pounds, or 4 ribs per person)

2 cups finely chopped roasted pecans

½ cup bread crumbs

1 teaspoon chopped fresh marjoram

¼ cup olive oil

salt and pepper to taste

Combine the mustard, honey, molasses, and garlic, and marinate the lamb in this mixture in refrigerator at least 4 hours, preferably overnight. Reserve marinade.

Bring lamb to room temperature (allow 4 to 6 hours). Preheat oven to 400°. Place meat on a sheet pan and roast for 8 minutes. Remove and let sit for 10 minutes. Meanwhile, combine the pecans, bread crumbs, marjoram, oil, salt and pepper. Dip lamb in marinade and then dredge in dry ingredients. Bake in the middle or bottom of the oven for a further 6 minutes until medium rare, or until internal temperature reaches 130°. Remove from oven and let sit for 2 minutes before carving.

PAPANTLA PORK
with Manchamantel Sauce

For this recipe, the meat needs to marinate overnight. This process magnifies the natural sweetness of the meat and helps keep it moist. This is particularly important since most modern pork is fairly lean internally, with little fat to moisten it as it cooks. I use this basic technique in the next three recipes, too. The combination of pork and fruit is classic: all the pork dishes in this chapter have fruit in some form. In this one, it is Manchamantel Sauce, which is made with pineapples, bananas, and apples.

Yield: 4 servings

Pork Marinade

½ cup sugar

1½ tablespoons salt

1 tablespoon dried thyme

½ tablespoon ground cumin

1 tablespoon crushed bay leaf

1 teaspoon crushed black pepper

1 teaspoon roasted ground Mexican oregano

3 tablespoons chile caribe

4 allspice berries

4 cloves

1 stick cinnamon

6 cups water

4 double pork loin chops

salt and pepper to taste

3 tablespoons olive oil

3 cups Manchamantel Sauce (see page 28)

Mix the marinade ingredients together, add the pork, and marinate overnight. Remove pork, bring to room temperature, and season with salt and pepper. Preheat oven to 400°. In a skillet over high heat, bring olive oil to almost smoking, and reduce heat to medium. Sear pork in olive oil until browned, about 1 to 2 minutes per side. Remove from pan, place in oven, and cook for about 20 minutes or until internal temperature reaches 140°. Alternatively, grill over a medium-low fire. Place sauce on plate and serve pork on top of sauce.

BRAZILIAN PORK

I used to prepare this dish in my student days, and while it may not exactly replicate the authentic "feijoada" flavor, the recipe brings together the essential elements in a lighter version. The combination of orange, ginger, and clove makes a great glaze, and red chiles can be added to make it spicier. Note that the pork should marinate for three days.

Yield: 4 servings

1 pork loin (about 4 pounds)

Pork Marinade (see preceding recipe)

4 cups fresh orange juice

1 cup chopped fresh ginger

1 cup brown sugar

2 teaspoons ground cloves

Place pork in marinade and refrigerate for about 72 hours. Remove pork and bring to room temperature. Preheat oven to 350°. Purée together ¼ cup orange juice and the ginger, and place purée in a saucepan together with remaining juice, sugar, and cloves. Cook for 10 to 15 minutes over medium heat to reduce glaze to the consistency of maple syrup. Remove from heat and brush pork with glaze. Place pork in a roasting pan and bake for 50 minutes to 1 hour or until internal temperature reaches 140°. If glaze gets too dark or begins to blacken, lower oven to 275°. Baste frequently with glaze to build a coating. Remove pork from oven, let sit for 10 minutes before carving, and serve with black beans (see Black Bean Soup, page 32).

TENDERLOIN OF PORK
with Apple and Red Chile Chutney

The end of the summer is the time to use red chiles — before they lose their sweetness and dry out. Pimento or Anaheim chiles, or even sweet red peppers can be substituted. Using New Mexican apples and pine nuts makes this a delicious seasonal Southwestern dish. The pork should be marinated for 24 hours, and the chutney is best prepared the day before serving.

Yield: 4 servings

Apple and Red Chile Chutney

4 Granny Smith apples, peeled, cored and coarsely chopped

4 fresh red chiles (or rehydrated dried chiles), diced

½ cup brown sugar

⅓ cup cider vinegar

8 cloves garlic, minced

1 cup water

1 tablespoon chopped fresh marjoram

½ cup roasted pine nuts (optional)

Pork Marinade (see page 117)

4 pork tenderloins, 6 to 8 ounces each

2 cups apple cider

3 tablespoons light brown sugar

2 tablespoons molido chile powder

To prepare the chutney, place apples and chiles in a heavy stainless-steel saucepan with sugar, vinegar, garlic, and water. Cook until apples are tender. Stir in marjoram and add pine nuts. Allow to cool and refrigerate.

Place pork in marinade and refrigerate. Remove pork and bring to room temperature. Combine apple cider, brown sugar, and chile powder. Grill meat over a hot fire for 7 to 10 minutes, or broil until internal temperature reaches 140°. Baste with a little apple cider mixture as meat cooks. Serve pork with chutney, and Tamale de Elote with Green Chile Sauce, if desired (see pages 61 and 26).

PORK TACOS
with Wild Mushrooms and Tamarind Chipotle Sauce

The idea for this dish came to me while leafing through a Chinese cookbook and studying a recipe for mu-shu pork and Chinese pancakes. This version uses corn tortillas instead of Mandarin pancakes, wild chanterelles instead of dried wood-ear mushrooms, and Tamarind Chipotle Sauce is substituted for hoisin sauce. As you can tell, I enjoy borrowing ideas from other cuisines and transposing the compositional features into the Southwestern style. While the results may not be strictly orthodox or traditional, Southwestern cuisine is nothing if not flexible; who knows, this very dish may have been created hundreds of years ago in a pueblo not far from here . . . .

Yield: 4 servings

2 pounds boned pork loin or tenderloin

Pork Marinade (see page 117)

1 cup corn oil

8 corn tortillas

12 cups coarsely chopped wild mushrooms

3 cloves garlic, smashed

4 tablespoons butter

4 tablespoons olive oil

2 cups Tamarind Chipotle Sauce (see page 27)

8 poblano chiles, roasted, seeded, and chopped into fine julienne strips

2 sweet red peppers, roasted, seeded, and chopped into fine julienne strips

2 cups shredded lettuce

1 cup finely chopped Roma tomatoes

1 cup coarsely chopped cilantro

Mix marinade ingredients together, add the pork, and marinate in the refrigerator overnight. Remove pork and bring to room temperature. Preheat oven to 375°. Place pork in a roasting pan and roast for 20 minutes or until internal temperature reaches 140°. Remove and let sit for 5 minutes. Cut pork into ¼-inch slices and finish on the grill, 1 minute per side. Cut pork into julienne strips.

Heat corn oil in a sauté pan and soften tortillas, about 30 seconds. Remove tortillas, dry excess oil with paper towels, and keep warm. Sauté mushrooms and garlic in olive oil and butter until tender.

To assemble tacos, place 2 tablespoons of Tamarind Chipotle Sauce on each tortilla and add pork, mushrooms, and garlic, poblanos, sweet peppers, lettuce, tomatoes, and chopped cilantro. Top with a further 2 tablespoons of sauce. Fold tortillas over to form a taco and serve two per person.

PORK LOIN
with Cascabel and Grapefruit Sauce

This dish, which originates in Veracruz on the Mexican Caribbean coast, again combines pork and fruit. At first sight this recipe may appear to yield simple flavors, but the cooked citrus juice and allspice create a complex taste. Cascabel chiles, literally "little rattles," are round and red, and have a pleasing warmth rather than a fiery heat, thus making excellent sauces.

Yield: 4 servings

24 dried cascabel chiles

3 cups water

6 cloves garlic

4 cups fresh grapefruit juice

1 cup fresh orange juice

3 teaspoons allspice

1 teaspoon salt

4 double pork loin chops

4 tablespoons olive oil

Remove stems and seeds from chiles. With a comal or black iron skillet, or in an oven at 250°, dry roast chiles for 3 to 4 minutes. Shake once or twice and do not allow to blacken. Add to the water in a covered pan and simmer very low for 20 minutes to rehydrate. Allow to cool. Taste the chile water, and if not bitter, add about ½ cup and the chiles to a blender (use plain water if bitter). Purée together with the garlic and strain. Add the fruit juices, allspice, and salt and mix together. Place pork in marinade and refrigerate overnight.

Remove pork and bring to room temperature, and reserve the marinade. In a skillet over high heat, bring olive oil to almost smoking, and reduce heat to medium. Sear pork in olive oil until browned, about 1 to 2 minutes per side. Pour off excess fat and set aside.

Preheat oven to 450°. In an ovenproof pan over medium heat, reduce reserved marinade by one-half. Then add meat and roast in oven for 40 minutes, or until internal temperature reaches 140°. Add a little water to pan if it gets too dry. Serve meat with sauce from pan, and black beans and fried sweet potato chips, if desired.

TAMARIND BARBECUED RIBS

This is my version of the old Tex-Mex favorite. The secret of great ribs is to marinate them to bring out more flavor, and to cook them very slowly to begin with. They should be tender to the bone and the meat should pull apart when cooked. Be careful not to add too much marinade as a glaze until the ribs have cooked, or it will caramelize and blacken. Finishing the ribs on a grill at a higher heat will give them an appealing crusty exterior.

Yield: 4 servings

2 cups olive oil

1 cup fresh lime juice

12 cloves garlic, chopped

8 teaspoons chile caribe

4 teaspoons sugar

2 racks spareribs (6 spareribs or ½ rack per person)

3 cups Tamarind Chipotle Sauce (see page 27)

Mix olive oil, lime juice, garlic, chile caribe, and sugar, and marinate pork ribs in this mixture overnight. Remove ribs, and reserve marinade. Bring ribs to room temperature. Preheat oven to 200°. Place ribs in an oven pan and bake for 1 hour to 1½ hours or until tender and cooked through to the bone. Transfer ribs to a very low grill and cook for a further 45 to 60 minutes to finish. Brush ribs with marinade while on grill; in the final 10 minutes, brush with a little Tamarind Chipotle Sauce. Cook until crusty, but do not let the ribs or sauce burn. Place remaining Tamarind Chipotle Sauce on plate and serve ribs on top.

DESSERTS & BREADS

Southwestern desserts should share the style of the rest of the meal: they should be simple, hearty, and expressive, like most of the recipes we have presented in this book. Southwestern cuisine reflects the "family" style of eating, where different courses may be served at the same time, like they were on the ranch. This contrasts with European cuisine, in which a series of courses leads on to the grand finale. Southwestern desserts represent less of a counterpoint and are more integrated into the rest of the meal.

If desserts are to complement the rest of the meal, they need strong flavors and personalities of their own. Ideally, they should emphasize a single flavor. If cinnamon is used, for instance, then other spices should be avoided, and the amount of sugar reduced to allow the sweet tones of the cinnamon to come through.

The flavor of desserts is more important than texture: our recipes tend to include two or three times the amount of spice or flavoring than is generally used in Continental-style desserts. Our churros, for example, are bathed in cinnamon and filled with flavored pastry creams. Some of the stronger, less refined, and more earthy Southwestern dessert flavors are anise, clove, *cajeta* (goat milk caramel), cinnamon, and nuts. All of these stand on their own and can feel refreshing after the hot and spicy dishes that come before.

Most Southwestern food is spicy and hot, so that desserts should be cooling and refreshing to the palate. Sorbets and tropical fruit flavors are perfect, but the ingredients are not available year-round; come to that, neither is the warm weather associated with them! In winter (and Santa Fe has a long, cold winter), I prefer heartier, comforting, almost New England-style desserts that I grew up with, such as rhubarb or apple crisps, or mincemeat tarts. On a chilly night, they go perfectly with a little brandy or aged bourbon.

Much of this chapter is the work of Kimberley Sweet, my very aptly named pastry chef. She deserves great credit, especially for her wonderful breads, which are always a favorite with our customers.

CHILE CORN BREAD

If you are yearning for a corn bread with a twist, look no further. The red and green ingredients and bright colors make this a festive bread at any time of the year. Intense and delightful, this yeasted corn bread juggles chiles, cheese, and cilantro in a rich corn dough.

Yield: Two loaves

Chopped Ingredients

½ cup finely diced sweet red onion

1 tablespoon corn oil

¾ cup grated medium Cheddar cheese

½ bunch chopped cilantro, no stems

3 serrano chiles, finely minced with seeds

5 to 8 jalapeño chiles, finely minced with seeds (the two chiles together should equal about ½ cup)

1 sweet red pepper, finely minced

¼ teaspoon cayenne

½ to 1 tablespoon ancho chile powder

Sponge

1½ tablespoons dry yeast

¾ cup warm water

1 tablespoons sugar

1 tablespoon all-purpose flour

Dough

1 cup buttermilk

1 cup regular milk

1 tablespoon salt

4 tablespoons sugar

¼ cup melted sweet butter

¼ cup corn oil

5 cups all-purpose flour

1 cup whole wheat flour

1⅓ cup coarse cornmeal

1 cup fine cornmeal

1 tablespoon corn oil

Grease two 4½ x 8½-inch loaf pans. Sauté onions in corn oil until soft and translucent. Combine with remaining chopped ingredients and set aside.

To make the sponge, add yeast to warm water. Let sit until it is bubbling. Add sugar and flour, and stir vigorously.

Scald both milks and add the salt, sugar, butter, and corn oil. Add the all-purpose flour to the milk mixture and mix thoroughly with a wooden spoon or use a mixer with a dough hook. The consistency should be very wet. Add the sponge to this mixture, along with the whole wheat flour and 1 cup each fine and course cornmeals. Mix until dough is firm and silky.

Remove to floured board and knead the chopped ingredients into the dough. Add extra flour as necessary to keep the dough from sticking to the board. Once chopped ingredients are well blended, place dough in a bowl greased with corn oil. Rotate the dough in the oil until it is well covered. Cover with plastic wrap and let the dough rise in a warm place for 45 minutes, or until it doubles in volume.

Preheat oven to 375°. When the dough has risen, divide in half and form into logs. Sprinkle loaf pans with remaining ⅓ cup cornmeal. Place dough in pans and bake for 50 to 60 minutes or until crust is a dark golden brown and the bottom of the loaf is hollow sounding when tapped. Turn loaves onto rack to cool.

CINNAMON BUCKWHEAT BREAD

This is one of our most popular breads at Coyote Cafe. The combination of cinnamon and buckwheat intrigues and satisfies, and provides a good foil for hot and spicy food. The rich, earthy aroma of the bread is captivating. Buckwheat is not in fact a grain at all, but an herb that was brought to Europe from China by the Dutch. Its dark coloring and coarse texture, in combination with the cinnamon, results in a fragrant rustic loaf with a hint of sweetness.

Yield: Two loaves

2 tablespoons plus 1 teaspoon dry yeast

2 cups warm water

½ cup dry milk

⅔ cup sugar

¼ cup buckwheat flour

5¼ to 6 cups bread flour

2 tablespoons cinnamon

2½ teaspoons salt

1 tablespoon corn oil

2 egg whites, lightly beaten

Grease two 4½ x 8½-inch loaf pans. Sprinkle the yeast over the warm water. Let sit approximately 10 minutes until bubbling. In a mixing bowl, combine dry milk, sugar, buckwheat flour, 5¼ cups of the bread flour, cinnamon, and salt. Add yeast mixture, and beat vigorously with hook attachment or by hand for 8 to 10 minutes until the dough is silky and resilient, adding more flour as necessary to keep the dough from sticking.

Place dough in a bowl greased with corn oil. Rotate the dough in the oil until it is well covered with oil. Cover with plastic wrap and let the dough rise in a warm place for 30 minutes, or until it doubles in volume. Punch the dough down and let rise for another 30 minutes.

Divide the dough in half and form into logs. Place into the prepared loaf pans, brush with whisked egg whites, and allow to rise further until bread reaches just over the lip of the pan (approximately 30 to 40 minutes). Make two diagonal cuts in the top of each loaf with a sharp knife and sprinkle lightly with 2 tablespoons bread flour.

Bake in a preheated 400° oven for 30 to 40 minutes or until crust is a dark golden brown and the bottom of the loaf is hollow sounding when tapped. Turn loaves onto rack to cool.

ORANGE CUMIN BREAD

Cumin is an indigenous spice that is frequently used in Southwestern cooking. This recipe features one of my favorite combinations: the sweetness of orange with its zesty citrus freshness, balanced by the pungent, woodsy quality of cumin. This combination also works well with other foods, seafood in particular. Toasting the cumin seeds and grinding them beforehand will bring out their flavor even more.

Yield: Two loaves

2 tablespoons dry yeast

2 cups warm water

2 tablespoons ground roasted cumin seed

6 tablespoons dry milk

½ cup sugar

5 tablespoons vegetable oil

½ cup orange juice concentrate

¼ cup plus 2 tablespoons fine cornmeal

1 cup whole wheat flour

4 cups all-purpose flour

1 tablespoon salt

2 egg whites, lightly beaten

Grease two 4½ x 8½-inch loaf pans. Sprinkle yeast over 1 cup warm water and set aside. Using a mixer with a dough hook, combine the cumin, milk, sugar, 4 tablespoons oil, orange juice concentrate, ¼ cup cornmeal and whole wheat flour. Add the remaining cup warm water, mix slightly and add the yeast. Then mix well to incorporate.

Stop the mixer and add the all-purpose flour and salt. Mix the dough either by hand or in the mixer until it becomes silky and resilient, adding extra flour as necessary to keep the dough from sticking to the surface. Place dough in a warm greased bowl with 1 tablespoon of vegetable oil. Rotate the dough in the oil until it is well covered. Cover with plastic wrap and let the dough rise in a warm place for 30 minutes or until it doubles in volume. Punch the dough down and let rise for another 30 minutes.

Divide the dough in half and form into logs. Place into the prepared loaf pans, brush with whisked egg whites, and allow to rise further until bread reaches just over the lip of the pan (approximately 30 to 40 minutes). Make two diagonal cuts in the top of each loaf with a sharp knife and sprinkle lightly with 2 tablespoons cornmeal.

Bake in a preheated 400° oven for 40 minutes or until crust is a dark golden brown and the bottom of the loaf is hollow sounding when tapped. Turn loaves onto rack to cool.

IBARRA CHOCOLATE CAKE
with Chocolate Glaze

Even though there is no Ibarra chocolate in it, this cake contains everything that Mexican Ibarra chocolate contains — chocolate, almonds, cinnamon, and sugar. Hence the name. The glaze for this torte-like dessert has twice as much chocolate as the cake, making this concoction a choco-holics delight.

Yield: One 8- or 9-inch cake

1 tablespoon cinnamon

zest of 2 oranges

4 tablespoons (2 ounces) bittersweet chocolate, grated

1½ cups (6 ounces) unblanched almonds, toasted and ground

4 eggs, separated

½ cup sugar

2 tablespoons fresh orange juice

2 tablespoons Grand Marnier

Chocolate Glaze (recipe follows)

Preheat oven to 325°. Grease, flour, and paper an 8- or 9-inch cake pan. Combine cinnamon, orange zest, grated chocolate, and ground almonds in a mixing bowl and set aside. Beat egg yolks with ¼ cup sugar; stir in orange juice, and set aside.

In another bowl, beat egg whites to soft peaks while gradually adding ¼ cup sugar. Stir egg yolks and orange juice into the chocolate-almond mixture, then fold in half the beaten egg whites. Blend well, and gently fold in remaining egg whites.

Spread mixture evenly in prepared cake pan and bake for 35 to 40 minutes or until cake pulls away from sides of pan. Let cool for 10 minutes and invert onto cake rack.

When cool, paint with Grand Marnier, and cover with Chocolate Glaze.

CHOCOLATE GLAZE

10 tablespoons (5 ounces) bittersweet chocolate

1 tablespoon (½ ounce) unsweetened chocolate

¾ cup softened butter

1 tablespoon corn syrup

1 tablespoon water

¼ cup chopped candied orange peel (optional)

Place both chocolates, ½ cup of the soft butter, corn syrup, and water in a double boiler over simmering (not rapidly boiling) water. Stir gently until just melted. Remove from heat, and stir in remaining ¼ cup soft butter. The glaze is ready to pour when it reaches the consistency of maple syrup (between 86° and 96°).

Place cake rack over pan or wax paper, and pour glaze over cake, tilting to coat evenly. Decorate with candied orange peel if desired.

ANISE POUND CAKE

This buttery pound cake highlights the licorice flavor of anise. We serve this cake with ripe summer strawberries soaked in Sambuca (an Italian anise-based liqueur), and a dollop of freshly whipped cream, or with blueberries, raspberries, or blackberries. The combination of naturally sweet fresh fruits mixed with sweet spices, such as anise or cinnamon, is irresistible. This is a great cake to serve at a picnic on a hot summer day.

Yield: One 10-inch cake

3 cups all-purpose flour

¼ teaspoon salt

1 pound butter

2 cups sugar

1 teaspoon vanilla extract

4 tablespoons ground roasted anise seed

5 eggs

⅔ cup sour cream

Preheat oven to 350°. Grease and flour a 10-inch tube pan. Sift together flour and salt, set aside. Cream the butter with sugar, vanilla, and anise seed until light. Add the eggs to the butter mixture, one at a time, beating well after each addition. After all the eggs are incorporated, add the dry ingredients alternately with the sour cream. Scrape the bowl well and mix until blended.

Pour into prepared pan and bake for approximately 1 hour until the cake is golden and springs back to the touch.

ALMOND POLENTA POUND CAKE

Polenta is usually associated with the famous Italian dish of the same name, but here refers to the rough cornmeal used extensively in Southwestern cooking. Polenta gives this cake a crunchy texture — you can bite into it and almost taste the sweet corn. When combined with almond paste, as in this recipe, a golden, sweet, tender cake is created. We serve it dusted with powdered sugar and accompanied by fresh ripe berries in season.

Yield: One 9-inch cake

¾ cup butter

½ cup (4 ounces) almond paste

1¼ cups sugar

1 teaspoon vanilla extract

6 large eggs, separated

1½ cups cake flour

¾ cup coarse cornmeal (polenta)

1 teaspoon baking powder

1 cup heavy cream

Preheat oven to 350°. Grease, flour, and paper a 9-inch cake pan. In an electric mixer, cream together butter, almond paste, 1 cup of sugar, and vanilla. Scrape down the sides of the bowl frequently. Add egg yolks to butter mixture and blend well.

Sift together cake flour, cornmeal, and baking powder, and add to the butter mixture along with the cream. Mix until well blended. Set aside.

Beat the egg whites with the remaining ¼ cup sugar until soft peaks form. Fold half the whites into the butter mixture and incorporate well. Gently fold in remaining whites and pour mixture into the prepared pan.

Bake for 30 minutes or until the top of the cake is golden and firm to the touch. Let cake cool on rack for 15 minutes before turning out.

CHRISTINE'S VENISON MINCEMEAT

Christine Wood's mincemeat is one of the best I have ever tasted. Christine was the butcher at Coyote Cafe when we started, and stuffs a mean sausage. This recipe contains a bit of rum, which gives it an added zip. The mincemeat can be stored in jars, keeps forever, and makes a great gift. You can use it for pies, tarts, and for a special sweet tamale. Make the mincemeat at least a month ahead of time.

Yield: Enough for three 10-inch pies

1 pound fresh venison

5 ounces fresh suet

3 pounds tart green apples

1½ cups packed dark brown sugar

1½ cups granulated sugar

1 pound golden seedless raisins

10 ounces raisins

5 ounces candied citron (preferably freshly made; available from an organic health food store)

⅓ cup candied orange peel

¼ cup candied lemon peel

2½ tablespoons ground cinnamon

1 tablespoon ground cloves

1 teaspoon ground nutmeg

1 tablespoon fine sea salt

⅓ cup cider vinegar

⅓ cup water

1 cup Myers's dark rum

1 cup bourbon

Carefully trim venison of connective tissue, and grind through the medium plate of a meat grinder. Grind the suet through the finest plate of your grinder, or grind twice (make sure that the suet has no smell of blood or it will spoil the mincemeat). Peel and core the apples, and chop roughly in a food processor. Place these ingredients in a large bowl, and mix together with the sugar, raisins, citron, and peel. Add the remaining spices, salt, vinegar, water and liquor and blend well.

Pack into a glazed earthenware or other nonreactive container. Cover mixture with a clean towel soaked in rum and then cover tightly with a lid or plastic wrap. Store in the refrigerator for at least one month to ensure that the flavors 'bind' together. The mincemeat will continue to develop for about four months, and can then be stored indefinitely.

To make mincemeat pies, prepare Pie Pastry (see page 141), and pre-bake shells according to directions. Pour filling into prebaked shells and cover with top crusts. Blend 1 egg and 1 tablespoon water, and brush top crusts with this egg wash. Cut four vent holes in each pie crust. Bake at 350° for 40 minutes or until golden brown.

WHITE CHOCOLATE BUTTERMILK TART

This is a traditional pie whose refreshing and tangy taste belies its creamy richness. We serve the White Chocolate Buttermilk Tart garnished with garden-ripe berries and curls of white chocolate. Try to find unpasteurized old-fashioned-style buttermilk, which is more tangy, and use good quality white chocolate such as Tobler or some other Swiss brand. The white chocolate should not be stored for too long, or else it will go off more quickly than regular chocolate because of its high fat content.

Yield: One 9-inch tart

3 ounces white chocolate

1 prebaked 9-inch tart shell (see page 141)

3 eggs

3 egg yolks

1½ cups buttermilk

4 tablespoons melted butter

juice of 1 lemon

zest of 1 lemon

1 teaspoon vanilla extract

½ cup packed brown sugar

1½ tablespoons all-purpose flour

Preheat oven to 350°. In a double boiler, melt white chocolate over simmering (not boiling) water. Remove from heat, let cool, and paint the tart shell with chocolate.

Whisk together eggs, yolks, buttermilk, butter, lemon juice, lemon zest, and vanilla. Mix sugar and flour together, then add to the buttermilk mixture. Pour into saucepan and cook over medium heat, stirring constantly, until slightly thickened.

Pour into tart shell and bake for approximately 30 minutes, until the custard is softly set. The custard will firm as it cools. Garnish with sweetened berries of your choice.

RHUBARB ANISE CRISP

Rhubarb and anise team up to create a new rendition of an old favorite. It's an unlikely combination, but a winning one. Even Coyote remembers this one, from back when he was a pup!

Yield: One 9-inch crisp

2 cups sugar

1½ cups all-purpose flour

3½ tablespoons coarsely ground roasted anise seed

7 ounces (1¾ sticks) cold butter

1½ pounds rhubarb

juice of half a lemon

zest of 2 oranges

¼ teaspoon vanilla extract

Preheat oven to 400°. Using an electric mixer with paddle attachment or a food processor with a metal blade, mix 1 cup sugar and flour together. Add coarsely chopped anise and cold butter. Mix just until large pea-size chunks form and crumbs hold together when a handful is squeezed. Set aside.

Trim off rough ends of rhubarb, cut into 1-inch lengths, and toss with lemon juice, orange zest, vanilla, and remaining sugar. Place in a 9-inch pie pan. Cover with sugar-anise topping. Bake for 45 minutes or until fruit juices are bubbling around the sides of the pan and the crisp is evenly golden.

COYOTE CHURROS

Churros are golden deep-fried pastries rolled in cinnamon sugar. The original churros are the famous Spanish breakfast pastries that are served with dark chocolate foamed with heavy cream. The dough, which is similar to cream puff dough, was introduced to Mexico by the Spanish. In Mexico, churros are sold by street vendors who make them to order in black kettles containing boiling oil. Filled with flavored creams, or sprinkled with sugar, churros are a delightful treat for dessert, a special brunch, or any time of day!

Yield: Two dozen churros

zest of 2 oranges, finely chopped

2 cups water

1 cup butter

1 teaspoon salt

½ cup plus 3 tablespoons sugar

2 cups all-purpose flour

8 eggs

2 quarts vegetable oil

1 tablespoon cinnamon

Pastry Creams (recipes follow)

To make the dough, combine orange zest, water, butter, salt, and 3 tablespoons sugar in a saucepan, and heat to a rolling boil. Quickly stir in flour all at once. Stir briskly over heat until all the ingredients are well incorporated and dough is silky and pulls easily away from the sides and bottom of the saucepan. Place the dough in a mixer and beat on medium speed with the paddle attachment. Add the eggs one at a time as dough cools. After the addition of all of the eggs, beat for 5 minutes.

Place dough in pastry bag with a large star tip. Pipe the dough onto a prepared sheet pan in tube shapes 3 inches long and 1 inch thick. Freeze the piped dough until firm so it can be more easily handled. Heat oil to 375° and deep-fry churros until golden brown, then flip to complete browning. Remove with slotted spoon to a plate lined with paper towels. Let cool.

To assemble the churros, push a tunnel through both ends of the churros, using the handle of a wooden spoon. Fill a small pastry bag with a flavored pastry cream and pipe into churros. Repeat for each flavor. Refrigerate for 30 minutes.

In a bowl, stir together ½ cup sugar and cinnamon. Toss the churros in the cinnamon sugar. Garnish the plates with a rosette of softly whipped cream, if desired. Each plate should get 3 churros, one of each flavor.

PASTRY CREAM

2 tablespoons all-purpose flour

3 tablespoons sugar

2 cups milk

½ vanilla bean, split and scraped

3 eggs

2 tablespoons butter

Chocolate Flavoring

2 tablespoons chopped bittersweet chocolate

1½ tablespoons butter

Almond Flavoring

1 teaspoon almond extract

1 tablespoon finely chopped toasted almonds

Espresso Flavoring

1½ teaspoons instant espresso powder

1½ teaspoons sugar

To prepare pastry cream, mix flour and sugar together. Heat milk and vanilla bean to scalding in a heavy saucepan. Add ½ cup hot milk to the flour and sugar. Beat until smooth and return to the saucepan. Beat the eggs lightly and temper by adding ½ cup of the milk mixture to the eggs, then beat well. Return the tempered eggs to the remaining milk mixture and cook over medium heat until the mixture reaches the consistency of thickened pudding. Remove from heat and add butter.

While the pastry cream is still warm, divide into three equal batches. Add chocolate flavoring to one batch, almond flavoring to another, and to the last, espresso flavoring, beating it well to dissolve the espresso and sugar. Cover with plastic wrap. Let cool and refrigerate.

KATHY WOLF'S CHOCOLATE KUMQUAT HELADO

Kathy Wolf created a lot of desserts when she was pastry chef at Fourth Street Grill in Berkeley. This ice cream is one of her special creations. The combination of chocolate, coffee, and kumquats (a tangy tropical fruit) gives this ice cream an unusual and distinctive flavor. This dessert provides a refreshing contrast to hot and spicy food.

Yield: One quart

1 cup kumquats, seeded and sliced into thin rounds

1¾ cup sugar

1 cup water

½ cup strong coffee

8 ounces grated bittersweet Swiss chocolate (preferably Tobler brand)

½ cup cocoa

2 cups milk

1 cup heavy cream

½ vanilla bean, split and scraped

3 strips lemon peel, thinly cut

6 extra large egg yolks

Cook kumquats with 1 cup sugar and water in a saucepan over medium-low heat for about 30 minutes, to marmalade consistency. Remove from heat. Cool, chop finely, and set aside.

Combine coffee, chocolate, and cocoa, and set aside.

Combine milk, cream, ¾ cup sugar, vanilla bean, and lemon peel, and cook in a saucepan over low heat until sugar dissolves. Whisk 1 cup of the warm milk base into the egg yolks. After it is thoroughly mixed, add this back to the base and cook in a double boiler over simmering water, making sure the pan does not touch the water. Cook until the mixture is a custard consistency (about 160°). Remove from heat and add chocolate mixture immediately. Stir to combine.

Add 6 tablespoons of the cooled kumquats to chocolate ice cream base. Place over bowl of ice water to chill. Pour into ice cream machine and freeze according to manufacturer's specifications.

VANILLA HELADO

To make real vanilla ice cream, you need to use real vanilla. Be sure to use very fresh, flexible Mexican or Tahitian vanilla beans that are moist and thick, and heavily perfumed.

Yield: One quart

2 cups heavy cream

1 cup milk

⅔ cup sugar

1 vanilla bean, split and scraped

4 large egg yolks

Heat the cream, milk, sugar, and vanilla bean to scalding. Temper the egg yolks by adding 1 cup of the hot cream mixture to the yolks, beating well, and returning it to the remaining hot milk mixture. It is important to stir constantly and not let the mixture boil. Cook over medium heat until bubbles appear and the custard is slightly thickened.

Remove from heat and pour into a clean container. Let cool completely, remove vanilla bean, and refrigerate. Pour into ice cream machine and freeze according to manufacturer's specifications.

CAJETA CARAMEL

Cajeta — goat's milk caramel — is used in many traditional Mexican desserts. Cajeta is less sickly sweet than the average caramel, and possesses a flavor and sense of the outdoors that is part of the aesthetic of Southwestern cooking. It is definitely a delightful surprise to those who have not experienced it. It can be flavored with chocolate, brandy, or coffee to create a variety of recipes.

Yield: 2 cups

4 cups evaporated goat's milk

2 cups milk

5 teaspoons cornstarch

½ teaspoon baking soda

1½ cups sugar

6 tablespoons water

juice of ½ lemon

To make the caramel, heat both milks to boiling and then simmer. Mix cornstarch and baking soda together in a small bowl. Add just enough of the hot milk to dissolve the dry ingredients. Beat well with a whisk and pour back into the remaining hot milk. Stir well with a whisk and continue to simmer.

Moisten the sugar with water and lemon juice. Cook over high heat to caramelize, until light golden brown. Wash down the sides of the pot frequently with a pastry brush dipped in water to prevent sugar crystals from forming. Let the sugar cool (until bubbles have subsided) and slowly add half of the milk mixture to the cooled sugar. Return tempered sugar to the remaining milk mixture and continue to cook at a low boil until caramel is thick and dark (approximately 1 hour). Remove from heat and let cool.

This recipe will make enough Cajeta Caramel for one large or two small Cajeta Tarts, several Cajeta Caramel Sundaes, or a few Blackberry Cinnamon Shortcakes (recipes follow). Once refrigerated, the caramel can be stored indefinitely.

CAJETA CARAMEL SUNDAE

Top our rich Vanilla Helado with Cajeta Caramel and pine nuts to make an ice cream sundae that's sure to be a winner. We have it on our menu year round.

Yield: 1 serving

1 tablespoon pine nuts

Vanilla Helado (see page 135)

Cajeta Caramel (see previous recipe)

Toast the pine nuts on a baking sheet for 15 minutes or until light golden in color. Pour some Cajeta Caramel into an ice cream sundae glass or wide wine glass. Add a scoop or two of Vanilla Helado, more caramel, and another scoop of the ice cream. Top it all with more caramel and toasted pine nuts.

CAJETA TART

In this dessert, Cajeta Caramel is used to flavor both the custard layer and the whipped cream topping. The chocolate layer is made with bittersweet chocolate and Ibarra chocolate, the special Mexican chocolate that is made with cocoa, almonds, cinnamon, and sugar. Ibarra chocolate has an enchanting taste, and it makes the best hot chocolate in the world, especially if you add a dash of brandy! You will need a prebaked 9-inch tart shell (see page 141).

Yield: One 9-inch tart

Praline
½ cup pecans
1 cup sugar
⅓ cup water
juice of ½ lemon

Custard
1 cup heavy cream
1 cup milk
7 eggs
¼ teaspoon salt
1½ cups Cajeta Caramel
   (see page 136)
⅔ cup sugar
1 teaspoon vanilla extract
1 prebaked 9-inch tart shell (see page 141)

Ibarra Layer
10 tablespoons (5 ounces) Ibarra chocolate
3 tablespoons (1½ ounces) bittersweet chocolate
⅓ cup heavy cream

Cajeta Whipped Cream
1½ cups heavy cream
¼ cup Cajeta Caramel
3 tablespoons sugar
½ teaspoon vanilla extract

To make the praline, preheat oven to 350°. Place pecans on a well-greased or sprayed cookie sheet. Toast pecans lightly in oven for 15 minutes. Meanwhile, cook 1 cup sugar with water and lemon juice until golden brown. Wash down the sides of the pot frequently with a pastry brush dipped in water to prevent sugar crystals from forming. Pour syrup over pecans and set aside. When cool, cut praline into small pieces with a knife and then crush with a rolling pin or grind with a food processor to a fine meal.

To prepare custard, preheat oven to 325°. Combine and mix the custard ingredients, and strain into a saucepan. Heat until thickened, stirring constantly with a whisk. Pour the thickened custard into the pre-baked tart shell, which has been placed on a papered baking sheet. Place tart shell in oven. Do not let the custard boil (if the oven is too hot, lower the temperature or set the oven door ajar). Bake for 20 minutes or until the custard is softly set (the custard will quake like Jello). The custard will firm as it cools.

To make the Ibarra layer, chop chocolate into pea-size pieces and place in a small mixing bowl. Heat ⅓ cup cream to boiling and pour over chocolate, stirring only to cover all of the chocolate with cream. Once the chocolate has melted, stir vigorously to incorporate the cream and chocolate to a smooth, silky consistency. If the mixture is still grainy, as is characteristic of Ibarra chocolate, return to a double boiler and stir until smooth or blend in a food processor until smooth. Let cool (a bowl of ice water under the chocolate will speed the cooling process) until chocolate has the consistency of frosting and can be spread on top of the cooled custard. Refrigerate.

To make Cajeta Whipped Cream whip 1½ cups cream until soft peaks form and then add Cajeta Caramel, 3 tablespoons sugar, and vanilla. Whip until stiff peaks appear. Put Cajeta Whipped Cream in a pastry bag with a large star tip (#7) and pipe attractive design; for example, shells around the perimeter of the tart. Refrigerate.

To serve, garnish with pecan praline.

CINNAMON SHORTCAKE

A tender rich biscuit, this short-cake will perfume your kitchen with cinnamon as it bakes. We use this recipe at Coyote Cafe to make the Blackberry Cinnamon Short-cake (see next recipe). It can also be used on its own, or with other fruits and sauces. If possible, try to use Mexican canela, which has a softer flavor than the regular Batavia cinnamon, which is darker and harder, although the recipe will work well with either. Best results will be obtained by grinding your own, whichever you use.

Yield: Six 3-inch biscuits

2 cups all-purpose flour

1/2 cup plus 2 tablespoons sugar

pinch salt

4 teaspoons baking powder

1½ tablespoons *canela* (or 2½ teaspoons cinnamon)

9 tablespoons (4½ ounces) butter

1/2 cup milk

Line a 9-inch cake pan with parchment paper. In a mixing bowl, combine the flour, 1/2 cup of sugar, salt, baking powder, and 1 tablespoon canela. Cut the butter into 1-inch cubes and add to the dry ingredients. With mixer or by hand, blend the butter into the flour until a rough coarse meal is formed. Do not overmix. Add the milk and blend until the dough just comes together.

At this point you can wrap dough in plastic and refrigerate it until you're ready. Preheat oven to 400°. To make the shortcakes, roll dough out on a floured board to 1/2-inch thickness. Cut out shortcakes with a 3-inch cutter and place on papered cake pan. Combine 2 tablespoons sugar with 1/2 tablespoon canela and sprinkle it over the shortcakes. Bake for approximately 20 minutes or until the tops are dark golden brown. Remove pan from oven and let cool.

BLACKBERRY CINNAMON SHORTCAKES
with Cajeta Caramel

Coyote's sweet tooth is always happy when presented with this spectacular yet homey dessert. This recipe combines the traditional Mexican flavors of cajeta and cinnamon with the vibrant taste of ripe summer blackberries and rich Mexican Crema.

Yield: 6 servings

4 cups blackberries

1½ cups sugar

1½ teaspoons vanilla extract

1/2 cup blackberry brandy (or cassis)

1/4 cup water

2 cups heavy cream

3/4 cup Mexican Crema (see page 35)

6 Cinnamon Shortcakes (see recipe above)

1 cup Cajeta Caramel (see page 136)

6 sprigs mint (optional)

Toss the berries in a bowl with 1 cup sugar, 1/2 teaspoon vanilla, brandy, and water. Cover with plastic wrap and let sit at room temperature for at least 3 hours. This will draw the juices out of the berries. In an electric mixer, whip the cream to soft peaks. Add the crema, 1/2 cup sugar, and 1 teaspoon vanilla, and beat until firm peaks are formed. Refrigerate.

Cut the cooled shortcakes in half and place the bottom half on the dessert plate. Liberally pour the berry-brandy juice over the short-cake so that a pool of juice is formed around it. Generously scoop the blackberries on top of the shortcake base, letting some fall around the base on the ~~plate~~. Cover the berries with ~~a dol~~-lop of whipped ~~cream and~~ place the top ~~half~~ over the ~~berries. Then~~ sque~~eze~~ ... ~~acro~~ss the ... ~~caramel~~ to within ... ~~ream~~ of the pla~~te~~ ... a mint sprig ... ~~Ser~~ve immediately.

MANGO RASPBERRY BRÛLÉE

The classic crème brûlée is a silky custard with a hard, caramelized sugar topping. Our version is a rich and refreshing dessert with a surprise at the bottom. While this particular combination of fruit is one of Coyote's favorites, the brûlée can also be made with other low-acid fruits, such as blueberries, papayas, or peaches. These fruits help prevent the custard from curdling. The brûlée can also be served plain.

Yield: Six 6-inch ramekins

5 egg yolks

2 cups heavy cream

⅔ cup half-and-half

2 cups sugar

½ teaspoon vanilla extract

1 cup mango, chopped into ¼-inch cubes

1½ cups raspberries

Preheat oven to 325°. In a large bowl, lightly whip the egg yolks. Add the cream, half-and-half, ⅓ cup plus 1 tablespoon sugar, and vanilla. Blend well and strain.

Distribute combined fruits evenly between the ramekins. Pour the custard evenly over the fruit. Set the ramekins in a pan with at least 2-inch sides and fill the pan with hot water reaching halfway up the sides of the ramekins. Bake for about 30 to 40 minutes or until the custard is softly set.

Remove from oven and let sit in hot water for 20 minutes. Then place on rack to cool. At this point the brûlées may be refrigerated for use later that day, or overnight.

To serve the brûlées, sprinkle each ramekin with 1 to 2 tablespoons sugar and place under broiler until caramelized. Rotate the ramekins as necessary. (Some restaurants use a propane torch to facilitate this process!) The caramelization process is complete when a dark golden hard-crack surface is formed. The brûlées should not be caramelized more than 30 minutes in advance or the sugar will melt.

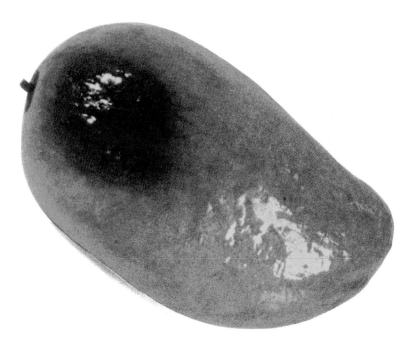

PIE PASTRY

This pastry offers the option of using butter or shortening. Butter will enhance the richness of the dough, while shortening will create a very flaky crust. In either case, this is a tender crust that works well with any filling.

Yield: One 10-inch double crust

2¼ cups all-purpose flour

¼ teaspoon salt

¾ cup vegetable shortening (or butter)

1 teaspoon vinegar

2 egg yolks

2 tablespoons ice water

Mix the flour and salt together in a bowl. Using two knives or a pastry cutter, cut in the shortening or butter until the mixture resembles coarse meal. In another bowl mix the vinegar, egg yolks, and water. Add to the dry ingredients and combine until the ingredients form a ball. Add more water (in teaspoon increments) if necessary. Wrap and chill the dough for at least 1 hour, or overnight before rolling it out.

If your recipe calls for a prebaked pie shell, preheat oven to 350°. Roll out half the dough until it is 2 inches larger than the pan. Fit the dough loosely into the pan and trim the edges. Prick the dough liberally with a fork or fill the shell with pie weights or beans after lining it with foil. Bake until golden brown (approximately 15 minutes).

TART SHELL

2 cups flour

3 tablespoons sugar

¼ teaspoon salt

1 cup butter, chilled

1 teaspoon vanilla extract

1 teaspoon lemon juice

4 tablespoons ice water

Mix flour, sugar, and salt together in a bowl. Using two knives or a pastry cutter, cut in the butter until the mixture resembles coarse meal. Using a fork, lightly toss the vanilla, lemon juice, and water together with the flour mixture. Be careful not to overwork the dough or the pastry will be tough. The dough will be crumbly, but should hold together when gathered into a ball. If necessary, add additional water in teaspoon increments. The dough can be rolled out immediately or you can wrap it in plastic and refrigerate or freeze it for later use.

To bake the shell, preheat oven to 350°. Roll out the dough and fit it into a 9-inch pie pan or tart ring. Fill shell with pie weights or beans, lining it first with foil, and bake until dry and golden, approximately 20 minutes. Let cool.

COYOTE'S BAG OF TRICKS

Here in his final chapter, Coyote pulls out some old favorites and standbys that he just loves to rustle up. These dishes, which make all his friends howl with delight, range from brunch items to last-minute side dishes to midnight snacks. Most of them are fairly simple; all express the underlying spirit of Coyote's food. They involve plenty of chiles (his favorite) and lots of spices.

These dishes are simple and relatively inexpensive to prepare. They have character, a completeness of expression, and satisfy in taste and tone. They have a simple soul and speak plainly and quietly (except of course for the chiles!). Their hominess belies their quality: once again, this is food from the ranch, the *cocina*, and the hearthside.

Some of these dishes may sound familiar. However, unless you've been very lucky, you've probably only had versions that were improperly prepared or watered down, and not treated with the respect due them. For example, Huevos Rancheros are often served with canned chile sauce and overcooked eggs. Chile Rellenos are all too often made with canned chiles and a watery tomato sauce, tasting bland and greasy. The recipes in this chapter better represent the true origins of these classics.

To appreciate these healthy, hearty foods with their nurturing qualities is to understand and carry with you the spirit of the Southwest. They represent its soul and spirit, and like Coyote himself, they take many disguises. These simple dishes bring us back to ourselves and nature. They create a bridge between today's world and the values and traditions of past times, and a way of life that should be perpetuated. In the modern age, these foods are hymns and prayers to another time, another earth, and other gods.

Now the Mother Earth
And the Father Sky,
Meeting, joining one another,
Helpmates ever, they.
All is beautiful,
All is beautiful,
All is beautiful, indeed.
And the white corn
And the yellow corn
Meeting, joining one another,
Helpmates ever they.
All is beautiful,
All is beautiful,
All is beautiful, indeed.

From: Song of the Earth (Navajo).
Songs of the Southwest.
In *American Indian Poetry:*
An Anthology of Songs and Chants.
Ed. George W. Cronin. Liveright, New York, 1934.

RED CHILE RICE

The ever-present, ever-tasteless, ever-mushy so-called Mexican or Spanish Rice: this poor soul has been bastardized to the point of having no identity, texture, taste, or character. With this recipe we snatch back the lost soul from the hell of combination plates and the purgatory of side dishes, and put it back where it belongs as one of the major elements in Southwestern cuisine. The real stuff has personality. It is crunchy, rather like Italian risotto, and not too fluffy. I prefer not to use stock, so the true, clean flavors of the chile and herbs will predominate. (The quality of this dish will depend directly on the quality of the chile powder, so don't try to get by with less than the best.) The rice goes very well with grilled chicken, fish, or seafood.

Yield: 4 to 6 servings

1 large clove garlic, minced

½ cup minced onion

4 tablespoons butter

2 cups long-grain rice

4½ cups water

1 teaspoon roasted ground Mexican oregano

1 tablespoon minced fresh marjoram

1½ teaspoons salt

1 teaspoon roasted, ground cumin seed

⅓ cup medium to medium-hot molido chile powder

In a large pan or skillet, sauté garlic and onion in the butter over medium heat for 6 to 8 minutes, until soft. Add remaining ingredients, bring to a boil and cook for 2 minutes. Reduce heat to lowest setting, cover, and simmer for 20 to 25 minutes until water just evaporates. Beat with a wooden spoon to fluff up, and add a little butter if desired. The rice can be kept warm and held up to 2 hours.

SPICY GREEN RICE

This dish is a great vehicle for expressing strong herbal flavors, and it always comes as a surprise because of its unusual appearance. The important thing is to be sure there are enough chiles to make it hot and spicy, and sufficient green ingredients for color and taste. In addition to the herbs and chiles given in the recipe, you can put in orange zest, avocado leaves, epazote, yerba santa, fresh basil, or marjoram. The rice goes well with grilled fish or pork dishes. It can also be served cold: mixed with chilled shrimp, it makes a great lunch or picnic dish.

Yield: 4 to 6 servings

4 leaves Romaine lettuce

6 roasted poblano chiles

2 roasted serrano chiles

1 large clove garlic

2 tablespoons minced onion

1 cup loosely packed cilantro leaves (about 1 small bunch)

½ bunch parsley

3½ cups water

4½ tablespoons butter

2 cups long-grain rice

2 teaspoons salt

In a blender, purée all ingredients except butter, rice, and salt. Melt 2½ tablespoons butter in a large saucepan and add rice. Cook for 3 to 4 minutes over medium heat until translucent, taking care not to scorch the butter. Add salt, and puréed ingredients, bring to a boil and cook for 2 minutes. Reduce heat to lowest setting, cover, and simmer for 20 to 25 minutes, until water just evaporates. Add remaining 2 tablespoons butter and fluff up with a wooden spoon. Garnish with fresh chopped cilantro or basil, if desired.

SWEET CINNAMON RICE

This dish acts as a foil to spicy and peppery food. At Coyote Cafe, we serve it with Yucatán Lamb and Smoked Rabbit Enchiladas. The strong cinnamon flavor suggests sweetness without the addition of sugar. The currants add to the sweetness, and provide a surprise for the palate.

Yield: 6 to 8 servings

4 tablespoons butter

½ cup finely diced carrots

½ cup finely diced celery

½ cup finely diced white onion

2 cups long-grain rice

½ teaspoon salt

4 sticks canela (or 1 tablespoon ground cinnamon)

½ cup dried currants

6 cups water

Melt 2 tablespoons butter in a large saucepan over medium heat. Add the carrots, celery, and onion, cover the pan and cook over low heat for 10 minutes, stirring occasionally. Add the rice, salt, canela, currants, and water and bring to a boil over high heat. When the water has reduced down to the level of the rice, reduce heat to low, cover, and simmer for 15 to 20 minutes, stirring occasionally. Remove canela, add remaining butter, and fluff up with a wooden spoon.

PECAN AND WILD BOAR BACON WAFFLES
with *Bourbon Syrup*

This dish is the result of a collaboration with Reed Hearon, my former sous-chef, who had a good feel for Texas country food. These waffles, served with chorizo and enchiladas, would make a welcome brunch after a long morning's horseback ride! They also go well with fowl, in which case a wild mushroom butter or Red Chile Honey would be preferable to the Bourbon Syrup. These waffles can alternatively be made with apple or pumpkin. Just add 1 cup apple or pumpkin purée to the batter and reduce the milk to ½ cup. (I served Pecan Pumpkin Waffles with Red Chile Honey as an accompaniment to quail at a food event in Philadelphia, and it proved a winning combination.)

Yield: 4 servings

½ cup chopped wild boar bacon (or regular bacon)

½ cup butter

3 egg yolks

1 cup milk

¾ cup roasted pecans

1 cup cornmeal

¾ cup all-purpose flour

1 teaspoon salt

1 teaspoon baking powder

4 egg whites

Bourbon Syrup (recipe follows)

To prepare the waffles, cook the bacon in a frying pan with the butter. Beat the egg yolks with the milk and add the cooked bacon and butter from the frying pan. Chop the pecans to a medium-coarse consistency. Mix together pecans, cornmeal, flour, salt, and baking powder, and stir into the egg yolk mixture. Beat the egg whites until they form soft peaks, then gradually fold them into the batter. Cook in a hot waffle iron until brown, but still moist inside. Pour Bourbon Syrup over waffles and serve.

BOURBON SYRUP

12 ounces dark brown sugar

1 cup water

¾ cup roasted pecans

⅓ cup sour mash bourbon whiskey

1 tablespoon vanilla extract

Bring the sugar and water to a boil in a pan and stir until all the sugar is dissolved. Continue to boil, without stirring, until the syrup thickens slightly and its surface becomes shiny. Pour syrup into a stainless steel bowl and stir in pecans. Carefully add the whiskey and vanilla. Keep warm.

GREEN CHILE CORN MUFFINS

These sweet muffins are great for breakfast, brunch, or lunch. The combination of corn and green chiles is a classic, while the molasses gives the muffins a "roundness." Don't worry about trying to achieve perfectly-shaped muffins as this is rustic fare.

Yield: 12 muffins

⅓ cup butter

2 eggs

1 cup all-purpose flour

1 cup stone-ground yellow cornmeal

4 teaspoons baking powder

3 tablespoons mild Chimayo chile powder

1 cup milk

1 tablespoon molasses

2 teaspoons finely minced orange zest

1 tablespoon minced fresh marjoram

2 New Mexico green chiles (or 1 poblano chile and 1 Anaheim chile), roasted, seeded, and chopped

Melt butter and lightly beat eggs. Sift together the flour, cornmeal, baking powder, and chile powder. Mix together the milk, melted butter, eggs, and molasses, and fold into the sifted dry mixture. Then add orange zest and fold in the marjoram and chiles. Let batter sit for 30 minutes.

Preheat oven to 400°. Pour batter into a buttered 12-muffin pan and bake for 12 to 15 minutes, until firm.

HUEVOS RANCHEROS

The best time to visit the markets in Mexico is early in the morning. It's cooler then, and the markets are bustling with activity and full of wonderful smells, colors, and sounds. Fresh produce is carefully arranged and displayed in the huge shaded sheds. There is always a part of the market set aside for cooked foods, and in the mornings you can count on finding three breakfast items at every market: delicious fresh coffee with hot milk, hot chocolate, served with foamed milk and cinnamon, and Huevos Rancheros, Mexican-style eggs cooked to order with hot chile sauce, and fresh warm tortillas. Huevos Rancheros with a hot chocolate or a cold beer is the perfect Mexican breakfast. Actually, there's no need to confine it to the morning hours. This delicious but inexpensive dish is commonly served at all times of day and night at roadside stands and cafes.

Yield: 4 servings

1½ cups dried black beans

2 large cloves garlic

1 canned chipotle chile in adobo sauce (or 1 dried chipotle chile)

2 quarts water

sea salt to taste

3 tablespoons lard (or duck fat or corn oil)

1 tablespoon butter

8 large eggs

6 cups Ranchero Sauce (see page 28)

4 tablespoons sour cream

12 sprigs cilantro

Place beans, garlic, and chipotle chile in a saucepan, cover with water and simmer until beans are very soft, about 1½ hours. Drain, season with salt, and discard the chile. Melt the lard over medium heat in a heavy skillet or frying pan. Mash the beans with a potato masher or large spoon, and add to the pan. Fry until beans have a firm but fairly smooth consistency; set aside and keep warm.

Melt butter in a skillet and fry eggs sunny-side up. Spoon 1½ cups of Ranchero Sauce on plates and place two fried eggs on top of each serving. Crisscross strips of poblano chiles (see Ranchero Sauce recipe) on top of eggs. Serve beans on the side, garnished with a tablespoon of sour cream and cilantro sprigs.

GREEN CHILE STEW
with Pork and Crema

This is a New Mexican staple that can be served on its own, or with beans, or with sopaipillas, a sweet deep-fried bread, and honey. Lamb can be used instead of pork, which would make the stew more like a Navajo dish (the Indians would have served it with fry bread). Once again, the quality of the dish will be determined by the quality of the chiles used. I prefer to brown the meat first, as this gives the sauce a richness. This dish makes a great snack, and can be frozen and reheated in an oven or microwave. Serve it with Green Chile Corn Muffins (see page 148).

Yield: 4 servings

2 tablespoons corn oil

2 pounds pork butt, trimmed and cut into 1-inch cubes

1½ cups chopped red onion

3 quarts plus 2½ cups water

15 Anaheim chiles, roasted, peeled, seeded, and chopped

8 cloves roasted garlic, roasted, peeled, and minced

1½ teaspoons roasted ground Mexican oregano

2 teaspoons salt

4 serrano chiles, roasted, peeled, seeded and chopped

2 cups cilantro leaves

1 cup Mexican Crema (see page 35)

Heat the corn oil over medium heat in a large heavy skillet and brown the pork. Add the onion and sauté until tender. Add 2 cups water and deglaze pan, scraping the bottom of the skillet. Add 3 quarts more water and gently simmer for 30 minutes. Add Anaheims, garlic, oregano, and salt. Simmer for a further 30 to 40 minutes until pork is tender. (Pork should be at least two-thirds covered with water throughout the add water if necessary). Purée serranos, cilantro, and ½ cup water in a blender, and add to stew. Adjust seasoning and cook stew for a further 15 minutes. Serve, garnished with crema.

CHIPOTLE SHRIMP
with Corn Cakes

This dish combines three of my favorites: shrimp, chipotles, and corn cakes. The corn cakes can also be served alone for breakfast or as an appetizer, or with fowl such as duck and quail. The buttermilk gives the batter an appealing tanginess.

Yield: 6 servings

1½ pounds medium shrimp (about 30)

3 tablespoons butter

1 cup softened butter

4½ tablespoons canned chipotle chiles, puréed

1½ dozen Corn Cakes (recipe follows)

2 green onions, chopped

1 cup Pico de Gallo Salsa (see page 13)

Peel the shrimp. On a griddle or in a frying pan, cook the shrimp in 3 tablespoons butter over low heat for about 5 minutes, turning them once.

To prepare chipotle butter, roughly purée together the softened butter and 1½ tablespoons chipotle purée and set aside at room temperature.

Place 3 corn cakes on each plate. Place 5 shrimp on top of the cakes and spread the chipotle butter liberally over the shrimp. Sprinkle the chopped green onions over the shrimp. Serve the Pico de Gallo Salsa at the side of the corn cakes.

CORN CAKES

¾ cup all-purpose flour

½ cup coarse cornmeal (polenta)

½ teaspoon baking powder

½ teaspoon baking soda

1 teaspoon salt

1 teaspoon sugar

1¼ cups buttermilk

2 tablespoons melted butter

1 egg, beaten

1 cup fresh corn kernels

2 green onions, chopped

Place the dry ingredients in a bowl and mix together. In a large bowl, whisk the buttermilk and butter together and then whisk in the egg. Gradually add the dry ingredients to the liquid and whisk until thoroughly incorporated. Purée ½ cup of the corn, and fold it into the batter along with the whole kernels and green onions. Add a little buttermilk if necessary to thin the mixture.

Using a nonstick pan over medium heat, ladle corn cake batter and form 3-inch cakes. Cook until golden brown (about 2½ minutes on each side). Batter makes about 18 to 20 corn cakes.

GRILLED CHEESE SANDWICH
with Poblano Chiles

Everyone loves a good grilled cheese sandwich, and Coyote is no exception. It is essential to use bread with great taste and texture, such as our Chile Corn Bread or Orange Cumin Bread. The sandwich should be cooked at medium-low and not hotter, or the bread will brown before the cheese melts. Also, the cheese must be thinly sliced, so it melts easily. Covering the pan with a domed lid—for example, a wok cover—will speed up the cooking process without drying out the bread. While roasted fresh poblano chiles work best, roasted green chiles or even canned green chiles can be substituted. Feel free to add some sliced roasted jalapeños if the poblanos are not hot enough! White Cheddar, Fontina or mozzarella may also be used. Be sure to put in the cilantro last so it keeps fresh.

Yield: 4 servings

11 tablespoons (5½ ounces) softened butter

8 slices bread, ½-inch thick

8 slices Monterey jack cheese, ¼-inch thick

4 large poblano chiles, roasted, peeled, seeded, and cut in half lengthwise

8 slices large red onion, ¼-inch thick

4 tablespoons chopped fresh cilantro leaves

1 cup Pico de Gallo Salsa (see page 13)

Spread 1 tablespoon butter on both sides of each slice of bread. Melt 2 tablespoons butter in a large pan or skillet and add the bread. Over medium-low heat, toast both sides until golden brown. Lightly sauté onions in 1 tablespoon butter or grill for about 1½ minutes, so they are still crunchy. Place a slice of cheese (cut to the same size as the bread) on each slice of bread. Place a poblano over the cheese on

4 of the slices, cover with 2 cooked onion slices, and close each sandwich. Reduce heat to low, cover the pan, and cook until cheese is melted, about 5 to 7 minutes. Remove sandwich from pan, open, and fill with cilantro leaves. Reclose, and serve with a garnish of Pico de Gallo Salsa.

OYSTER PO' BOY
with Green Onion Mayonnaise

Another of Coyote's favorite grilled sandwiches, this one comes from New Orleans. The mayonnaise can be made with either green onions or green chiles as the base. This sandwich goes well with roasted red peppers, corn, and okra, either as side dishes or in the form of a soup.

Yield: 4 servings

4 8-inch Italian or French baguettes (or soft rolls)

1¼ cups clarified butter

1½ cups yellow cornmeal

2 tablespoons cayenne

¾ teaspoon pepper

3¾ teaspoons salt

24 large shucked oysters

Green Onion Mayonnaise (recipe follows)

2 cups finely sliced Romaine lettuce

4 Roma tomatoes, finely sliced

Slice the baguettes or rolls in half and toast the cut sides in a skillet with 4 tablespoons of the butter until golden brown. In a bowl, combine the cornmeal, cayenne, pepper, and salt, and mix thoroughly. Heat one cup butter in a skillet, dip each oyster in the corn-

meal mixture, and fry oysters in the skillet over medium heat until tender, about 5 minutes. Remove oysters and pat dry.

Place fried bread open-face on plate. Spread each side liberally with Green Onion Mayonnaise. Place Romaine on one side of the bread and tomatoes on the other side. Put 6 oysters per sandwich on top of the lettuce and serve open-face.

GREEN ONION MAYONNAISE

3 egg yolks

2 tablespoons water

3 teaspoons fresh lemon juice

1 tablespoon Tabasco sauce

½ teaspoon salt

1½ cups light olive oil

½ cup very finely sliced green onion (or green chiles)

Whisk the yolks and water until light. Beat in the lemon juice, Tabasco, and salt and gradually add the oil, whisking constantly. Mix in the green onion.

CHORIZO

*My mother has always been an
adventurous spirit (no doubt I
inherited this trait from her!) as
well as a great cook, and she constantly exposed my brother,
Wayne, and me to new tastes as
we grew up. She once took a trip
to Mexico, and came back with a
bilingual Mexican cookbook. I
remember her making chorizo and
eggs for us because it was my first
taste of the spicy Mexican sausage. I loved it then, and I love it
now, especially my own recipe. It
takes a little patience to make, but
the results are worth it.*

*It is important to add enough
water to allow the chorizo to cook
before it browns too quickly and
becomes tough. The pork should
not be too lean or the chorizo will
be too dry. The natural oil produced in the cooking process
should turn red from the chiles,
and will contain the delicious flavors exuded by the ingredients. As
Coyote has been overheard
remarking while rustling up a
batch of chorizo, "If it ain't got
grease, it ain't nothing to howl
about."*

*Serve chorizo as a side dish for
breakfast or brunch, or in burritos
with beans and chiles, or add it to
scrambled eggs at the end. Chorizo also makes a great filling for
empanadas, quesadillas, enchiladas, and tacos, and goes very well
with grilled scallops.*

Yield: 4 servings

1 pound fresh ground pork butt

½ pound fresh ground lean beef

2 small cloves garlic, finely minced

**4 tablespoons ancho chile powder
(or New Mexico chile powder)**

½ teaspoon cayenne

⅛ teaspoon ground cloves

**½ teaspoon freshly ground black
pepper**

2 teaspoons cinnamon

1 teaspoon cumin

1 teaspoon sea salt

3 cups water

In a heavy skillet, fry the pork and
beef over medium heat. Break up
with a wooden spoon and do not
allow to brown. Add garlic, spices,
salt, and 1 cup of water. Cook
slowly over low heat for at least 1
hour to "smooth out" and blend the
flavors. Add extra water as needed,
though the finished mixture should
not be wet; all the excess water
should have evaporated and the
chorizo should be cooking in its
own fat. Adjust the final seasoning
to taste.

YUCATÁN WHITE SAUSAGE

*This recipe was born one day at
the Fourth Street Grill when we
ran out of veal sausage. We made
up a new version with chicken,
pork, and about five times the
amount of chile we used in the
veal sausage, and we served it
with black beans. It proved so popular that we were obliged to make
20 to 30 pounds of it every other
day thereafter. Many customers
would buy packages of them to
use at home for weekend brunch.*

*I christened it "Yucatán Sausage"
because the original recipe called
for a sauce made with green
Habanero chiles, which come
from that region. We use serrano
chiles now, because they're much
easier to get, but the name
remains. If you are making this
recipe ahead of time, bear in mind
that the heat of cooked fresh green
chiles dissipates after a day or
two. When grinding the pork, try
to ensure that it is not too streaky
by cutting and cubing it first and
then freezing it for about 15 minutes. This technique applies to all
sausage-making: it helps the grind
to be more even and less mushy.
This dish can be served as sausages or as breakfast patties.*

Yield 6 to 8 servings

CHILES RELLENOS

1¼ pounds pork butt with fat, cut into 1-inch cubes

¾ pound chicken breast meat, no skin or fat, cut into 1-inch cubes

⅓ pound fat back, cut into 1-inch cubes

10 serrano chiles, coarsely chopped

¼ cup white wine

1 clove garlic, minced

1 cup cilantro leaves, well packed

1 tablespoon sugar

1 tablespoon salt

½ teaspoon ground allspice

1 egg

In a stainless steel bowl or pan, combine all ingredients except egg. Mix well, cover with plastic wrap, and place in freezer for 1 hour. Meanwhile, chill all parts of the meat grinder in the freezer or in iced water.

Grind meat mixture and toss with the egg. Form into patties or force into casings. Heat skillet and cook patties or sausages over medium-low heat until well browned and cooked through, about 5 minutes per side.

Note: You can use a food processor, although the results will not be quite as good. Be sure to cut fat into small pieces and to chill it thoroughly. Be careful not to over-process the meat.

Literally "stuffed chiles," rellenos are probably the most popular item in Southwestern cuisine besides fajitas. The test of a really good kitchen is a great chile relleno. When you find one, you are in for a memorable meal. The key to this recipe is a high-quality green chile. Poblanos, with their thick walls and subtle smoky flavor, and long New Mexico green chiles work best. Likewise, it is important to use very good cheese and fresh marjoram, while the sauce should be made with the best red chile you can find. The batter should be very light and the deep-frying oil clean. This recipe can be augmented by stuffing the chile with shrimp, pork, or smoked duck, in addition to the cheese.

Yield: 4 servings

2 quarts corn oil

4 large poblano chiles (or long New Mexico green chiles)

2½ quarts water

5 ¾ teaspoons salt

3 cups fresh corn kernels

2 cups grated jack cheese

¼ cup grated white Cheddar cheese

¼ cup grated Fontina cheese

3 teaspoons finely chopped fresh marjoram

6 eggs, separated

⅔ cup Mexican beer

1¾ cups all-purpose flour

2 cups Mark's Red Chile Sauce (see page 25)

½ cup Mexican Crema (see page 35)

Heat oil in a deep-fryer to 375°. Deep-fry poblanos for about 3 minutes or until skin blisters. Place in a stainless steel bowl, cover with plastic wrap, and sweat for 20 minutes. Reserve oil and keep warm.

Meanwhile, boil water and add 4½ teaspoons salt. Add corn and blanch for 2 minutes. Drain corn through a sieve and refresh with cold running water. Set aside. Mix cheeses, marjoram, corn (when cool), and ½ teaspoon salt, and divide mixture into 4 portions. Gently peel poblanos, cut a slit lengthwise in each, and carefully remove seeds. Stuff with cheese mixture and roll between the fingers to close the opening.

To prepare the batter, whisk egg whites until stiff. In a separate bowl, beat egg yolks, beer, and ¾ teaspoon salt together. Gradually add flour, beating constantly, and whisk until smooth. Add half of the egg whites and mix well to incorporate. Gently fold in the remaining whites to form a light batter.

Reheat oil to 375°. Dip poblanos in batter and deep-fry until exterior is firm and golden, about 8 minutes. Serve over Mark's Red Chile Sauce and decorate with crema from a squirt bottle, drawn in a Southwestern zigzag design.

BLUE CORN
BLACK BEAN
RELLENOS

The sum of this recipe is greater than its parts. You take three great Southwestern ingredients — blue corn, green chile, and black beans — and presto! you have this elegant relleno. The filling always comes as a surprise, and it really is a very attractive way of serving black beans. It can be served on its own or as a side dish with pan-roasted salmon and Gazpacho Salsa or Squash Salsa. Placed over crema drawn in a Southwestern zigzag pattern, this dish is spectacular.

Yield: 4 servings

2 quarts plus 3 tablespoons corn oil

4 Anaheim chiles

1 cup wild boar bacon (or Amador, Smithfield, or Harrington's corn cob smoked bacon), chopped into ¼-inch cubes

4 tablespoons finely chopped white onion

3 cups cooked black beans (see Black Bean Soup, page 32)

½ teaspoon ground cumin

½ teaspoon salt

6 egg yolks

1 cup coarse blue cornmeal

Heat 2 quarts oil in a deep-fryer to 375°. Deep-fry Anaheims for about 3 minutes, or until skin blisters. Place in a stainless steel bowl, cover with plastic wrap, and sweat for 20 minutes. Reserve oil and keep warm.

Heat 3 tablespoons of corn oil in a skillet and sauté bacon and onion over medium heat until tender. Drain beans and mash to a rough purée. Mix together with cumin and salt and add to skillet. Stir constantly and cook for 5 to 7 minutes. Remove from heat and allow to cool. Divide mixture into 4 portions. Gently peel Anaheims, cut a slit lengthwise, and carefully remove seeds. Stuff with black bean mixture and roll between the fingers to close the opening.

Reheat oil to 375°. Dip the anaheims in the egg yolk and then roll in the cornmeal. Deep-fry until exterior is dark blue, about 4 to 5 minutes.

REFRIED BLACK BEANS
with Mint and Goat Cheese Crema

This great dish is a gift from the gods! If I could only choose one dish to take away with me to a desert island, it would be this one! The key to this simple dish is to cook it in enough fat or oil to keep the beans moist. The beans should be cooked until crusty and smooth, preferably to order, and in a nonstick pan. As Coyote also quips, "Don't stint on the mint" — it must be noticeable. The mint not only livens the beans up, but it also provides an interesting contrast and freshness, making the beans much more adaptable if served with lamb, goat, or salmon. I presented this dish with cabrito and goat cheese sausages at a dinner for California Deutz vineyards, which produces one of the best American sparkling wines.

Yield: 4 servings

2 tablespoons lard

1½ teaspoons finely chopped garlic

4 teaspoons finely chopped white onion

2 cups cooked black beans (see Black Bean Soup, page 32)

½ teaspoon canned chipotle chile, puréed

½ teaspoon salt

2 tablespoons chopped mint

4 ounces goat cheese

⅓ cup heavy cream

Melt lard over medium-low heat, preferably in a heavy-bottomed nonstick pan, and sauté garlic and onion until tender and cooked through, about 10 minutes. Drain beans and mash to a rough purée and mix together with chipotle, salt, and mint, and then add to pan. Constantly flip in pan, like an omelet, and occasionally scrape bottom of pan to keep beans from sticking. Cook for about 10 minutes until beans become dark, dry, and crusty. Turn beans out of pan like an omelet, rolling them out in one piece.

Mix goat cheese and heavy cream together until smooth, and serve on top of each serving of beans.

Glossary

This glossary of ingredients most commonly used in Southwestern cuisine is organized in alphabetical order so that it will be easy to check from any point in the text. For many of the ingredients the Spanish name is also given. Following the main glossary, chiles are treated in their own separate glossary, as are special techniques and terms, equipment, wine, beer and spirits, and sources.

Achiote (Annatto) This spice, which takes the form of small brick red seeds, is a trademark of the Yucatán cuisine and the markets of that region. It is usually available in solid blocks of red paste and has a distinctive, iodine-like flavor that gives an earthiness to chicken, pork, and fish. It is used commercially to dye Cheddar cheese and butter to make them look more appetizing. Before grinding them, soften the seeds by boiling them for 1½ hours, but care should be taken as their natural dye will stain.

Acorn Squash Dark green, with bright yellow flesh, and "shoulders" tapering to a point, the acorn squash is about 8 inches long and 12 inches around. Rich and very sweet, it is best stuffed or baked and puréed. It was often baked whole by the Indians, who used fat and honey for seasoning. It is harvested in the fall.

Adobo An adobo is a vinegary sauce that may also be used for pickling. Meat, vegetables, or chiles prepared in adobo sauces are described as being *en adobo*. For example, *chiles chipotle en adobo* are canned dried, smoked jalapeño chiles stewed with onions, tomatoes, vinegar, and spices. Pork *en adobo* refers to pork served with a red chile sauce.

Allspice *(Pimienta inglesa; pimienta de Jamaica)* A cousin of clove and black pepper, allspice is a berry native to the Yucatán. Well named, it tastes of a combination of cloves, pepper, cinnamon, and nutmeg. It makes an excellent seasoning for meats and game.

Anise *(Anís)* Anise is used in sweet and savory dishes. Its sweetness, like that of allspice and canela, acts as a good foil for spicy dishes. We use it in desserts and bread and in red chile sauces. Roasting and grinding the seeds before use imparts a toasty flavor with an interesting licorice finish that matches the natural flavor of certain chiles, such as ancho and mulato. Chinese star anise is stronger and more perfumed. We use it in marinades rather than directly in cooking.

Annatto See Achiote

Antelope *(Antílope)*. See Venison

Apples *(Manzanas)* We are fortunate that the area around Chimayo that produces New Mexico's best red chiles also grows some of the best apples in the entire country. Older varieties of apple such as Gravenstein, Winesap, and Cox's orange pippin are still grown here, rather than better-known commercial varieties such as Granny Smith, Red Delicious, and McIntosh. The local apples taste much better, and besides, Chimayo chiles and Chimayo apples have a startlingly natural affinity for one another. Try them together in a salsa or a sorbet.

Arugula (Rocket; Roquette) A salad green that is native to the Mediterranean, arugula has a soft texture, and mustardy, sharp, green taste. It is best used plain, with a simple dressing.

Atole A beverage dating from pre-Columbian times, *atole* is made from finely ground roasted corn that is mixed with water and boiled until thickened. It is often flavored with fruit, sugar, cinnamon, or chocolate and, in southern Mexico, chiles. *Atole* makes a great breakfast drink.

Avocados *(Aguacates)* I prefer the purplish black, bumpy-skinned Haas avocados with their rich, buttery flesh, to the smoother, green-skinned Fuertes, which are more watery. The Haas variety, which is in peak season in the first half of the year, also keeps better. Buy ahead of time, as avocados are usually sold before they are ripe. For an unusual Mexican-style twist, use avocados in desserts — for example, avocado ice cream.

Baby Corn Very small — between 2 and 3 inches at most — whole corn cobs, with kernels not much larger than a pinhead. Eaten cob and all, they are generally available canned in the supermarket. However, unless they are available fresh, I prefer to substitute the kernels cut off a fresh, albeit full-grown, cob.

Bananas and Plantains *(Plátanos)* We routinely eat bananas, as we do so much other produce, before they are ripe. Rather than eating them when they are yellow-green or yellow, wait until they are evenly covered with black spots: then their full flavor emerges. Use bananas, or their cousins, the plantains, as a starch or in salsas. Plantains should be bought when deep green and then ripened. They are particularly wonderful twice-fried and served as a vegetable garnish with tuna and black beans.

Banana Leaves *(Hojas de Plátano)* Large, tropically flavored banana leaves are used extensively in the Yucatán and on the Gulf Coast of Mexico for wrapping food before it is steamed or baked and are commonly used for tamales. They were used to pit-cook wrapped meat for *barbacoas,* the forerunner of the modern barbecue. Banana leaves are usually available in Thai or Oriental markets and can be kept indefinitely in the freezer. Before using, steam them or pass them over a flame for a few seconds to bring out their aroma.

Basil *(Albahaca)* Basil has a natural affinity for tomatoes, mint, and cilantro and has a cooling, fresh effect when used with chiles and hot spices, although it is not a traditional ingredient in Southwestern cuisine. The variegated purple basil gives an unusual decorative effect in Southwestern salads.

Beans *(Frijoles)* After corn, beans are historically the most important ingredient in the Southwestern diet. There are a great many varieties available and they are all inexpensive, nutritious, and tasty. Soaking beans only makes them more gaseous; cooking them with a little epazote will mitigate their infamous effect. Beans are best cooked covered in a heavy pot, very slowly (just below a simmer), and in a minimal amount of liquid. They will then be meltingly tender and well flavored.

Anasazi Bean The Anasazis — "the old ones" — were the original progenitors of the Pueblo cultures of the Southwest and date back to the fifth century A.D. The bean that bears their name was cultivated by them and is one of the oldest existing Indian beans of the region. It is a piebald dark cranberry and white color.

Black Bean *(Frijol negro)* Actually a very dark purple, black beans are also called turtle beans. They are native to Central and South America and are used widely in the Caribbean. With their strong, smoky flavor and overtones of mushroom, they are my favorite beans. I especially like them refried with mint and serrano chiles, in the Yucatán style.

***Bollito* Bean** This is the wild progenitor of the pinto bean (see below) and is native to the Southwest. It is smaller than the pinto, has a better flavor, and is beige in color. *Bollitos* take a little longer to cook than pintos and are usually boiled. Try them in a Southwestern cassoulet with sausage and game.

Pinto Bean The pinto is the most used bean in this country and one of the most nutritious. It is native to the Southwest and is a variety of the common kidney bean. Literally meaning "painted," the pinto is beige with brownish pink streaks. When cooked, the mottled skin becomes a uniform pink. Because they are a little bland, I like to wake them up by cooking them with diced bacon and onions that have been fried together, roasted garlic, pickled jalapeños, oregano, and lots of beer.

Tepary Bean *(Tepari)* The tepary bean was domesticated by prehistoric Southwestern Indians and was of particular ceremonial importance to the Zuni. It is also known as the Mexican haricot bean. Unlike the *bollito,* the tepary is rarely cultivated because it can harbor a mold spore that is deadly to other varieties of bean. They are variegated in color and come in a number of shapes and sizes. Tepary beans have an excellent earthy flavor that goes well with green chile stew.

White Bean *(Frijol blanco)* This is the familiar Navy bean of Boston baked bean fame. Instead of smothering them in molasses, cook them with garlic and sage in duck stock and serve as an accompaniment to poultry.

Beef *(Carne de vaca)* At Coyote Cafe, we use dry-aged, corn-fed, prime New Mexican certified Black Angus beef, which is low in fat. Our customers have told us after trying our cuts, that they realized they hadn't tasted good beef in a long time. I think this reflects a general decline in quality, which is one factor behind the slump in beef sales over the last few years. Thanks to downgraded standards, tough, flavorless grades of beef are sold to the consumer as choice cuts. Instead of being dry-aged to allow the natural enzymes to provide flavor and tenderness, beef is all too often stored for weeks in airtight plastic packaging that prevents oxygen from activating the all-important enzymes. As a result, beef can take on a dry and mushy texture and a slightly sour flavor. Much of the responsibility for this situation lies with the consumers. We have sent the message to the ranchers and packers that we are not willing to pay for better meat. Seek out local sources and demand the best. Look for an old-fashioned butcher shop that has carcasses hanging in a meat-aging locker. Fine beef will have a creamy white, dry, waxy cover of fat, a soft but not mushy texture, and a robust aroma.

Bell Peppers See Sweet Peppers

Black Beans See Beans

Bollito Beans See Beans

Buckwheat Buckwheat flour is ground from the seeds of plant that is not a cereal at all, but a member of the family that includes rhubarb, dock, and other plants native to Europe and Asia. Traditionally used for blinis in Russia and for pancakes in America, buckwheat flour contains very little gluten.

Buffalo *(Bufálo)* Buffalo tastes something like beef, with an earthier and more intense flavor, but is leaner. It is at its best when served very rare or braised and makes superb sausages, burgers, and barbecue.

Butter, Clarified *(Mantequilla Aclarada)* Clarified butter has a higher smoking point than regular butter. It is better for browning meat, especially poultry, and I prefer it to olive oil for this purpose. It is prepared by melting butter over a gentle heat; a milky residue — the whole fats — collects on the bottom of the pan. After you skim off any surface foam, the clear oil may be poured off and used.

Buttermilk *(Suero de la leche)* Traditionally the liquid (whey) left over from making butter, buttermilk is now made by adding a culture to skim milk. Buttermilk has a refreshing sourness and can be used as a drink, in salad dressings, desserts, and as a base for Mexican crema (see below). It also goes very well with fresh fruit.

Butternut Squash Yellow and bell-shaped, being narrower at the stem than at the base, the butternut is native to tropical America but is now commonly grown in this country and in Europe. Harvested both in the summer and fall, this squash becomes sweeter as it matures. It can be used as a vegetable or in pies, and in pickles and jams.

Cactus *(Nopales; Nopalitos)* Cactus paddles (the "leaves" of the *Opuntia* cactus) are common in the American Southwest and in central Mexico. They have a wonderful flavor when cooked, grilled, or used in salsas and taste of a cross between green beans and okra. Use them as a vegetable and cook covered, either for a very short or a very long time. If you are blanching them in water, add some tomatillo husks, which will magically prevent the paddles from becoming slimy and losing their color. Before you cook them, put on garden gloves and remove all of the very thin spines that cover the paddles.

The prickly pear *(tuna)*, which is the greenish-yellow, egg-sized fruit of the cactus, has a bright red flesh and tastes somewhat like sour cherries. It too should be handled carefully and the spines removed. Ripen it at room temperature until it exudes a perfume. It can be used in salsas, sorbets, or in sauces, especially for venison. Cut the prickly pear in half and scoop out the flesh.

Bottled prickly pear juice is available in the Southwest. You can make your own by puréeing prickly pears and straining out the juice. Pomegranate juice can be used as a substitute and is available in Middle Eastern Markets.

Canela *(Canela)* There are over 150 varieties of cinnamon, which is the inner bark of the *Cinnamomum* tree. Canela, originally from Sri Lanka, is a lighter brown and has a softer texture and milder, sweeter flavor than does the more common Malabar cinnamon from India. Canela is also thinner and more fragile and usually comes in sticks 3 to 5 inches long and $\frac{1}{4}$ to $\frac{1}{2}$-inch wide. I prefer canela in most recipes as it more closely matches the warm, earthy tones of Southwestern cuisine. Because canela is regarded as a lower grade of cinnamon, it is less expensive; however, it may be harder to find. You can substitute regular cinnamon if you can't get canela.

Carnitas Carnitas are small pieces of pork that have been sautéed slowly and become deliciously flavored and tender. Sometimes sold at stands and market stalls in parts of Mexico, carnitas are most commonly prepared as a filling for tacos, tamales, or enchiladas.

Chayote Ranging from cream to dark green in color, the chayote squash is about the same size and shape as a very large pear. The skin is usually fairly smooth, the flesh crisp, and the flavor a combination of cucumber and zucchini. It was cultivated in pre-Columbian times in Central America and is also now grown in Africa and the Far East. Chayote is native to the Southwest. It is excellent when stuffed with savory ingredients.

Cheese *(Queso)*

> ***Quesillo de Oaxaca*** is a soft, slightly acid cheese that is sold in braids and turns to strings when cooked. Thus it makes a good filling and is used frequently. Fresh mozzarella is similar, but milder. Monterey jack or Muenster may be substituted, as may Fontina.

> ***Queso fresco*** is a fresh, unripened, moist cheese made from partially skimmed milk. It is mildy salty, somewhat sharp, and has a pleasant creamy color. It may be replaced by a moist farmer's cheese, dry cottage cheese, or a mild feta cheese; all of these substitutes might be improved with the addition of some cream and salt.

Chicken *(Pollo)* At Coyote Cafe, we use free-range chickens, which are firmer, have more flavor, and are healthier than commercial chickens, because they have significantly lower levels of antibiotics. They are well worth the difference in price. Free-range or organic chickens are usually about 100 days old, compared with an average of 55 days for commercial fryers. Their sturdy flavor stands up well to hearty Southwestern salsas and sauces, and the more mature, juicy bird will braise well and not turn to string and fall apart as fryers tend to do. Do not believe any studies or articles you read about there being no difference between free-range and other types of chicken: there is.

Chicory, Red *See* Radicchio

Chicos Dried whole corn kernels, *chicos* are available in all the variegated colors of Indian corn. Unlike posole, *chicos* are not treated with lime, but they are cooked in the same way and used interchangeably. They are soaked before cooking to soften them and they take a long time to cook, but make an excellent winter vegetable. *Harinilla* is a meal made of finely ground chicos.

Chocolate *(Chocolate)* Mexican dark chocolate, of which Ibarra chocolate is a representative brand, is based on the Aztec drink made from cocoa, chile, and almonds. It is a little rough both in texture and its cocoa flavor and should be used unsweetened. In Oaxaca, you can buy chocolate made to order, with more or less cinnamon or almonds, according to taste. Never substitute Dutch chocolate which is alkalized and has higher solubility and a different fat content.

Cider *(Sidra)* Apple cider is useful as a sauce base for quail or to braise venison. Unfiltered fresh cider is best and it is often frozen to prevent it from fermenting. See also Apples.

Cilantro *(Cilantro)* Also known as fresh coriander and Chinese parsley, cilantro is common in Asian cuisines and is the most widely used herb in the world. We use it by the case at Coyote Cafe. An aromatic member of the parsley family, its pungent, sweet, and intense flavor "brightens" salsas and it is an important element, both for its flavor and color, in sauces such as pipiáns and moles that use green chiles. It is best bought with the roots still attached and it should look fresh, green, crisp, and unwilted. Cilantro should be stored with water covering the roots. Discard any yellow or discolored leaves, and do not use the tough stems. Cilantro and coriander seed are not interchangeable.

Cinnamon *See* Canela

Clam Juice *(Jugo de almejas)* Clam juice, or clam broth, is the by-product of cooking clams and is usually bought bottled or in cans. It makes a perfectly acceptable substitute for fish stock, and can be used instead of *fumet*.

Clove *(Clavo de especia)* Clove, which is indigenous to Madagascar and Zanzibar, matches the other spicy flavors of central Mexican cooking. It is a very strong spice and is best when it is not detectable, but used as a background ingredient. If you want an especially mild flavor, discard the bulb at the end of the clove berry and use only the remaining stem.

Coconut *(Coco)* Fresh tropical coconut is far preferable to the grated and sugared products commercially available. Coconut has volatile oils that are released when it is grated. Buy heavy coconuts that slosh when shaken. Pierce the eyes, empty out the liquid, and reserve it for sauces or stews. To extract the meat, place the coconut in a 350° oven for between 20 and 30 minutes. The shell should crack; if it doesn't, a sharp hammer blow should do the trick. Separate the flesh from the shell and peel it. Grate in a food processor or by hand as required, and refrigerate in an airtight container or freeze for later use.

Coconut Milk *(Leche de coco)* Canned coconut milk is available in oriental markets, but fresh coconut milk is better. Prepare it by puréeing fresh coconut meat with about 2 cups of warm water, depending on the size of the coconut, until the mixture is relatively smooth. Strain and use the liquid. If you are using the canned version, make sure that it is unsweetened and not something like Coco Lopez, which is best used in cocktails.

Coriander *(Cilantro)* It is the dried seed of the cilantro plant that is known as coriander. It is worth growing cilantro to use the green berries instead, as they combine the flavors of both herb and spice. Coriander goes well in fish marinades and makes an excellent seafood sauce when mixed with olive oil, lemon juice, orange juice, and basil.

Corn *(Maíz)* Corn is one of the sacred plants of the Southwest and has been cultivated by the Hopis for over 2,000 years. Further south, in Mexico, corn had been cultivated for at least 3,000 years before that. The maize plant originated in the central highlands of Mexico and was worshipped as the source of mankind, from which we were created. Corn is still an important and ever-present staple in both the Mexican and Southwestern cuisines and takes a variety of forms. Dried corn is starchier and less sweet than fresh corn. Indian corn is highly variegated and occurs naturally in many colors including blue, red, yellow, white, and purple.

Corn, Blue *(Maíz azul)* At Coyote Cafe, we are often asked, "Why is the corn blue — did you dye it?" The blue color occurs naturally in Indian corn, which is commonly variegated. When ground, it becomes blue gray. The blue color indicates a higher lysine content in the corn, making it more nutritious. The higher protein content makes it softer and less starchy than are other Indian corns. Thus it must be handled more carefully. Blue corn has more flavor than does regular cornmeal, yellow or white. It has particular religious significance for the Hopi and other Southwestern Indians.

Corn Flour Corn flour is a very finely milled cornmeal that is often used for dredging food before it is fried. It is not cornstarch, but this confusion is only likely if you are working from an English cookbook in which cornflour (one word) does, indeed, mean cornstarch.

Corn Husks *(Hojas de maíz)* No part of the maize plant is wasted. Dried corn husks, after they have been soaked in warm water to make them soft and pliable, are used for wrapping tamales (see General Instructions for tamales, page 59). They will keep for up to a year if stored in a dry place.

Cornmeal *(Harina de maíz)* Cornmeal is used as a thickener and as a filling or principal ingredient. Commercial cornmeal is processed with metal rollers that extract the germ and its natural oil, making it less moist and less flavorful. Stone-ground cornmeal retains the germ and has a superior flavor, especially when used in corn bread or polenta. However, it also has a shorter shelf life as the germ can become rancid, and it is usually less evenly ground. Cornmeal is ground in two consistencies: fine and coarse.

Corn Salad See Mâche

Crema A soured cream equivalent to crème fraîche, crema is made from heavy cream, preferably unpasteurized, and a culture such as that in buttermilk. The flavor is more interesting than that of sour cream. Crema adds a richness to beans and has a pleasant, cooling effect on hot spicy dishes.

Crème Fraîche See Crema

Cucumbers *(Pepinos)* Members of the squash family, cucumbers are soothing and cool, and have a natural affinity for serranos and mint. They are useful in salads and salsas and make a wonderful summer garnish for grilled fish. Buy the longer English or hothouse varieties, which are sweeter and less bitter.

Cumin *(Comino)* The cumin plant is indigenous to the Southwest and Mexico and is also used in Asian curry powders. The flavor of roasted and ground cumin seeds is better than that of cumin powder. This is a pervasive, earthy spice that combines wonderfully with dried chiles. Lamb cooked with a paste of cumin, garlic, and onions is terrific, and whole cumin seeds can be used in potato empanadas, much as they are used in the *pakoras* of Indian cuisine.

Duck *(Pato)* A great favorite of mine and of our customers at Coyote Cafe, duck is too often neglected in home kitchens. It has one of the most versatile and consistently enjoyable flavors and has a richness that goes perfectly with a great Pinot Noir. In confits, braised with chiles and spices, its flavors are picked up easily. The legs and breasts should be cooked separately: the legs should be braised slowly until well done; the breasts should be grilled rare to medium-rare. Wild duck is available in certain parts of the Southwest, but be careful not to bite down too hard!

Duck Fat *(Manteca de pato)* The rendered by-product of cooking duck or making confit (see Special Techniques, below), duck fat has a richer flavor than that of lard or butter. It is available in cans from gourmet specialty stores.

Epazote Also known as wormseed, Mexican tea, and stink weed, epazote grows wild and is most easily bought in potted form from nurseries. But beware: it propagates with abandon and can spread like wildfire if not carefully controlled. It is most frequently used in southern Mexico. Do not be put off by the aroma of this herb, which is reminiscent of kerosene. It has an untamed flavor that I am partial to, and once you get used to it, you'll love it. The young, small leaves are best. It goes very well in stews and with seafood. It is also cooked with beans of all types to reduces their gaseousness.

Fat Back The pure white fat from the back of pork loins, fat back should be ordered fresh from your butcher. Use it to make fresh lard or for adding to sausages — pork does not have enough fat of its own.

Flour, High-gluten High-gluten flour made from strong winter wheat — the type extensively grown in Canada — is the best type to use for bread because of its gluten content, that makes the loaves rise well. Flour made from soft wheat contains less gluten and is more suitable for cakes and pastry.

A product known as gluten flour, most easily obtained at health food stores (because it is used in special diets), is a flour made after the starch has been washed out of the wheat berry. Its extremely high protein content makes it useful for adding to low-gluten flours, such as oat flour and buckwheat flour.

Frisée Frisée, a member of the escarole family, has curly green leaves with white or light green outer edges. It is crunchy and slightly bitter, and we use it for warm, wilted salads.

Garlic *(Ajo)* One of the foundations of Southwestern cuisine, garlic is used almost exclusively at Coyote Cafe in its roasted form. Dry-roasting (see Special Techniques, below) brings out its sweetness and eliminates any harshness. Garlic provides the bass notes or earthy tones that mix well with cumin and other roasted spices and herbs, and roasted peppers and tomatoes. Along the Gulf Coast of Mexico — in the Veracruz region and the Yucatán — garlic is caramelized in brown butter until crisp and served in large spoonfuls as a condiment. When using fresh garlic, make sure that it is as fresh as possible. If you must chop it ahead of time, cover it with olive oil as garlic will oxidize when exposed to air. I strongly dislike garlic in guacamole: it is far too overpowering for the delicate, fresh, green fruit flavor of avocados. Contrary to common belief, garlic is not at its peak the year around. It is harvested in the spring and, in some areas, in the fall. We buy red Mexican garlic, when available, because of its sweet pungency. See also Wild Garlic.

Ginger *(Jengibre)* Ginger is a rhizome or root that is native to Asia and is now grown in the Caribbean, where it is more commonly used than it is in Mexico or the Southwest. It comes in both fresh and powdered forms. I prefer fresh young ginger, which usually comes from Hawaii and is small, with a reddish brown papery skin. It is very tender, has a delicate floral flavor, and is much less tough and fibrous than older, regular fresh ginger. Fresh ginger gives a wonderful tropical accent to Caribbean salsas and seafood stews. Good-quality dried ginger should be used sparingly in spiced Mexican desserts, usually in combination with clove and allspice. It can be also used to make a ginger flan, and at Coyote Cafe we include it in our cheesecake crust.

Goat *(Cabra)* Traditionally, goat meat is used for celebrations or feasts throughout the Southwest and Mexico. It has its own particular flavor and is best cooked slowly for a long time, on a spit or in a horno oven. Older goat is used more for milk and cheese products; young goat — *cabrito* — tends to be favored for its meat. Its flavor is stronger and more interesting than that of baby lamb, but it is less strong and the meat is not as tough as that of older goat. As goat cheese becomes more popular and more farms are established, we are likely to see more top-quality goat meat on the market.

Goat's Milk *(Leche de cabra)* The essential ingredient for the sweet, syrupy cajeta, a caramel sauce, goat's milk is rich. It can be bought from goat farms or health food stores or pharmacies where it is stocked for those who are allergic to cow's milk.

Green Onions Also known as scallions and spring onions, green onions have a fresh, peppery taste and are highly versatile. They are used extensively in Mexican cuisine and are often grilled with lime juice and salt and used in soft tacos. They are also tasty in salads and vegetable soups. The green tops can be used in crab cakes and stuffings, a Creole influence. See also Wild Garlic.

Harinilla Finely ground *chicos* (see above) used for making tortillas and tamales.

Hibiscus Blossoms *(Flores de Jamaica)* The dried blossom of the hibiscus flower is dark purple and is commonly used in Mexico to flavor *liquados* (see page 9). *Flores de Jamaica* take about 20 minutes to rehydrate. They have a wonderful intense taste of dried cherries or blackberries. They are also used in teas and marinades and make a refreshing drink when mixed with lemonade.

Honey, Red Chile Red chile honey is a specialty product from the Taos area of northern New Mexico. You can make your own from wild honey, New Mexican red chile powder or crushed chile caribe, and a little crushed, roasted garlic. Let the ingredients sit for 1 or 2 weeks. It can be used not only as a honey (it is especially good with blue corn pancakes) but also as a sauce, butter, or marinade.

Ibarra Chocolate See Chocolate

Jamaica, Flores de See Hibiscus Blossoms

Jícama Jícama is a tropical root that looks like a large turnip and has a thin brown skin. The crisp white flesh has the texture of an apple or a radish, but the taste is considerably milder — more like that of a water chestnut, for which it may be substituted. In the Southwest, it is usually peeled and eaten, uncooked, in salads; I prefer it seasoned with chile powder and citrus juice.

Juniper *(Enebro)* Like sage, juniper brings to mind the natural range flavors of the Southwest — Santa Fe is surrounded by juniper and piñon trees. The berries are gray-blue, with an aromatic, woodsy fragrance, and were traditionally used in teas and as medicines by the Southwestern Indians. An ingredient of the classic marinade, juniper is a natural match for venison, since the deer commonly graze on the bushes. Bunches of juniper will flavor meat deliciously when added to a grill.

Lamb *(Cordero)* Sheep have long been used by the Navajo for meat (especially in stews) and wool. The images created by Laura Gilpin in her book, *The Enduring Navajo* of the Navajo sheep grazing on sparse land is symbolic of the landscape and history of the Southwest. Lamb has an excellent flavor and, in my opinion, is much underused. Lamb picks up the flavor of the plants the sheep graze on, which in this region include wonderful, aromatic herbs such as sage, thyme, rosemary, and juniper. At Coyote Cafe, we are now using Churro lamb, a historic and very healthy breed of sheep that is being reintroduced as commercial livestock in northern New Mexico. We also use choice fresh baby lamb from Sonoma and Vermont and always sell out whenever it appears on the menu. The outside fat and the fell (a thin, tough membrane covering the flesh) contain strong flavors that can be overwhelming. For a more subtle and delicate taste, these should be removed.

Lard *(Manteca)* Melted and clarified pork fat, Mexican lard is made from fresh fat back (see above), water, and salt. Lard is best made at home and can be flavored with chile or garlic. Lard has a lower fat content than butter and less than half the cholesterol. Its flavor makes it good for frying or refrying Southwestern foods.

Lavender, Dried Dried lavender is used in Middle Eastern or Provençal cooking, and should be used sparingly. It has a penetrating, somewhat sweet, lemony flavor and is usually part of a mixture of spices. It is obtainable from Middle Eastern markets or shops that sell dried flowers for potpourri.

Leeks, Wild See Wild Garlic

Lettuce *(Lechuga)* We use a number of greens at Coyote Cafe. Most of them have a stronger flavor than the more common Iceberg lettuce and go better with Southwestern food, even though not all are native to the region. (See also other individual names)

Bibb lettuce has a tender texture and a sharp flavor and goes well in salads with richer dressings such as cream or mayonnaise, or with ingredients such as crab. It is also good mixed with other greens. At Coyote Cafe, we use it in our house salads.

Butter lettuce has similar qualities and uses.

Oak leaf lettuce comes in red and green varieties and has lobed leaves the same shape as oak leaves. It has a medium, garden-green flavor and a semisoft texture. It is useful as an attractive garnish around the edge of salads.

Red leaf lettuce is grown commercially and is best when small. It has a medium green flavor, a mild sweetness, and a soft texture. It is best used as a filler.

Romaine lettuce comes in red or green varieties and we use it for our Caesar Salad, pipián sauces, and Green Rice. It has a sweet, green flavor and a crunchy texture. It is the best lettuce for shredding and using in tacos or in Southwestern fillings.

Limes *(Limas)* Our recipes call for Mexican limes whenever possible. These are basically the same limes as the more familiar Florida Key limes. Both types are egg-sized, fragrant, and sweet and are picked ripe, when the fruit turns a mottled yellow. Historically however, the market in the United States has shown a preference for the large, immature Persian lime and, in deference to this, Mexican limes for shipment to this country are usually picked immature. Unripe Persian limes tend to have a very sour juice and little perfume. Allow green Mexican limes to mature at room temperature for about a week and use them when they turn yellow and sweeten in flavor. They will make all the difference in margaritas and other recipes.

Mâche (Corn Salad; Lamb's Lettuce) This is a delicate European lettuce with downy medium to dark blue-green leaves. It has a sweet, nutty flavor and is very good served simply with a dressing of olive oil, vinegar, and fresh herbs.

Mangoes *(Mangos)* The mango with its mixture of banana, pineapple, papaya, and melon flavors seems to symbolize perfectly the tropics. Choose ripe, fragrant, and slightly soft mangoes for eating, and just underripe fruits for salsas. Add a little lime to bring out their full flavor and to cut their richness.

Marjoram *(Mejorana)* Related to mint and thyme, marjoram has a sweetness that goes particularly well with corn, cilantro, and ripe tomatoes. We most often use fresh marjoram when a subtle, fresh, herbal flavor is called for, and oregano would be a little too strong. Wild marjoram is available in New Mexico and in other parts of the Southwest.

Masa The cornmeal dough made from posole (see below) and used to make tortillas and tamales is known as masa.

Masa harina The cornmeal that is known as *masa harina* is finely ground posole (see below). It is used to prepare masa. Because posole (unlike *chicos*) is treated with slaked lime, *masa harina* has a slightly less delicate flavor than does *harinilla*, but is rather easier to use.

Mint *(Menta)* Mint is frequently used in the Yucatán, where it is used to balance the sometimes "soapy" aftertaste of cilantro. We use peppermint most often at Coyote Cafe and find it gives spicy dishes a deliciously clean finish in the mouth. I love mint in fresh salsas with tomatoes and cilantro and with lamb, goat, or black beans.

Mint Marigold, Mexican *(Yerbanís)* This pungent herb has a flavor similar to that of French tarragon with anise undertones. In Mexico, it is primarily used to make a medicinal herb tea. It works well with robust meats and in sauces and has a natural affinity for squash and corn.

Mizuna New to the Southwest, mizuna is a medium green Japanese lettuce with a pointed leaf and a mild, peppery flavor that gets stronger as the plant matures. It is slightly crunchy and can be substituted for watercress.

Mushrooms, Wild *(Hongos)* Wild mushrooms were used in pre-Columbian times. Varieties such as chanterelles, cèpes, morels, and porcini grow in the mountains of New Mexico. They have an intense flavor and go well with hearty Southwestern ingredients, especially game. Cook wild mushrooms as you would the domestic variety. If you cannot find fresh wild mushrooms, use dried cèpes or morels but avoid the shiitakes and oyster mushrooms as they have a flavor that does not blend well in Southwestern recipes. As a last resort, buy domestic mushrooms with opened caps. They have a full mature flavor that white button mushrooms lack.

Mustard Greens Mustard greens have bright, light green leaves with frilled, scalloped edges and a soft texture. They have a sharp, pungent mustard flavor. We use them with shrimp tamales and serve baby mustard greens in salads accompanying heavier foods such as beef. They can also be sautéed as a vegetable with Southern-style dishes such as chicken or crab cakes.

Nopales; Nopalitos See Cactus

Olive Oil *(Aceite de oliva)* I like to cook Southwestern food and dress certain salads with olive oil. Use a pure or light olive oil that has been pressed from olive pulp when you want little olive flavor in cooking or for salads. Extra virgin olive oil is made from the first pressing and has the strongest, heaviest flavor —

use it for salads rather than cooking. Virgin olive oil is made from second and subsequent pressings. It has a rather nutty flavor and a higher acidity (more than 3 percent) than does extra virgin oil.

Onions *(Cebollas)* We use different types of onion at Coyote Cafe. White onions are most commonly used in Southwestern and Mexican cooking. Yellow onions are large, firm-fleshed, and strongly flavored, and have a high sugar content. Red onions come in various sizes and are usually mild. They can more easily be eaten raw and are also useful for their color. In season, sweet varieties such as Maui, Vidalia, and Texas are good when eaten raw.

Wash cut onions under hot running water for 2 to 3 minutes if they are to be used raw; they oxidize easily and can quickly develop a musky flavor after being cut. This procedure is unnecessary if you are cooking them, unless you plan to hold them for a time. See also Wild Garlic.

Oranges *(Naranjas)* Always use fresh oranges when recipes call for orange juice. We use sweet juice oranges, such as Washington navel and Valencia, because their natural sweetness goes best with hot chiles. The combination of oranges and chiles is successful in marinades and sauces for pork. We also use sweet blood oranges (so-called for their purple-red flesh) when they are in season.

Oregano, Mexican *(Orégano)* We use Mexican oregano only in its dried form, never powdered. Drying seems to narrow its strong and sometimes overwhelming range of flavors. Mexican oregano is more pungent and "weedier" than is regular dried oregano and should be dry-roasted before it is used. If substituting regular dried oregano, use a little more. In Tex-Mex cooking, Mexican oregano is often used in soups and sauces and is an important element in red chile sauces and beef chile.

Palm Oil *(Aciete de dendê)* Also known as *dendê* oil, the palm oil that is used extensively in West Africa and the Bahia region of Brazil is a bright orange red and solidifies at room temperature. It has a distinctive flavor and imparts a vivid color to any food with which it is cooked. There is no good substitute.

Papayas *(Papayas)* Another evocatively tropical fruit, the papaya can grow as large as a watermelon, but those we see in this country tend to be relatively uniform and small. Buy them slightly underripe, colored yellow with greenish tinges like bananas. Allow them to ripen at room temperature until they are a golden yellow all over and then use quickly. Like mangoes, papayas are best served with fresh lime juice to bring out their flavor and counter their richness.

Parsley *(Perejil)* The wonderful flavor of parsley adds liveliness and freshness, especially to heavier dishes. We use the flat-leaved Italian variety for garnish and the curly-leaved variety for stocks.

Passion Fruit *(Granadilla)* Dark purple to brown, with an uneven, lumpy skin, passion fruit are about the size of a large golfball. The skin wrinkles up as they ripen, and the flesh is a yellow-green mixture of juicy pulp and seeds. I think they have one of the most incredible perfumes of any fruit — flowery and citric, like the scent of mangoes, oranges, and lilies all rolled into one. They can be used in sauces and make lovely sorbets, ice creams, or garnishes for desserts.

Pecan Nuts *(Pacanas)* The pecan is probably the most important North American nut tree and is native to New Mexico, most Southern states, and Mexico. The pecan was improved by European settlers and is related to the hickory and walnut. Pecan nuts were ground by the pre-Columbian Indians to be used as a thickening agent and flavoring and were pressed whole for oil. Pecans are used for their flavor, color, and consistency in a variety of baked goods and desserts, especially, of course, in pecan pie, as well as in praline and ice cream. We use pecan wood at Coyote Cafe for grilling; it is a sweeter wood than mesquite.

Pepper, Black *(Pimienta negra)* Different kinds of black pepper have very different qualities and nuances; some are hotter, others are more perfumed. It pays to learn the differences; inferior pepper is notable for its heat but poor flavor. Best bought in specialty stores or coffee shops, peppercorns should have a strong, fresh aroma. I avoid using black pepper in most chile sauces because the flavors compete and do not blend well together.

Peppers See Sweet Peppers

Pheasant *(Faisán)* This is a kingly bird, deserving of a feast! It is also a festive treat that I associate with Christmas, truffles, and fine old Burgundies. Come to think of it, when preparing pheasant, invite only good guests with fine old Burgundies. Pheasant has a dark-meat flavor, and I especially like the new Californian variety that has more internal basting fat and is less stringy. Pheasant should be browned quickly and pan-roasted. Allow half a bird per person. Save the bones to make a soup with wild mushrooms.

Piloncillo Unrefined processed brown sugar, *piloncillo* is sold in the form of tapered cones, measuring about 3 inches high with a 2-inch base. It has a better flavor and contains more nutrients than regular sugar and can be purchased from Latin markets. Substitute dark or light brown sugar.

Pine Nuts *(Piñones)* Pine nuts are a native staple crop of Southwestern Pueblo Indians, and especially of the Pima of southern Arizona. I have a study published by the Bureau of Indian Affairs showing that, in the nineteenth century, more than 200 recipes from the region called for pine nuts. They were mostly used ground in breads and porridges. Native pine nuts, which have a more marked taste of resin, are scarcer now. Increasingly, the nuts are being imported from Europe and China. They are terrific eaten raw and, when ground, make a delicious flour for desserts. Evergreen piñon trees cover the landscape in many parts of the Southwest, including New Mexico. They tend to be small and grow mostly at elevations above 5,000 feet.

Pineapples *(Piñas)* Pineapples, too, were discovered in the New World by Columbus. Good pineapples are really hard to find outside the tropics because they do not ripen well after they have been picked and then are very perishable once they are ripe. Try to find pineapples that feel heavy and have an even yellow coloration and a strong perfume — those that smell sweet and fresh will taste that way. Pineapples with little perfume will likewise have little taste. They ferment easily, so do not buy them too ripe. If possible, buy the air-expressed Hawaiian fruit. Always skin and core pineapples. Use the fruit in salsas, relishes, desserts, and cocktails.

Pinto Beans See Beans

Plantains See Bananas

Polenta Polenta is a very even, coarse grind of corn used for making the Italian dish of the same name. Polenta can be full-flavored, but it can also be old and stale, so it is worth tasting a little before you use it. Grits, or ground hominy, makes an adequate substitute, although its finer grind gives the polenta a sweeter, less cornlike flavor.

Pork *(Carne de puerco; Cerdo)* Pork is used more in Spanish and Mexican cuisine than any other meat. It is now bred leaner than it used to be, so needs to be marinated to preserve moisture and cooked for a shorter time. Corn- or peanut-fed pork is superb. It is worth bearing in mind that, contrary to what you might expect, pork lard has only 60 percent of the cholesterol that butter contains, and adds a wonderful flavor to whatever is cooked in it.

Posole (Pozole) Posole is dried whole corn kernels that have been treated with slaked lime and boiled until they become soft and the husks discarded. Very similar to hominy, it is used in the South as a vegetable or starch. Posole is also the main ingredient of a famous Southwestern soup of the same name (see page 38).

Prickly Pear and Prickly Pear Juice See Cactus

Pumpkin *(Calabaza)* The familar orange pumpkin ranges in size from that of a softball to that of a watermelon. Its flesh is neutral or slightly scented in taste, and orange, yellow, or white in color. The pumpkin originated in Central and South America. The Southwestern Indians prepared it in every conceivable way: baked, cooked in broth as a vegetable, mashed and served with butter as a starch-like mashed potatoes, or combined with other ingredients in soups. It can be used in salads and soups, as a vegetable or sweet pickle, and of course in pies and desserts. Pumpkin seeds are also used as ingredients in chile sauces, pipiáns, and moles and are rich in protein.

Quail *(Codorniz)* Quail, a native Southwestern bird, is my favorite fowl. The subtle, desert flavor should not be overwhelmed by sauces that are too strong or spicy. The birds are best roasted or fried or, ideally, browned in clarified butter and then roasted so that they do not cook too quickly on the outside. Smoked quail are terrific for picnics.

Radicchio (Red Chicory) A crisp lettuce that originated in Italy, radicchio is primarily used for its maroon or purple color. It has a slightly bitter flavor and a crunchy texture. It should be used sparingly in salads, preferably mixed with other lettuce, and is wonderful grilled as a vegetable with garlic, oil, herbs, and balsamic vinegar.

Radishes *(Rábanos)* Little red radishes with the tops still attached are a true delicacy. We don't eat these versatile vegetables enough, relegating them instead to mere decoration. They have a terrific fresh flavor with a stimulating hotness. Use them in salads or cooked as a vegetable with meats. I particularly like radishes with oranges and rare tuna in a summer salad.

Rice *(Arroz)* Beans and rice, like beans and corn, together form a complete protein. The latter combination was important in the diet of Southwestern Indians and contributed to their survival. Rice was introduced by the Spanish and heavily influenced the cuisine. Use basmati varieties (such as the Texmati brand) when you want a separate grain and short risotto *(arborio)* varieties when you want a creamy dish.

Rocket (Roquette) See Arugula

Sage *(Salvia)* Sage grows wild throughout New Mexico and in parts of Texas, where it is a primary source of grazing for Churro lamb and venison. Wild sage is much stronger than the garden variety and is a wonderful herb, especially with game, fowl, and meat, when used sparingly. Related to mint, wild sage may be added to a wood fire when grilling.

Salt *(Sal)* Sea salt has a clean taste. Is is especially good with seafood, matching as it does its natural habitat. Undersalting poached fish will extract the flavors rather than preserve them: the salinity of the water should be the same as that of sea water. I also like the coarseness of sea salt with carpaccio and the flavor it gives to a court bouillon. Kosher salt should be used when you are looking for a less salty taste.

Sassafras *(Sasafrás)* Used in medicinal teas in Mexico, sassafras has a sweet, root beer flavor. The powdered leaves of the plant (filé) have been removed from the market by the United States Department of Agriculture because they might be carcinogenic, but the bark is excellent when ground and used with dried chiles, allspice, anise, and black pepper. Sassafras is wonderful in ice cream and cookies.

Scallions *(Cebollitas)* See Green Onions

Shallots *(Chalotes)* Originating in the Middle East, shallots are members of the onion family and have small elongated bulbs, usually with a papery reddish-brown skin. They have a subtle, complex flavor, stronger than onions but less pronounced than garlic; sometimes we use them as a substitute for wild garlic.

Shrimp, dried *(Camerónes secos)* Dried shrimp are soaked before being used. Like dried herbs and spices, they can also be toasted briefly before being rehydrated. Good dried shimp will be an attractive pink color (if they are too pale a pink or somewhat gray, avoid them) and whole, including heads, tails, and shells. They should be simmered gently in water for 5 minutes before being trimmed and shelled. If they are already shelled, simply soak them in warm water for about 5 minutes before using. They have a strong, fishy flavor. You can find them in Oriental grocery stores.

Spaghetti Squash Also known as vegetable spaghetti, this squash ranges from cream to yellow in color, is oval to round, and about the size of a football. When cooked it yields crisp, tender strands resembling spaghetti. It has a slightly sweet, bland taste. It originated in the Southwest and Mexico and is now grown in most temperate climates around the world.

Spanish Squash Pale green with stripes, small and round, about 6 inches across, the Spanish squash has a rich flavor almost like that of avocado. The sweetest summer squash, it is a native of the Southwest and a favorite of the Hispanic community, especially in New Mexico.

Spring Onions See Green Onions

Squab *(Pichón)* Squab are domesticated pigeons, not the type you would encounter in the park. With their subtle, dark, rich flavor that is a little like veal liver and combines well with rosemary and garlic, they are best served with assertive stuffings, such as roasted garlic. Because of their richness, serve half a squab per person. Grill or roast them but always cook them medium-rare.

Squash *(Calabacita)* Squashes are native to the Southwest and were cultivated as a mainstay by a number of Southwestern Indian tribes. Like both corn and beans, squash was of ceremonial importance. It was eaten in all stages of development, and was sun-dried for winter. The Spanish settlers introduced new varieties to the region.

Squash is best eaten young when the skin is tender and the flavor is strongest. Buy them firm and with unblemished skin, and store them in the open. Ideally, squash should be home-grown; it tends to be tastier and less starchy.

Summer squashes are often available in winter as well as in the spring and fall, but summer is their prime season. They are more perishable than are winter squashes, are eaten immature, and are edible raw. If left to grow, they will develop thick, hard skins and become winter squashes. Use only specially grown hybrid versions of baby squash; ordinary squash when eaten while still immature is often bitter. Zucchini and yellow crookneck are the most common summer squashes. Winter squashes are planted during the summer and are usually harvested during the fall or early winter. They are mature vegetables and are always cooked. Most have an orange flesh that is usually sweet and nutty in flavor. Acorn, butternut, turban, Hubbard, and spaghetti are the common winter squashes. (See also individual names.)

Squash Blossoms *(Flores de calabaza)* Squash blossoms have been a feature of Mexican and Southwestern cuisine for thousands of years. These deep yellow, fragrant flowers, between 4 and 6 inches long, are commonly used deep-fried, stuffed with goat cheese, sautéed as a vegetable, added to quesadillas, soups, and raviolis, or as garnish. The male flowers are best and they should be used immediately; they are in season throughout the summer.

Stocks *(Caldos)* It is best to make your own stocks. Use a high proportion of bones and brown them in the oven first. Add vegetables and simmer for between 8 and 24 hours. Fish stock, however, becomes bitter if cooked longer than 45 minutes. Never boil stocks and be sure to skim them constantly. Do not add salt, except sparingly to chicken stock, as most meats are naturally salty.

Sugar See *Piloncillo*

Sweet Peppers *(Pimientos dulces)* Also referred to as bell peppers, sweet peppers come in a variety of colors — red, yellow, green, purple, or orange. They vary greatly in sweetness and flavor, though most are crisp and refreshing. They should not be substituted for fresh chiles, although they may be combined with them. The green sweet pepper, which has an overpowering taste, tends not to marry well with other Southwestern flavors. Roasting and peeling sweet peppers gets rid of the tough outer skin and improves their flavor. Red and yellow peppers are especially decorative.

Tamarind *(Tamarindo)* These coffee brown, sticky pods, about 4 inches long, can be found in Latin or Asian markets and possibly in the specialty produce section of your supermarket. To buy ripe ones, look for large, heavy, dark pods and break one open; if it is not sticky inside, the pod is not ripe and cannot be used. If they are not heavy, they are too old. To prepare tamarind, peel off the outer bark-like husk and simmer the pulp and seeds in enough water to cover until the pulp separates from the seeds. This will take at least 1 hour. Push the pulp and water through a sieve or food mill. Tamarind is also available as a bottled ready-made paste. It is a flavoring used most often in Mexico in *liquados* (see page 9). It is also used as a flavoring in Worcestershire sauce and cola drinks. We use it at Coyote Cafe in sauces, marinades, and as a dessert flavoring.

Tepary Bean See Beans

Thyme *(Tomillo)* The flavor of thyme reflects the aromas of open range land and complements lamb and venison particularly well. Used both dried and fresh, its wild taste makes it a great ingredient in soups, sauces, and stocks.

Tomatillos *(Tomatillos; Tomates verdes)* A plum-sized, bright green fruit that was cultivated by the Aztecs, the tomatillo is covered with a light green papery husk. It is not related to the tomato, even though it looks like a green one and has a taste that is not dissimilar. Actually, it is a member of the Cape gooseberry family. Its tart flavor, that includes tones of unripe apple, rhubarb, or green plum, marries perfectly with serrano chiles, cilantro, and garlic. Tomatillos develop a toasty sweetness when blackened on a comal or roasted. They complement green chiles. After the tomato, the tomatillo is the most widely used salsa ingredient and forms the base of most green Mexican sauces.

Tomatoes *(Tomates)* Tomatoes originated in Central and South America and were brought back to Europe by the early explorers. We usually use the versatile pear-shaped Roma tomato at Coyote Cafe. It has thicker pulp and less juice and goes best with Southwestern ingredients. Buy firm, red tomatoes; they should not have any green or yellow color. Do not refrigerate them, as their flavor disappears when they are cold. The best way of preparing Roma tomatoes for cooking, especially in sauces, is to cut their tops off, quarter them, and place them on a baking sheet in a single layer. Bake at 325° for about 1 hour or until most of the moisture has evaporated. This procedure will yield a sweet, tasty tomato that is superior to the canned version.

Tumbleweed Shoots *(Renuevos de rastrojo)* Anyone who has watched Westerns will recognize the tumbleweed, which is native to the Southwest and northern Mexico. The shoots were used by the Southwestern Indians, and they are a rare and exotic ingredient. They are related to *romelitos,* another wild shoot that grows in Mexico. Tumbleweed shoots have a wild bean flavor and can be used in salads or as a vegetable.

Turban Squash Distinctively double-deckered or cottage-loaf-shaped, turbans are brightly multicolored, round squashes. The larger base of the turban, nearest the stem, is usually red or orange; the smaller, tapered part is usually orange and green with yellow stripes. Often used for ornamental purposes, it may be cooked in the same ways as the Hubbard squash. Extravagantly colored turban squashes are much in evidence at roadside stands when you drive through the Rio Grande Valley in October.

Turkey *(Pavo; Guajolote)* Ben Franklin wanted the native turkey to become the national symbol rather than the eagle. It has been used extensively in Southwestern and Mexican cuisine for thousands of years, and is often served with mole sauces. Fresh organic birds have the best flavor. If you order ahead from a good butcher, you should be able to get fresh, additive-free turkeys the year around. Wild turkey is far more difficult to obtain. It is moister and has a richer and gamier flavor than that of domestic turkeys. The differences between the two are similar to those between free-range and commercial chickens.

Vanilla *(Vainilla)* Native to the New World and cultivated by the Aztecs, who used it to flavor chocolate and other foods and drinks, the vanilla plant is a member of the orchid family. Probably the best vanilla comes from Tahiti and it is also grown in Madagascar and Indonesia as well as in Mexico. Buy whole vanilla beans (rarely used now in Mexico) or pure liquid extract. Vanilla is mostly used to flavor desserts, ice cream, and drinks.

Venison *(Venado)* Images of hunters stalking venison and returning to their cliff dwellings or pueblos with their trophies are among the historic tableaux symbolic of the Southwest. Ranchers in open range areas throughout the Southwest have discovered that there is a burgeoning market for game animals. Black-buck antelope is a great delicacy and, in my opinion, one of the finest meats available in this country. It has a rich, nutty, complex flavor and, like the nilgai antelope, offers more flavor than venison. Together with axis and sika deer, it is raised by the Texas Wild Game Co-operative in Ingram and by other suppliers.

Vinegars *(Vinagres)* Vinegar is used in a number of ways in Southwestern cuisine: in marinades and sauces and for grilling and salads. At Coyote Cafe we generally use four main types of flavored vinegar:

Balsamic vinegar, made from Italian red wine, is full, flavorful, but relatively mild. It is aged in wooden casks for between two and forty years. We use it mainly for salad dressings and with sautéed tomatoes and vegetables to complement grilled fish and chicken.

Cider vinegar, made from apple cider, is the most common in Southwestern cuisine. Good quality cider vinegars that smell of apple are available from health food stores. Cider vinegar is particularly good for giving chile sauces a lift, without using salt.

Rice vinegar is a light, mild Japanese vinegar with a lower acidity than that of cider vinegar, making it better for fish, pickling, and escabeche dishes. Buy only the unseasoned version. Its natural sweetness complements hot chile flavors. It is available in the Oriental sections of stores and markets.

Sherry vinegar, made from Spanish sherry, is also aged. It has a subtle sweetness and a rich flavor that goes well with heavier sauces, especially those based on tomatoes. We use it in our Caesar salad dressing.

White Bean See Beans

Wild Boar *(Jabalí)* Beware — these do not make good pets! Wild boar has a very rich flavor, akin to pork but more herbaceous. As our recipes suggest, we use a lot of wild boar bacon at Coyote Cafe. It can be an inconsistent product and there is no way of predicting the quality. The meat is best hung and used in hams, sausages, and bacon.

Wild Garlic, Leeks, and Onions All these plants are related undomesticated herbs resembling their culivated counterparts; only the wild onion is native to the Southwest. All were used by Indians as a food source, either raw or with corn dumplings or bread. The bulbs of these plants can be roasted or sautéed and used to flavor soups, sauces, and salads, or eaten, sparingly, on their own as vegetables. They are all fiercely strong, both in flavor and aroma.

Yellow Crookneck Squash Bright yellow, with a narrow, curved neck, and averaging about 6 inches long, this summer squash is sweeter than zucchini. The flavor is better the younger it is used. It has a pleasant perfume when cooking and is good in soups. It can also be used in salads, sautéed, fried, or stuffed and combines very well with other vegetables, especially tomatoes, garlic, and onions.

Yerba Santa Yerba Santa is a highly aromatic leaf that has strong anise, sassafras, and root beer flavors. It is said to be useful as a medicinal herb in the treatment of bronchial conditions.

Zucchini Also known as the courgette, the zucchini is cucumber-shaped, averages about 6 inches long, and is medium to dark green in color with yellow to brown mottling on the skin. The flavor is best when the vegetables are tiny. The small, round zucchini that are grown in the Southwest are sweeter and are excellent when stuffed. The zucchini is closely related to the pumpkin and vegetable spaghetti and is usually available the year around. It originated in Central America, not in Europe as popularly believed.

Chiles

All chiles, including the milder ones that are usually known as peppers, are members of the Capsicum family. The misnomer came about because Columbus and other European explorers who came to the New World were searching for the East Indies, the source of the much sought-after black pepper and other spices. The chiles they brought back from the Americas were referred to as *peppers,* though they are not related botanically or by taste. One of the best sources of information on chiles is the book, *Peppers: The Domesticated Capsicums,* by Jean Andrews (University of Texas Press, 1984). Coyote Cafe and Ten Speed Press will shortly be publishing a poster identifying more than seventy-five fresh and dried chiles.

Descriptions of the chiles most commonly used in Southwestern cuisine may be found below, according to whether they are used fresh, dried, or powdered. Some varieties are used in all three forms and may have different names in each!

Fresh Chiles *(Chiles frescos)*

It is common to roast, peel, seed, and devein fresh chiles when cooking with them (see Special Techniques, below). It may be necessary to use rubber gloves when preparing chiles as their natural oils can irritate and burn the skin. Be particularly careful not to touch your face or eyes when working with chiles. Buy chiles that have bright, smooth, unbroken skins and are firm and unblemished, with a fresh, sharp smell. Store them wrapped in paper towels in the refrigerator and not in plastic bags where moisture can accumulate and hasten the spoiling process. Besides providing the wonderful flavors that are the essence of Southwestern cuisine, fresh chiles are high in vitamins (especially A and C) and are believed to aid digestion.

Anaheim Pale green (sometimes red), tapered, and about 6 inches long and 2 inches around, the Anaheim is the mild-flavored cousin of the New Mexico green and is believed to have been introduced to New Mexico from Mexico in the sixteenth century by the founder of Santa Fe, Don Juan de Oñate. It can be found most of the year in the Southwest and in Latin markets elsewhere. The Anaheim is the mildest of the fresh green chiles and it is favored for chiles rellenos and chile stews. Its flavor can be much improved by roasting it over a fire, allowing it to sweat for half an hour under a cloth, and peeling it carefully, leaving the odd bit of burnt skin to add flavor. Never substitute green bell peppers for this, or any other, chile.

Ancho A fairly large chile, about 5 inches long and tapering from 3-inch-wide shoulders, this chile is graced with several names. Known as *ancho* in both its fresh and dried forms, it is called *poblano* (apparently because it originally came from the Puebla Valley near Mexico City) when green, and in some areas, *pasilla* (although the true pasilla chile is very different, being long, narrow, a dark brownish black, and curved). For a description of the frequently used poblano, see below. See also ancho and mulato, under the descriptions of dried chiles.

Cayenne Bright red, thin, and pointed, the cayenne is between 4 and 6 inches long and ½ inch around. Fiercely hot, sweet, and intense, it is similar in flavor to red Thai peppers and is related to the tabasco chile. It is used fresh in salsas and, when dried, as cayenne pepper (see below).

Cubanelle Light green or yellow, tapered, and measuring between 4 and 5 inches long and 2 inches around, the cubanelle is a very mild, sweet chile widely available on the Eastern seaboard. It is an acceptable substitute for Anaheim chiles. When roasted and peeled, it makes a good eating chile and is also ideal for pickling.

Fresno A red chile that tapers to a point and measures about 2 inches long and between 1½ and 2 inches around, the Fresno is usually available only in the fall. This thick-fleshed, very hot chile is sometimes mistaken for a red jalapeño, although the two are of different varieties and the Fresno is broader at the shoulders.

Güero Güero is a generic term for yellow chiles — the name coming from a Spanish word meaning light-skinned or blond — and is usually applied to pale yellow, tapered chiles that vary from the size of a jalapeño up to between 4 and 5 inches long and 2 inches around. They are sometimes called wax or banana chiles or peppers, or Santa Fe Grande, which is one variety of güero (although I haven't seen any by this name in Santa Fe itself). This chile is slightly sweet, has a waxy taste, and varies in strength from medium-mild to hot. It is most commonly used in sauces or is pickled.

Habanero Green, yellow, or orange, lantern-shaped (like a small bell pepper), and measuring about 2 inches long and 2 inches around, the habanero ("from Havana") is used extensively in the Yucatán and is the hottest of those used commonly in Central America. I would estimate that the habanero is between 15 and 20 times stronger than the serrano, and it can have a caustic effect both internally and externally. The first one I ever ate in Mexico raised a blister on my lip. In spite of the fierce heat, it has a wonderful flavor. Two bottled table sauces, one red and one green, based on the habanero are imported into this country under the El Yucateco brand. They are not easy to obtain, but they really wake up a timid dish. Users beware! Sometimes I'm surprised that the spoon does not melt.

Hatch The hatch chile is a variety of the New Mexico green.

Jalapeño Medium to dark green or (more rarely) red, tapering to a rounded end, and measuring about 1½ inches long and 1 inch across the shoulders, the jalapeño is the best known and most widely eaten hot chile in this country. It may be used fresh or roasted and is excellent in quesadillas, salsas, and soups, or with cheese on nacho chips. It is commonly pickled. Fresh, ripe jalapeños, when dried and smoked, are known as chipotles.

New Mexico Green Light to medium green, tapered, and measuring between 4 and 6 inches long and 2 inches around, the New Mexico green chile varies in strength from medium to very hot. This is the basic chile in New Mexican cuisine. The question, "Red or green?" when asked in a restaurant refers to the choice between dried red or fresh green chile sauce. The flavor is unlike that of any other chile in North America: sweet, earthy, and with a clarity that seems to reflect the skies and landscapes of New Mexico. The New Mexico green is usually available fresh the year around, although anyone who has been to Santa Fe in the fall knows that these chiles are roasted in huge quantities so that they can be frozen and enjoyed through the winter. Fifty pounds of chiles are roasted at a time in large drum-sized squirrel cages of wire mesh that rotate in front of propane burners. They freeze well, and frozen New Mexican greens are better than canned. If they are unavailable, substitute a mixture of Anaheims and roasted jalapeños.

New Mexico Red A ripened version of the New Mexico green, the New Mexico red is a dark, deep, intense red. In northern New Mexico in early October, particularly in the Velarde Valley, much of the chile crop is left on the vine to turn bright red and ripen in the crisp fall sun. These chiles are then tied into bunches — the familiar *ristras* — to dry. During a few short weeks, we use as much fresh New Mexico red chile as possible at Coyote Cafe. They are fleshy, hot, and sweet and, like the green chiles, can also be roasted in drums and then used for sauces, soups, and chutneys. In fact, most chiles turn from green to red if left to ripen; all the same, I can't help but feel that the New Mexico chiles are different.

Pepperoncini Pale green or occasionally yellow, thin, pointed, and curved, pepperoncini are about 2 inches long and 1 inch across. They are mild, similar in flavor to the cubanelle, and widely available on the Eastern seaboard and in areas near Italian growers or markets. They are often pickled and, when roasted and peeled, are a good eating chile.

Pimento *(Pimiento; Pimiento dulce; Pimiento morrón)* Red, almost heart-shaped, and tapered to a point, pimentos measure about 4 inches long and between 3 and 4 inches around. Fleshy, wonderfully sweet, and slightly hot, this chile is grown widely in southern Spain, Hungary, and in the southern United States and California. The pimento has more flavor than does the sweet red bell pepper. In its powdered form it is known as paprika.

Poblano The poblano is the green form of the ancho chile (which is described under both categories, fresh and dried). It is dark green, tapers down from the shoulders to a point, and measures about 4 or 5 inches long and 3 or 4 inches around. It is medium to hot in strength. It is always used cooked or roasted and never eaten raw. Roasting gives the poblano a smoky flavor, and we use them all the time at Coyote Cafe. They are essential for chiles rellenos and any other stuffed chile dish as they have a thick flesh. Very hot poblanos should be seeded and deveined.

Serrano Bright green or red, cylindrical with a rounded end, and measuring about 2 inches long and ¼ inch across, the serrano — literally "highland" or "mountain" — is the hottest chile commonly available. With its clean, biting heat and pleasantly high acidity, the serrano is a favored ingredient in fresh salsas. This chile is good when roasted and pickled and will liven up a Bloody Mary.

Thai Bright red or dark green, long, thin, and pointed, and measuring about 4 inches long and ¾ of an inch around, Thai chiles are as hot as serranos and taste a little meatier. Available at oriental markets, they can be used instead of serranos. Their thin flesh and copious seeds make them awkward to skin and seed, so they are best used whole. One Thai chile is approximately equivalent to 3 serranos.

Dried Chiles *(Chiles secos)*

In Mexico there are perhaps 200 names for only twenty or twenty-five distinct chiles. However, they are worth getting acquainted with; Robert Mondavi has likened their complex and varied flavors to the layers of flavor in fine wines. When buying dried chiles, make sure that they are uniform in color. They should be dark and brilliant, not faded, and make sure that there are no white spots or other markings that indicate improper drying. Dry chiles should be unbroken, so that their flavors are intact. A degree of flexibility indicates freshness; they are likely to be less fresh when brittle. Dry chiles should have a good aroma and not be too dusty or dirty. Store them in a cool, dry place. At Coyote Cafe, we usually dry-roast and rehydrate dried chiles and then purée them for sauces (see pages 179 and 180 for directions).

Ancho Brick red to dark mahogany, wrinkled, with broad shoulders — the word *ancho* means wide — tapering to a point, and measuring about 4 or 5 inches long and between 2 and 3 inches wide, the (dried) ancho is the most widely used dried chile in Mexico. This chile is at its best when it is very flexible and aromatic — it has sweet fruit flavors, mainly of dried plum and raisin. The mulato (see below) is a variety of ancho. See also the entries under Ancho and Poblano in the section on fresh chiles and under Pasilla (below), a name by which the dried ancho is often sold.

California Burgundy to mahogany in color, smooth, tapered, and measuring about 6 inches long and 2 inches wide, the California chile is the dried form of the Anaheim chile. The sweet flavor blends well with those of other chiles.

Cascabel Dark red brown, smooth, globe-shaped, and measuring about 1½ inches in diameter, the cascabel is named for the rattling sound it makes. Medium-hot, its flavors of toasted tomato and plum are good in salsas, sauces, and soups.

Chinese Red The small, glossy red-brown chiles are about 1½ inches long and are sold in the Oriental sections of almost any supermarket.

Chipotle A light flat brown in color, wrinkled, tapered, and measuring about 2½ inches long and ¾ inch wide, the chipotle is the dried form of the fresh, ripe jalapeño chile smoked slowly over the dried foliage of the chile plant. It is extremely hot and has a wonderful toasted, smoky flavor that contains tones of leather, coffee, and mushrooms and a marked aftertaste of pure capsicum. The chipotle is also available canned in adobo sauce, prepared by stewing the chiles with onions, tomato, vinegar, and spices. I love the flavor of chipotle, and at Coyote Cafe we most often use them puréed in soups, sauces, and salsas.

De Árbol Bright red to orange, translucent, smooth, tapering to a point and measuring about 3 inches long and ½ inch wide, the de árbol — literally "tree" chile — is related to the fresh cayenne. It is pungent and extremely hot, with a toasty sweet flavor.

Guajillo Brick red to burgundy, smooth with some large folds or wrinkles, tapered, and measuring about 4 inches long and 1½ inches wide, the guajillo (literally "little gourd") is the dried form of the mirasol chile. It has a medium heat, an earthy flavor, and a dusty, fruity aroma of plum and raisin, with a slight tobacco finish.

Japones Orange to red, smooth, long, and pointed, japones chiles are about 2 inches long and ⅜ inch wide. Popularly thought of as dried serranos, they are actually a different variety. Similar in flavor to the de árbol, with toasty, dried red berry tones, the japones can be searingly hot.

Mulato Similar in shape and color to the ancho, of which it is a variety, but slightly larger and a little darker when held up to the light, the mulato (literally "dark-skinned") is the poblano dried. An essential ingredient in moles, it is medium-hot and has a full, smoky flavor that includes tones of licorice, currant, and tobacco.

Negro See Pasilla, below

New Mexico Green Very dark olive green, smooth, tapered, and measuring about 3 or 4 inches long by 1 inch wide, the New Mexico green chile is rarer in its dried form than is the New Mexico red. Dried, it provides another way of surviving the winter if you run out of the fresh and then of the roasted, frozen green chile. The wonderful sharp, pungent capsicum flavors of fresh green chile are captured in the dried product. Unfortunately, because of the labor involved, it is wildly expensive but, like dried wild mushrooms, a little goes a long way. Try it ground as a seasoning on steaks, chicken, or pork instead of black pepper.

New Mexico Red Dark brick red, smooth, and tapered, the dried form of the fresh New Mexico Red measures about 5 inches long and 1½ inches wide. At its best, this is truly the king of dried chiles. It has a variety of tones, ranging from those of toasty, dried corn and dried berry, to rich tomato; sometimes there are hints of apple and orange. This chile should be used on its own with a minimum of spice or herbal accompaniments.

Pasilla Very dark purple-black, wrinkled, and tapered, the true pasilla (as distinguished from the dried ancho, which may also be sold as the pasilla), is about 5 inches long and 1 inch wide. It is also called the negro. This chile has intense and smoky flavors with deep, rich tones that range from those of currant to tobacco to coffee. This chile makes a wonderful seafood sauce and is used in moles.

Pequín Orange, smooth, either round or slightly tapered, and measuring about ¼ inch in diameter, chiles known as the pequín may actually be any one of several different varieties that are all closely related. They are very hot and taste like cayenne.

Powdered Chiles *(Chiles en polvo)*

The quality of most dishes that include chile powder is directly related to the quality of the chile powder itself. When buying chile powder, make sure that the color is a bright brick red. The consistency should not be too powdery, but slightly lumpy, indicating that the natural oils are still fresh and present. These oils, which contain the flavor, should stain when a little chile powder is rubbed between the fingers. The aroma should be strong, intense, and earthy. Old or stale chile powder has a dull and dusty aroma and flavor. Chile powder should be refrigerated or stored in a cool, dark place.

Do not buy commercial chile powder mixes that contain black pepper, salt, sugar, cumin, garlic powder, cayenne, and paprika. These seasoned chile powders generally contain very little real chile powder, which is the essential ingredient. This product should not be used in Southwestern cuisine.

Different grinds of the same chiles have different flavors when cooked. This reflects the inclusion of seeds, for example, or the way in which the palate reacts to different grades or textures of ingredients. Chile powders are usually labeled mild, medium, or hot. Described below are the main types of chile powder used in Southwestern cooking.

Ancho Ancho chile powder, also called pasilla chile powder on the West Coast, consists of pure ground ancho chiles. It is not a blend. It is brick red, sweet, medium-hot, and makes a good base for a red chile sauce.

Caribe The crushed, flaky (rather than ground) version of the dried New Mexico red chile, the California chile, or other similar varieties is sold as chile caribe. These are the chile flakes that are used as pizza topping in Italian restaurants. Because of the seeds and coarse texture, the effect of chile caribe in a dish is very different from those of other red chile products. It is best used in dishes in which an earthy texture and flavor are called for. It is also used in New Mexico to make a winter salsa with garlic, tomatoes, vinegar, and sometimes sour apple cider.

California What is sold as "California chile powder" usually consists of pure ground Anaheim chiles. Brick red in color, it is sweeter, less earthy or complex than are New Mexico or chimayo chile powders, and milder.

Cayenne Pepper Ground from dried cayenne peppers, too often cayenne powder has plenty of heat but not enough flavor. In general, I prefer to use a really hot, freshly ground New Mexico chile powder.

Chimayo This is the best known and finest form of ground New Mexico chile. The chiles are grown in the beautiful mountainous area around Chimayo, which is about twenty-five miles north of Santa Fe. The dry and crisp high-altitude climate of the Sangre de Cristo range seems to produce the best chiles for this authentically hot New Mexico chile powder.

Molido A finely ground powder of New Mexico chiles that varies in heat from mild to medium to hot according to the amount of seed ground along with the dried chiles. Like paprika, chile molido is useful as a dry spice for seasoning. In fact, because it has an earthy sweetness that other chile powders do not share, I prefer to use mild chile molido instead of paprika, and hot chile molido instead of cayenne pepper. An acceptable red chile sauce can be made from chile molido instead of from whole seeded red chiles, though it will tend to have a grainy texture. A brief toasting in a skillet or on a comal will give a pleasant, nutty dimension to the flavor of chile molido and chile caribe.

New Mexico Chile Powder See Chimayo and Molido, above

Paprika Paprika (the name comes from a Balkan word for pepper) is the ground form of the dried European pimento and its cousins. The best paprikas, which can have a truly wonderful range of toasty, sweet, tomato, and hot flavors, are Hungarian. Unfortunately, much of the paprika sold in this country seems to be tasteless, dusty, and bitter. Instead, in most cases, I would recommend a mild, sweet chile molido made from New Mexico chiles. If you do find a good paprika, use it in dishes where mild chile molido is called for.

Canned Chiles

Except for chipotles in adobo sauce or chiles canned *en escabeche*, canned chiles should be avoided. Their texture and subtlety are obscured, and canned chiles are too flimsy for stuffing. It is better to use frozen chiles if fresh chiles are unavailable.

Special Techniques, Equipment, and Terms

The following glossary includes descriptions of special equipment that is useful for Southwestern cooking and explanations of techniques and terms that may not be familiar.

Bain Marie A pan that sits in a bath of warm (not boiling) water to keep sauces and mixtures warm, and to cook creams and custards (see Ramekin, below). It differs from a double boiler in that the latter is used to cook with on top of the stove, rather than in the oven.

Blacken A technique usually applied to tomatoes that imparts a rustic taste that duplicates the flavors derived by traditional cooking methods, over outdoor fires or grills. The tomatoes, preferably Romas because of their lower liquid content, should be stemmed and placed under a broiler or on a rack over a high gas flame until the skin blisters, cracks, and blackens. A hand-held butane torch can also be used. Take care not to overblacken the tomatoes or they will become bitter.

Blender Perfect for preparing chile sauces and some salsas, among many other uses, the blender is the most common appliance used in Southwestern and Mexican cuisine. It is better than a food processor for small amounts, and emulsifies ingredients to a finer consistency. Most blenders have a glass or stainless steel bowl which is preferable to plastic. A recent innovation is the hand-held wand-type mixer which has blender blades on the end of a rod and will turn your pot into a blender. The advantage is being able to purée a hot sauce without having to ladle it back and forth from a blender, while the slightly rough texture these mixers give is sometimes more appealing than the perfect smoothness of a blender, and gives a more rustic feeling. Just how useful are blenders and food processors? I suggest making a mole sauce the old-fashioned way, with a lava mortar and pestle or metate. Then you'll swear by them!

Butane Torch A hand-held butane torch is useful for blackening tomatoes, roasting chiles, and caramelizing desserts such as crème brûlée. It is useful in a kitchen without a gas range.

Cazuelas Glazed or unglazed Mexican pots that are ideal for long, slow cooking, either in the oven or on top of the stove, *cazuelas* add subtle, earthy nuances that metal pots cannot give. They can also be used as serving dishes. Some concerns have been raised about the lead content of the glazes; it is preferable to buy glazed *cazuelas* from reputable dealers. The unglazed pots do not present this problem.

Chiffonnade See Julienne

Chinois A fine sieve for straining sauces and purées, especially those containing chiles. It is especially important to always strain mole sauces to obtain an even texture. The best types are made from stainless steel.

Comal The comal is the all-purpose Mexican cooking surface. It is traditionally large and round (between 12 and 30 inches in diameter), about 1/2 inch thick, and made of unglazed, fired clay. It is common to season it before use with salt or garlic. Its slightly porous surface absorbs moisture and gives a better crust. In more recent times, metal or cast-iron versions have replaced the clay comal. A cast-iron skillet or a flat cast-iron griddle are recommended as alternatives. The main requirement is a thick-bottomed, even-tempered, and relatively large cooking surface, so there are no uneven hot spots to scorch or burn ingredients. A comal is particularly useful for toasting spices and herbs and for making tortillas.

Confit The result of a traditional French technique for preserving food, usually fruit or meat, confit was invented before refrigeration. To make confits of meat, the fattier varieties, such as pork, duck, or goose, are cooked slowly in their own fat and seasoned with herbs and spices. When cooled, the fat solidifies and covers the cooked food, preventing oxygen from spoiling it. This method also results in a finely textured seasoned meat that is especially useful for tamale and other fillings. Fruit confits are made, using an entirely different process, with brandy or other spirits.

Deep-Fryer The best type for the home is a large stable pot with a fitted basket, which can be bought at specialty hardware, gourmet, or restaurant supply stores. In general, use high-quality peanut oil, available in Oriental markets. It has a clean, nutty flavor, and a high breakdown point, and tastes greaseless.

Never fill your fryer more than half-full, and filter the oil through cheese-cloth or a fine strainer after each use. Cleaning the oil will make it fresher and keep it longer. A deep-fryer thermometer is necessary to precisely control cooking and browning.

Dry-Roast To roast or toast dried chiles, garlic, herbs, or spices most commonly on a comal or in a heavy-bottomed skillet or frying-pan without any liquid or fat. Garlic should be dry-roasted over low or very low heat; a medium to medium-low heat is best for herbs and spices.

Escabeche Most commonly refers to vegetables, but meat, fish, eggs are also to be found *en escabeche*, which means that they have been pickled or soused, usually in a mixture of vinegar, chiles and spices.

Food Mill A stainless steel mill with varying grates is perfect for puréeing fruit or vegetables for stuffings or desserts, and especially for large amounts of garlic, bean, or tamarind purée. The French Mouli-type food mill is particularly recommended.

Food Processor The modern-day life-saver for the average cook. A food processor can do much of the necessary preparatory handwork formerly done by a metate, or mortar and pestle, as well as mixing, slicing, chopping and puréeing. Excellent for preparing pipiáns and rough-textured sauces, but as it tends to mash rather than cut, salsas are often best prepared by hand. Remember, a food processor is no substitute for a sharp knife.

Grill There are many types of grills on the market. The purpose is to reduplicate the technique of cooking over open fires, a tradition used for thousands of years in Southwestern cuisine. It is important to get a grill that is convenient to use, easy to clean and made out of as heavy a grade of metal as your budget allows. Look for heavy and carefully made cast-iron or aluminum grates, and adjustable dampers. Avoid using commercial charcoal, especially briquets (which include petroleum based products), as it can give an unpleasant tar flavor and contains a great deal of carbon monoxide. Instead, find a source for hardwood or hardwood chips, and grill over them. Make sure, if you are building a grill, that it is large enough to accomodate regular cord-size wood, and that the wood you buy is aged at least one year and is dry. Experiment with the different flavors that local woods give. At Coyote Cafe, we use pecan wood for its mild sweet flavor and hot flame.

Julienne To cut fruit or vegetables into thin, even strips, usually measuring 3 inches by ¼ inch. This can be done by hand, with a food processor, a French *mandoline,* or a Japanese variable slicer. The term, *chiffonnade is* used to describe fine, thin slices of leafy greens, such as lettuce or fresh herbs.

Metal Rack A cake-cooling rack or something similar is ideal for roasting chiles or blackening tomatoes over the gas burners of your range. This enables you to roast several at once. Buy a heavy-duty rack available from restaurant supply or gourmet supply stores; flimsier supermarket versions will bend and melt.

Mortar and Pestle The Japanese versions *(suribachi)* are ideal for grinding herbs or spices. The Mexican types *(molcajete* and *tejolote)* are usually made of unglazed terracotta and have ribs in the bottom; marble versions are also fine. The traditional, more picturesque mortar and pestle made out of lava or basalt is also highly recommended and can be used to serve salsas at buffet or party tables.

Parchment Paper Used for lining baking trays, pounding out carpaccio, and to separate layers of thinly sliced food (such as carpaccio). Use firm-textured, heavy-quality paper, which has the advantage of not burning easily. Available in baking sections of specialty gourmet stores or through mail-order companies such as Williams-Sonoma.

Rajas Long, thin, even strips. In Southwestern cuisine, the term usually applies to roasted, skinned, and sliced chiles. *Rajas* generally measure about 3 inches by ⅜ inch — thicker than julienne strips — and are used in soups or as garnish.

Ramekins Straight-sided dishes, usually with walls of 1½ inches to 2½ inches, and a diameter of 2½ to 4 inches. Used for custards, such as crème brûlée or caramel flans, and stuffings or timbales. Ramekins for custards are usually placed in a bain marie (see above) which keeps their contents moist and crust-free, and prevents curdling while cooking in the oven.

Refry A technique for providing flavor and texture for cooked foods such as beans or sauces. The ingredients are puréed or mashed and fried in fat, usually with fresh herbs to add flavor. Refrying gives beans a crustier consistency and brings the flavors of chile sauces together, while smoothing and balancing the tones of the individual ingredients.

Rehydrate Dried fruit or, more commonly in Southwestern cuisine, dried chiles are soaked so that they will more nearly resemble their fresh form. The chiles are then puréed and usually used for sauces. First, they should be stemmed and seeded and dry-roasted in a single layer on a comal or in a skillet (or in an oven at 250°) for 3 to 4 minutes. Shake once or twice and do not allow to blacken or burn, otherwise they will taste bitter. Cover the chiles with water and bring to a boil. Let them simmer at the lowest setting or turn the heat off and let the chiles sit for 15 to 20 minutes until they are soft. Taste the water and, if it is not bitter, add it with chiles to a blender and purée. If the water is bitter, purée the chiles with plain water.

Roasting In Southwestern cuisine, the ingredients most commonly roasted are chiles, garlic, and tomatoes. Fresh chiles should be roasted on a rack over an open gas flame, under a broiler, on a wood grill, or with a hand-held butane torch until they blister and blacken all over, but without burning the flesh. The chiles should then be placed in a bowl, covered with a clean kitchen towel or plastic wrap, and allowed to cool. Pull the skins off with your fingers or the edge of a knife. Do not wash the chiles under running water as you will dilute the natural oils and hence the flavor. Split the chiles open and scoop out the seeds and pith with the tip of a knife. Chiles can be roasted ahead of time and kept in the refrigerator for 2 to 3 days.

Fresh garlic should be roasted unpeeled, broken up into individual cloves, on a comal or in an iron skillet over low heat until the garlic softens, about 45 minutes. If the garlic begins to brown, lower the heat. When the garlic is done, you should be able to squeeze it out of the clove. Roasted garlic has a sweeter, more subtle flavor than does fresh garlic.

Tomatoes should be stemmed, cut in half, and placed on a wire rack, cut-side up. Roast in an oven at 300° for 1½ hours. This procedure dries out the excess moisture and concentrates the flavor of the tomatoes.

Smoking Smoking adds the traditional flavors of outdoor cooking to meat, fish, chiles, and other vegetables and ingredients. I prefer the smoke of apple or some other sweet fruit wood. Sometimes, to bring out its full flavor, seafood is marinated with spices before being smoked. Smokers are available from gourmet or specialty hardware stores. Cold smoking refers to the use of this process at a very low temperature so that delicate, drier foods, such as rabbit or seafood, do not dry out too much.

Spice Mill Small electric spice mills cost between $10 and $20, and are a great investment for the kitchen: they just happen to be better known as coffee grinders! If you're also using it to grind coffee beans, make sure you wash it out thoroughly, or better still, buy one for each purpose. Types with clear plastic tops are preferable so you can see the consistency of the grind. Spices are far fresher and more flavorful if they are ground at the last minute. A whole range of perfumes are lost only hours after grinding, as volatile oils evaporate. In addition, to bring out their sweetness, we often toast spices on a comal or in a skillet. Since some spices are very hard, make sure you buy a durable mill. Alternatively, use a sturdy hand coffee grinder, or a mortar and pestle.

Squirt Bottles At Coyote Cafe squirt bottles are indispensible for making Southwestern designs with cremas and sauces to decorate certain dishes. Buy extra tops as it's useful to cut different sized openings (thin, medium and thick) to vary the designs. Beware though: squirt bottle tops seem to be like socks — you're always mislaying them! Or maybe our dishwasher eats them; I'm not sure.

We bring out the artistic sides in our kitchen staff by letting them loose with plastic squeeze bottles filled with cremas, chile sauces, and mayonnaise sauces. These budding de Koonings and Pollocks decorate some of our dishes with festive or traditional designs and most commonly draw series of large, open Z-shapes under or over the food.

Steamers Steamers are used for cooking tamales or vegetables. Try to find the multi-layered steamers made with heavy stainless steel that are available from Oriental cooking supply stores. Bamboo or inexpensive Mexican galvanized steamers are also fine. In Mexico, especially in the border towns, you can buy special galvanized tamale steamers that resemble old-fashioned milk cans with internal baskets.

Tortilla Press Used to press out and flatten masa dough into tortillas, the tinned tortilla presses you see in Mexican markets are often porous castings that will easily break. Try to find a steel press, or one made of aluminum or wood.

Zester These little hand-held gadgets are invaluable for zesting citrus fruits. The small, round, sharpened circles remove only the colored, flavorful part of the citrus peel, and leave the white, bitter pith behind. Available in better department store gourmet sections.

Wine, Beer, and Spirits

WINE

Good wine and chiles? Definitely. Many customers at Coyote Cafe order the cold beers or margaritas that seem to be the accepted beverages for Southwestern or Mexican food, but modern Southwestern cuisine, with its more complex and fresher ingredients, is very well matched with wine. Often, when asking for advice, people express trepidation that the "hotness" of chiles will overpower a good bottle of wine. On the contrary, a fine wine is highly compatible with the taste of foods that are flavored with chiles. At Coyote Cafe, we use chiles for their flavor, rather than for their heat. The earthy flavor of a great New Mexican red chile sauce with its sweet tones and fiery ring is reason enough to seek out complex wines with character.

We carry more than 200 wines on our list at Coyote Cafe, and most of them are from California. We also keep a number of older vintages on our reserve list. Below are some suggestions of varieties that match Southwestern cuisine best and vineyards that I particularly favor and recommend for the food we serve here.

Good food has many levels of flavor tones, and wine can complement these flavors in the same palate range and on the same levels. For example, one of my favorite combinations is game accompanied by an aged full-bodied Pinot Noir with its earthy, slightly smoky, stemmy quality. Grilled venison in particular, with its smokiness and herbaceousness, perfectly matches a good Pinot Noir or burgundy. One of the rules I have discovered is never to marry a young tannic Cabernet, Merlot, or Zinfandel with foods or sauces made with red chile. The tannin in the wine will make the chile seem harsh and bitter, and vice versa.

Rosé or blanc de noir champagnes go well with seafood dishes. The rosé champagnes have a little more forward fruit that goes well with salsas. The hint of Pinot Noir in blanc de noir gives the champagne a little more flavor so that it stands up well to more intense flavors. In general, younger champagnes, especially those showing spriteliness and vitality, match Southwestern food best. At my fortieth birthday party this year, we imbibed my favorite domestic rosé champagne, Iron Horse Rosé, which comes from Barry and Audrey Sterling's winery and is made by my good friend Forrest Tancer who is responsible for some of the best sparkling wines anywhere. Some of my other favorite sparkling wines from California are the Schramsberg blanc de noirs and Maison Deutz. Among French champagnes, those of the house of Veuve Clicquot Ponsardin have a full-bodied elegance and a yeastiness that marry well with the intense flavors of Southwestern cuisine, and especially seafood. Thanks to our friend Madeleine Dickinson, we have had a number of festive food and wine pairings with Veuve Clicquot at Coyote Cafe.

Chenin Blancs and Northern Italian country white wines such as Pinot Grigio have natural floral and fruity qualities and a light flavor that is well suited to the garden herbs and fresh spices used in Southwestern food. Good Californian Chenin Blancs such as that made by Chappellet are dry, with some oak, and have a wonderful simplicity that matches the philosophy of Southwestern food and shares a similar depth of flavor.

Sauvignon Blanc is another particularly good variety for Southwestern food. In fact, this is probably one of the most natural pairings of food and wine in any cuisine, as they are parallel in complexity and depth. The fresh grassy green tones of Sauvignon Blancs have a natural affinity for green salads, squash salsas, and dishes with cilantro (which means most of the recipes in this book). The best are from Napa, Sonoma, and the Central Coast region of California, and include Vichon's Chevrignon (which also contains some Semillon), Quivera, and Sanford. I prefer Californian Sauvignon Blancs to Loire wines as they taste fresher and have less sulphur.

Vin Gris is rosé wine made in the Burgundy style from Pinot Noir grapes. A high-quality Vin Gris or blush wine is fermented dry and has a fruity flavor with no residual sugar. Rosé wines are often snubbed as simple or unsuitable; however, they can be complex and are highly appropriate with Southwestern food. They are very attractive and festive in color and have a frivolous nature: they should be taken neither too lightly nor too seriously, but enjoyed. Vin Gris goes particularly well with grilled salmon and tuna, pan-roasted chicken or quail, and grilled stuffed pork. Served chilled on a hot day, Vin Gris and blush wines will stand up to Southwestern food refreshingly. I recommend the vin gris wines made by Bonny Doon, Sanford, and Domaine Laurier, and the white Zinfandel made by Green and Red.

The spicy flavors and full fruitiness of Gewürztraminers and Reislings make these the perfect wines to accompany spicy dishes such as chorizo quesadillas with anise, or steamed clams with chipotle and orange. They have little residual sugar, so their slightly sweet taste makes hot food seem less fiery. Their spicy varietal character complements the zestiness of the seasonings in salsas and most Southwestern dishes. Some of my favorite Gewürztraminers and Reislings come from the vineyards of Navarro, Fetzer, and Joseph Phelps.

Chardonnay wines are probably the most popular varietal wines today. They have undergone a change in style, so that now it is their fruit character rather than a heavy oakiness that predominates. Chardonnays are grown in cooler regions and contain hints of citrus and tropical fruit flavors. Better Chardonnays usually have a mixture of undertones, including those of new and used Limousin oak (from barrel fermentation and barrel aging), and a flavor of vanilla in the finish. The new style of Chardonnay makes a much better match for salsas, especially those with tropical ingredients such as mango and banana or pineapple. Californian Chardonnays are consistent in style and, in my opinion, are underestimated in terms of aging potential; many are as good and as complex as fine white burgundies. The better, richer Chardonnays go well with richer and naturally sweet dishes such as lobster, scallops, shrimp, and soft-shell crab. Older Chardonnays take on a corn-like quality that can be a good match with intense first courses that contain corn. Among my favorite Chardonnays are those made by Burgess, Mondavi, Sonoma-Cutrer, Neyers, Perret, Chappellet, Morgan, Flora Springs, Hanzell, Kistler, and La Crema. Australian Chardonnays have a distinctly more intense bouquet of banana and pineapple and are well worth investigating for their fruity and fresh quality. They also tend to be less expensive and of good value.

Pinot Noir is definitely my favorite wine for matching with Southwestern food. The subtle, light, smoky, and earthy herbaceousness of Pinot Noir mirrors the wild, outdoors flavors of game and especially venison. Older Pinot Noir, with its velvety texture and subtle yet complex flavors, goes perfectly with roasted quail and pheasant. The light tannic quality of Pinot Noir means that it will not interfere with the flavors of food or sauces containing red chile. It is important not to serve the wine too warm as the delicate perfumes will evaporate; it should be drunk cool, but not cold. If necessary, ask for an ice bucket for a few minutes to cool the wine down. Among my favorite Pinot Noirs are those from Carneros Creek, Stemmler, Mondavi (the older reserves), Saintsbury, Hanzell, Calera, Chalone, and Acacia.

Cabernet Sauvignon has some of the most complex flavors of any wine. Robert Mondavi has commented that it shares a lot in common with chiles. The anise, tobacco, smoky dried plum, and cassis tones of Cabernet are also present in ancho and mulato chiles in particular. Because young Cabernets are usually tannic, they do not taste good with red chile; they are much better with simply grilled or roasted beef or game. Older Cabernets, with their range of flavors and toned-down tannins are especially suited to game with more complex flavors and subtle richness, such as sika venison, buffalo, and wild duck. My favorite Cabernets are made by Mondavi (including Opus One), Duckhorn, Rutherford Hill, Sequoia Grove, Chappellet, Iron Horse, Joseph Phelps, Flora Springs, Niebaum-Coppola (Rubicon), Caymus, and Heitz.

Merlot is a softer cousin of Cabernet that has many of the same qualities but is not as intense in tannins or as structured. Merlots can be drunk younger and have a softer, fruitier quality than do Cabernets. In fact, Merlot is often blended with Cabernets to soften them and allow them to be drunk earlier. I recommend Merlot for accompanying Churro lamb and venison. I am particularly partial to Duckhorn and Rutherford Hill Merlots.

Syrah or wines labeled Petite Syrah are made from a variety of grape that originates in the warm Rhone valley. Syrah has an intensity of character, with cherry, blackberry, and black currant flavors and a pleasing spiciness. It is often overlooked, but is a very good match with Southwestern foods. Until recently, Syrahs tended to be too tannic to drink until they were at least five years old; now they are softer and more well balanced. I would recommend those from Qupé, Guenoc, Foppiano, and Stag's Leap.

Zinfandel, with its accentuated berry and spicy flavors and "black pepperiness" goes very well with meat or poultry that is marinated, or with sauces containing fruit. Young, tannic Zinfandels do not combine well with red chiles, and older vintages with their overripe fruitiness or "portiness" can take away from the freshness of Southwestern food. My particular favorites are the well-balanced, well-made Zinfandels from Green and Red and Storybook Mountain.

A number of Southwestern wines are excellent. The flavors of sagebrush, piñon, and juniper seem to perfume the wines delicately. They are wonderful when paired with food marinated with wild herbs and grilled over pecan wood. Some of the varieties to look for are a wonderful sparkling wine from Domaine Cheurlain in New Mexico, a very good Sauvignon Blanc from Fall Creek in Texas, and an excellent Cabernet Sauvignon from Pheasant Ridge, also in Texas.

BEER

Most of the Mexican beers popular today were first produced in the 1920s by German immigrants to Mexico, hence the predominance of the lighter, pilsner styles. The commonly available brands I prefer are Dos Equis, Pacifico, Superior, Bohemia, and Corona. Tecate, which, unlike the others, usually comes in cans, is traditionally served with a slice of lime and salt. These beers vary in hoppiness and dryness, but all are pilsners.

Two of my other favorites are dark beers, Negra Modelo and Negra Leon, that are specialties of the Yucatán. Both are creamy with a hint of chocolate, which makes them a perfect match for mole sauces. When traveling in other parts of Mexico, you might look for some of the interesting regional beers. One that is well worth trying is Indio Oscura, from southern Mexico. All the beers mentioned above, both pilsner-types and dark beers, are produced by the three main breweries in the country.

A new local micro-brewery has just opened up in Galisteo, a few miles outside Santa Fe. The inaugural product, Santa Fe Pale Ale, is a high-quality ale that we stock at Coyote Cafe and that has proved very popular in the area. They tell me they are even exporting it; one destination is Great Britain — now that really is sending coals to Newcastle!

TEQUILA AND MEZCAL

Tequila, which is named after the village in the state of Jalisco where it originated, is a liquor made only from the blue agave plant, also known as the maguey. Mezcal can be made from the same plant, as well as from other types of agave, of which there are over 400. Mezcal is less refined and lacks the distinctive subtle flavor of tequila. To make tequila, the blue agave plants are harvested between 8 and 12 years of age. The hearts *(piñas)* of the plant, which can weigh up to 200 pounds, are chopped and then roasted or steamed. The juice is pressed out, mixed with cane sugar, fermented, and double-distilled.

Tequila is produced in only three states: Jalisco, Nayarit, and Michoacán, all to the northwest of Mexico City. Mezcal is produced over a far wider area. As one writer summarized it, all tequila is mezcal, but not all mezcal is tequila. The distinction is similar to that between cognac and brandy. Tequila that has been aged in wood casks for at least one year and up to seven years is called *añejo*. Among the premium brands of tequila are Tres Commemorativo, Herradura Añejo, Herradura Gold, and Chinaco. If you are drinking just one shot, choose an *añejo*. If you are planning on more and, like Coyote, howling at the moon all night, try Hornitos tequila, made by Sauza, which is smooth and flavorful.

Mezcal has a strong country flavor that is more rustic and rough edged and less distilled. One of my favorite brands is Gusano Rojo, from Oaxaca. Mezcal is probably best known for the worm at the bottom of the bottle. Traditionally, this denotes the ripeness of the agave from which it is made. When in Mexico, look for the different varieties of tequila and mezcal, such as the orange mezcal that is a specialty of Oaxaca, and other premium aged tequilas not commonly available in the United States. Some of these tequilas are sold in beautiful hand-blown glass bottles.

Finally, a note on the correct etiquette for taking lime and salt with a shot of tequila. First, lick the area between the thumb and forefinger, and sprinkle a little salt there. Grasp a lime wedge between the thumb and forefinger. Lick the salt, knock back the tequila, and bite (do not squeeze) the lime. The salt opens up the taste buds, and the lime smooths out the alcoholic edge of the tequila.

Sources

Chiles

Los Chileros, PO Box 6215, Santa Fe, NM 87501, (505) 471-6967

Josie's, 1130 Agua Fria, Santa Fe, NM 87501, (505) 983-6520

The Chile Shop, 109 East Water Street, Santa Fe, NM 87501, (505) 983-6080

Bueno Foods, 2001 Fourth Street, S.W., Albuquerque, NM 87102, (505) 243-2722

Casados Farms, PO Box 1269, San Juan Pueblo, NM 87566, (505) 852-2433

Mi Rancho, 464 Seventh Street, Oakland, CA 94607, (415) 451-2393

Casa Lucas Market, 2934 Twenty-fourth Street, San Francisco, CA 94110, (415) 826-4334

La Palma, 2884 Twenty-fourth Street, San Francisco, CA 94110, (415) 647-1500

Dean and Deluca, 560 Broadway, New York, NY 10012, (212) 431-1691

Mercado Latino, 148-C Common Drive, El Paso, TX 79901, (915) 595-3195

Midwest Imports, 1121 South Clinton, Chicago, IL 60607, (312) 939-8400

Vegetables, Herbs, and Spices

A-One Produce, PO Box 5062, Santa Fe, NM 87504, (505) 471-5400

Elizabeth Berry, 144 Camino Escondido, Santa Fe, NM 87501, (505) 982-4149

San Francisco Herb Co., 250 Fourteenth Street, San Francisco, CA 94103, (800) 227-4530

Lucinda Hutson, 4612 Rosedale, Austin, TX 78756, (Consulting expert on herbs of the Southwest)

The Fruit Basket, PO Box 4, Velarde, NM 87582

Pacific Spice Co., 722 Stanford Ave., Los Angeles, CA 90021, (213) 626-2302

Game, Meat, and Fowl

Texas Wild Game Co-operative, PO Box 530, Ingram, TX 78025, (512) 367-5875

Preferred Meats, 2050 Galvez Street, San Francisco, CA 94124, (415) 285-9299

Night Bird Game and Poultry, 650 San Mateo Avenue, San Bruno, CA 94066, (415) 543-6508

Native Game, 1105 West Oliver Street, Spearfish, SD 57783, (605) 642-2601

Cheese

Bountiful Cow, 1521 Center Drive, Box B, Santa Fe, NM 87501, (505) 473-7911

The Mozzarella Co., 2944 Elm Street, Dallas, TX 75226, (214) 741-4072, (Southwestern-style cheeses)

Laura Chenel's California Chèvre, 1550 Ridley Avenue, Santa Rosa, CA 95401, (707) 575-8888

Supremo, V & V Food Products, 1234 West Cermak Road, Chicago, IL 60608, (312) 421-1020

Pecans, Cherries, and Preserves

Midwestern Pecan Co., Business Highway 71 North, Nevada, MO 64772 (417) 667-6333

American Spoon Foods, 411 East Lake Street, Petoskey, MI 49770, (800) 327-7984

Country Ovens, 123 Main Street, PO Box 195, Forestville, WI 54213, (414) 856-6767

Miscellaneous

Taos Honey Berry Farm, PO Box 2255, Taos, NM 87571, (505) 758-4350, (Red chile honey)

Mercado Latino, 148-C Common Drive, El Paso, TX 79901, (915) 595-3195, (Ibarra chocolate and piloncillo sugar)

Madame Chocolate, 1940-C Lehigh Avenue, Glenview, IL 60025, (312) 729-3330, (Ibarra chocolate)

Josie's, 1130 Agua Fria, Santa Fe, NM 87501, (505) 983-6520, (Blue cornmeal)

Blue Corn Connection, 3825 Academy Parkway S. N.W., Albuquerque, NM 87109, (505) 344-9768, (Blue cornmeal)

Madame Mushroom, 3420 West Malaga Road, Malaga, WA 98828, (Dried wild mushrooms)

Pacific Gourmet, PO Box 2071, San Raphael, CA 94912, (415) 641-8400, (Dried wild mushrooms, vinegar, and other products)

Talavaya Seeds, PO Box 707, Santa Cruz Station, Santa Cruz, NM 87567, (Seeds)

Santa Fe Bite-Size Bakery, 1364 Rufina Street, Suite 6, Santa Fe, NM 87501, (505) 473-3580, (Southwestern cookies, etc.)

Williams-Sonoma, PO Box 7456, San Francisco, CA 94120, (415) 421-4555, (Cooking equiment and seasonings)

Kitchen Bazaar, 4455 Connecticut Avenue, N.W., Washington, D.C. 20008, (202) 363-4600, (Cooking equipment)

Other Sources

Whole Chile Pepper Magazine, Outwest Publishing, PO Box 4278, Albuquerque, NM 87196, (505) 268-0288, (For information and further sources)

After June 1990, everything you will ever need to cook Southwestern food, including items from all of the categories listed above, will be available at our new store. Contact through our office address:

Coyote Kitchens
102 West San Francisco Street, Suite 1
Santa Fe, NM 87501
(505) 988-7124

Index

A

Achiote
  discussed, 62
  paste, 43
  seeds, 105
  in tamales, 62
Aïoli, Rosemary-Serrano, **116**
Albóndigas de Camarónes
  (shrimp dumplings), **38**
Almond(s)
  in cake, 130
  paste, in pound cake, 131
  Pastry Cream, **134**
Anise, in rhubarb crisp, 133
Apple cider
  Chimayo, discussed, 4
  in chutney, 120
Apples
  in chutney, 120
  for mincemeat, 132
Artichokes, timbales of, 99
Avocado, crema of, 86

B

Bacon, wild boar, 83, 85, 96,
    104, 112, 154
  discussed, 96
  with quail, 96
  substituting for, 96
  with venison, 96
  in waffles, 147
Baguettes, for po'boys, 151
Banana, salsa of, 77
Banana leaf, 61
  for tamales, 62
  to prepare, 62
Beans, black. *See* Black beans
Beef
  brisket, for rellenos, 114
  fillet of
    with Smoked Oysters, **112**
    with Tomato-Chipotle Sauce,
      113
  lean, for chorizo, 152
  steak, 112
  tenderloin of, seared, with Green
    Chile Jerky, **113**
  top round, for jerky, 113
  top sirloin, for steak tartare, 47

Beer, Mexican, 13, 79, 94, 114,
    153
Berry, Elizabeth, 52, 107
Black beans
  in chiles rellenos, 154
  discussed, 94
  in enchiladas, 79
  with fish, 86, 87
  in Huevos Rancheros, 148
  Refried, **155**
  in salsa, 16
  soup of, 32
  tamales of, 62
  with turkey, 105
  with venison, 94
Blackberries
  in shortcakes, 139
  tamales of, 71
Bloody Maria, **3**
Blue corn. *See* Corn, blue
Bourbon
  in mincemeat, 132
  syrup of, 147
Brandy, blackberry, 139
Bread
  Cinnamon Buckwheat, **128**
  Orange Cumin, **129**, 151
Brochette, Shrimp, **83**
Brûlée, Mango Raspberry, **140**
Buckwheat
  bread of, 128
  discussed, 128
Buttermilk, in chocolate tart, 133

C

Cactus. *See* Nopales
Cajeta. *See* Caramel, Cajeta
Cajeta Whipped Cream, **138**
Cake
  Almond Polenta Pound, **131**
  Anise Pound, **130**
  Ibarra Chocolate, with Chocolate
    Glaze, **130**
Canela
  discussed, 139
  substituting for, 28
  in tamales, 70
Caramel
  Cajeta, **136**
    in shortcakes, 139

Cardini, Alex-Caesar, 55
Carnitas, **51**
  discussed, 51
  Duck, **102**
  Raviolis, **51**
  in tamales, 63
Carpaccio, beef for, 113
Cassis, 4, 139
Cèpes
  with duck, 102
  with quail, 97
  in sopes, 49
Ceviche, discussed, 46
Champagne Padre, **8**
Chanterelles
  with duck, 102
  in sopes, 49
Chard, soup of, 34
Chayote, with duck, 101
Cheese
  Cheddar, 127, 153
  discussed, 52
  farmer's, 52
  feta, in soup, 36
  Fontina, 52, 113, 153
  goat, 52, 155
    with chicken, 104
    dry, with fish, 86
    in salad, 54
    tamales of, 70
  Grilled Sandwich, **151**
  grilling, 151
  Monterey Jack, 62, 151, 153
    dry, 68
  substituting, 104, 113
  see also Queso fresco
Chicken
  breast, 104
    Grilled, **104**
    for sausage, 152
    in soup, 36
    tamales of, 62
  free-range, discussed, 104
  legs, 104
  Roulade, **104**
  tamales of, 61
Chile
  Anaheim
    in green chile stew, 149
    in muffins, 148
    in salad, 54
    in sauce, 26
    in soup, 34

stuffed, 154
with venison, 96
ancho
    in carpaccio, 47
    with seafood, 75
    dried
        with beef, 114
        with duck, 101
        in dumplings, 38
        in sauce, 25, 28, 29, 30, 95
cascabel, 105
    with beef, 114
    discussed, 121
    with pork, 121
    in sauce, 25
Chimayo, in salsa, 17. *See also*
    Chile powder, Chimayo
Chinese red, 105
chipotle
    canned, 36, 78, 114, 115,
        149, 155
    in adobo sauce, 14, 18,
        25, 26, 27, 30, 31, 38,
        69, 83, 94, 105, 148
    dried, 25, 36, 148
    with lamb, 115
coloradito, 114
dried red, in crema, 34
fresno, in salsa, 16
green
    with fish, 85
    for mayonnaise, 151
    in soup, 34, 37
guajillo
    with beef, 114
    crêpes of, 79
    dried, in sauce, 30
    sauce of, 49
    in sopes, 49
güeros, canned *en escabeche*, 53
Habanero, 152
jalapeño
    canned *en escabeche*, 46, 53
    in chutney, 20
    in corn bread, 127
    dried, 82
    en escabeche, 17
    with quail, 100
    in salad, 54
    in salsa, 16
    in sauce, 26, 27
    in soup, 32, 34
    to smoke, 27
    with venison, 94
mulato, dried
    with duck, 101
    in sauce, 29
negros, dried, in sauce, 29. *See
    also* Chiles pasilla
New Mexico
    green
        in chutney, 20
        discussed, 153
        in muffins, 148
        in sauce, 26

with seafood, 75
stuffed, 153
substitution for, 75
in tamales, 61
red
    dried, broth of, 46
    in mayonnaise, 79
    in salsa, 17
    in sauce, 25
    roasting en masse, 26
pasilla, dried, with duck, 101.
    See also Chile negro
pequin red, with fish, 87
poblano
    with chicken, 104
    discussed, 15, 153
    with duck, 102
    in enchiladas, 79
    with fish, 45, 86, 88
    for grilled cheese sandwich,
        151
    in muffins, 148
    in Queso Fundido, 52
    in rice, 146
    in salad, 54, 55
    in salsa, 14, 15, 16, 19
    in sauce, 28, 30, 51
    in soup, 35, 36
    stuffed, 153
        in tamales, 61
    in tacos, 120
    with venison, 96
red
    in chutney, 120
    in posole, 39
serrano
    in aïoli, 116
    in cocktails, 3, 4
    in corn bread, 127
    in empanadas, 43
    with fish, 86, 88, 89
    in green chile stew, 149
    in mayonnaise, 86
    with pheasant, 103
    in pickling liquid, 54
    in relish, 20
    in rice, 146
    in salad, 54
    in salpicon, 44
    in salsa, 13, 14, 16, 17, 18,
        19, 20, 77
    in sauce, 26, 28
    for sausage, 152
    with seafood, 82
    in soup, 35, 36
    in steak tartare, 47
smoked, discussed, 83
substituting, 26, 120, 151
venison, **94**
Chile caribe, 20, 49, 51, 97, 106,
    117, 122
Chile Mignonette, **16**
Chile powder
    discussed, 76

ancho, 127, 152
Chimayo, 85, 113
    in carpaccio, 47
    with duck, 102
    in duck confit, 64
    in muffins, 148
    with quail, 97
    in squash blossoms, 52
dried red New Mexico, in sauce,
    25
green, 113
medium, for tamales, 65
molido, 100, 120, 146
    with beef, 112
    in confit, 49
    with seafood, 76
New Mexico, 101, 152
New Mexico hot, 76, 94
red, in tamales, 62
Chile Rellenos, **153**
Chocolate
    bittersweet
        in cake, 130
        in glaze, 130
        in ice cream, 135
    cake, Ibarra, **130**
    Ibarra
        in Cajeta Tart, 138
        discussed, 130, 138
        in sauce, 29
    and kumquat helado, **135**
    in sauce, discussed, 29
    unsweetened
        in glaze, 130
        in sauce, 29
    white
        discussed, 133
        tart of, with buttermilk, **133**
Chocolate Glaze, **130**
Chocolate Pastry Cream, **134**
Chorizo, **152**
Chowder, Green Chile and
    Oyster, **37**
Chung, Chris, 97
Churros
    Coyote, **134**
    described, 134
Chutney
    Apple and Red Chile, **120**
    Green Chile, **20**, 80
Cider, unfiltered, sauce of, 97
Cilantro, in mayonnaise, 86
Cinnamon, in buckwheat bread,
    128
Citron, candied, 132
Clams
    discussed, 39, 76
    Manila, in Red Chile Broth, **46**
    Red Chile Pesto, **75**
    Red Chile Risotto, **76**

in seafood stew, 89
soup of, 29
Clay, potter's, for cooking, 107
Cocktail
 Chimayo, **4**
 Coyote, **4**
Cocktails, making, 2
Coconut cream, 53
Coconut milk
 discussed, 53
 in salad, 53
 in seafood stew, 89
Confit, discussed, 64
Corn
 baby
  discussed, 54
  salad of, 54, 55
 blue, for tamales, 65, 71
 in corn cakes, 149
 discussed, 36
 in dumplings, 38
 in enchiladas, 79
 in relish, 20
 in salsa, 14, 16, 17
 in soup, 36, 37
 tamale of, 61, 65, 68
Corn Bread, **99**
 Blue, **103**
 Chile, **127**, 151
  with soup, 38
Corn Cakes, 102, **149**
Corn flour, in crêpes, 48
Corn husks, seafood cooked in,
 80. *See also* Tamale
Cornmeal
 blue, 103
  in chile rellenos, 154
  with trout, 85
 in corn bread, 127
 in corn cakes, 149
 in muffins, 148
 white, in tamales, 68
 yellow, 99
Crab
 fresh, 44
  with trout, 85
 Salpicón of Texas Blue, **44**
 soft-shell, 82
  discussed, 82
 Spicy Soft-Shell, **82**
 Texas Blue, 44, 80
 to clean, 82
Crab Cakes, Texas Blue, **80**
Crab Cushions, **44**
Crema
 Avocado, **86**
 Chipotle, 62, **83**
 discussed, 35
 Mexican, **35**, 83, 86, 94, 149, 153
  in crab cushions, 44

Red Chile, **34**, 62
Crêpes
 Guajillo, **79**, 106
  with roast duck, 48
Crisp, Rhubarb Anise, **133**
Croutons, **55**
Cucumber, in soup, 35
Cuisines of Mexico, The
 (Kennedy), 36
Currants
 in rice, 147
 in tamales, 70
Curry powder, for oysters, 77
Custard, for Cajeta Tart, **138**

D
Daiquiri, Brazilian, **3**
del Grande, Robert, 97
Dressing, Caesar, **55**
Drinks, measurements for, 22.
 See also Cocktails
Duck
 Barbecued Cakes, **48**
 Braised, **101**
 confit of, **64**
 Sautéed, with Wild Mushrooms
  and Corn Cakes, **102**
Duck Carnitas Rellenos, **102**
Dumplings, shrimp. *See*
 Albóndigas de Camarónes

E
Eggs, in Huevos Rancheros, 148
Empanadas, Oyster, **43**
Enchiladas
 Lobster, **79**
 Smoked Rabbit, **106**, 147
Epazote, 30, 31, 44
Escabeche, discussed, 45
Espresso Pastry Cream, **134**

F
Fearing, Dean, 78
Filling, Chanterelle, **49**
Fish, for ceviche, discussed, 46
Fish Fumet, **77**
Flour, high-gluten, 51
Forgione, Larry, 48, 82
Fowl, to cook, 93

G
Game, to cook, 93
Garlic, Confit of, **49**
Gathering the Desert (Nabhan),
 70
Goat, Horno-Style Leg, **107**
Goat's milk, caramel of, 136
Grapefruit juice, sauce of, 121
"Great Chefs of San Francisco"
 (PBS), 43
Green onion, mayonnaise of, 151
Green Pipián. *See* Pipián Verde

H
Ham, wild boar, 104
Harissa, 100
Hash, Scallop, **82**
Hearon, Reed, 147
Helado (ice cream)
 Kathy Wolf's Chocolate
  Kumquat, **135**
 Vanilla, **135**, 136
Hibiscus (jamaica) blossoms,
 with quail, 100
Honey, red chile, 70, 84, 96, 101
 discussed, 84
Horno oven, 107
Huachinango (red snapper), **88**
Huevos Rancheros, **148**
Huitlacoche, 14

I
Ice cream. *See* Helado

J
Jamaica blossoms. *See* Hibiscus
Jerky
 discussed, 113
 Green Chile, **113**

K
Kennedy, Diana, 36
Koscomb, Jeff, 116
Kumquat
 and chocolate helado, **135**
 liquado, 9

L
Lamb
 baked in clay, 107

Churro, 13
Rack of
    with Pecan Crust, **116**
    with Rosemary-Serrano Aïoli,
        116
    Yucatán, **115**, 147
Lime, liquado, **9**
Liquado
    discussed, 9, 100
    kumquat, **9**
    lime, **9**
    mango, **9**
    orange, **9**
    strawberry, **9**
    tamarind, **9**
Lobster
    in cushions, 44
    enchiladas of, 79
    salad of, 55
    sauce of, 79
    and Scallops in Corn Husks, **80**
    in seafood stew, 88, 89
    tamale of, 68
Louisiana hot sauce, 79

M

Mango
    in brûlée, 140
    in cocktails, 5, 9
    in salsa, 20
Margarita
    Coyote, **4**
    Watermelon. *See* Sunburnt
        Senorita
Marinade
    dry rubbed, **113**
    for lamb, **115**
    for pork, **117**, 120
    for quail, **100**
    for squab, **100**
    for venison, **95**
Martinez, Zarela, 19
Martini, Coyote, **4**
Masa
    discussed, 49
    dough, for tamales, **61**, 62, 63
    fresh
        described, 59
        in empanadas, 43
        in sopes, 49
        for tamales, 69
    harina
        blue corn, 71
            for tamales, 65
        described, 59
        in empanadas, 43
        in ravioli, 51
        in tamales, 61, 63, 64
        for tamales, 69, 70
    preparing, 59

Mayonnaise
    Cilantro, **86**
    Green Onion, **151**
    Orange, **78**
    Red Chile, **79**, 113
Measurements, for drinks, 2
Meat, temperature of cooked,
    110
Melon, cantaloupe, in salsa, 18
Mincemeat
    Christine's Venison, **132**
        in tamales, 63
Mint, 155
    discussed, 70
    in tamales, 70
Mole Rojo (Red Mole Sauce), **29**
    in tamales, 64
Mole Verde (Green Mole
    Sauce), **30**
    in tamales, 65
Monkfish, in seafood stew, 88
Morels
    dried, tamales of, 69
    with duck, 102
    in salsa, 14
Muffins, Green Chile Corn, **148**,
    149
Mushroom, powder
    discussed, 69
    to make, 69
Mushrooms
    dried, with duck, 102
    tamales of, 69
    wild
        discussed, 102
        with duck, 102
        with quail, 99
        for tacos, 120
Mussels
    Chipotle, **78**
    preparing, 78
Mustard greens
    with fish, 87
    in tamales, 64

N

Nabhan, Gary Paul, 70
Nopales
    discussed, 17
    with lamb, 115
    in salsa, 17

O

Octopus
    discussed, 53
    salad of, 53
Onion Rings, Red Chile, **112**

Orange
    blood, in salad, 54
    bread, **129**
    liquado, **9**
    in mayonnaise, 78
Oysters
    appetizer of, 43
    Black Pepper Yucatán, **43**, 112
    chowder of, 37
    Curried, **77**
    discussed, 37
    empanadas of, 43
    fresh, to smoke, 112
    po'boy of, 151
    smoked, with beef fillet, 112
    timbales of, 99
    in turkey stuffing, 105

P

Palm oil, 77
Pastry
    for pies, **141**
    for tarts, **141**
Pastry Cream, **134**
    almond, **134**
    chocolate, **134**
    espresso, **134**
Peanut butter
    discussed, 31
    in sauce, 31
Pecan(s)
    discussed, 116
    praline, **138**
    with roast lamb, 116
    in syrup, 147
    in tamales, 71
    in waffles, 147
Pepper, sweet red, sauce of, 87
Pesto, Poblano, **15**, 46, 51
Pheasant, with Chorizo and Blue
    Corn Bread Stuffing, **103**
Pickling, liquid for, **54**
Pie, pastry for, **141**
Pig's feet, in posole, 39
Piloncillo, 27
    discussed, 3
    in salsa, 18
    substitute for, 18
Pine nuts, in salsa, 15
Pineapple
    in cocktails, 3
    with quail, 100
    in salsa, 18
    in sauce, 28
    in seafood stew, 89
Pipián
    discussed, 30
    Rojo, **30**, 61, 100

Verde, **31**, 51

Pisco Sour, **5**

Planter's Punch, **5**

Po'Boy, Oyster, with Green
   Onion Mayonnaise, **151**

Polenta, pound cake of, 131

Pomegranate juice, 17, 95

Porcini mushrooms, 94
   with duck, 102

Pork
   Brazilian, **117**
   butt
      for carnitas, 51
      for Chorizo, 152
      in green chile stew, 149
      for sausage, 152
   fat back, for sausage, 152
   loin, 117
      for tacos, 120
   loin chops, 117
      with Cascabel and Grapefruit
         Sauce, **121**
   Papantla, with Manchamantel
      Sauce, **117**
   in posole, 39
   Tacos, with Wild Mushrooms
      and Tamarind Chipotle
      Sauce, **120-121**
   for tamales, discussed, 63
   tenderloin
      with Apple and Red Chile
         Chutney, **120**
      for tacos, 120

Posole, **38-39**
   discussed, 38
   with duck, 101

Potatoes, in soup, 37

Praline
   paste, 71
   pecan, **138**

Prickly pear
   juice, to make, 95
   sauce of, 94
   syrup, 17

Puck, Wolfgang, 88, 105

Pumpkin seeds, 52
   in sauce, 30, 31
   in turkey stuffing, 105

Pyles, Stephen, 103

Q

Quail
   discussed, 96
   Hibiscus, **100**
   Pan-Fried, **96-97**
   Pan-Roasted, with
      Artichoke/Oyster Timbales,
      99
   Red Chile, 70, **97**

Queso fresco, 52
   in soup, 36

Queso Fundido, **52**

R

Rabbit
   enchiladas of smoked, 106
   smoking, discussed, 106

Raspberries, in brûlée, 140

Ravioli Dough, **51**

Red Pipián. *See* Pipián Rojo

Refried Beans, **155**

Relish, Hot Corn, **20**, 48

Rellenos
   Blue Corn Black Bean, 83, **154**
   Chile. *See* Chiles Rellenos
   discussed, 102
   Duck Carnitas, **102**
   Oaxacan, **114**
   Tuna Tartare, with Cilantro
      Mayonnaise and Avocado
      Crema, **86**

Rhubarb, crisp of, 133

Rice, 105
   arborio, with clams, 76
   discussed, 76
   Red Chile, **146**
   Spicy Green, 89, **146**
   Sweet Cinnamon, 115, **147**

Risotto, Red Chile Clam, **76**

Rum
   in cocktails, 3, 5
   in mincemeat, 132

S

Salad
   Lobster and Corn, **55**
   Mark's Caesar, **55**
   Merida-Style Octopus, **53**
   Pickled Shrimp and Corn, **54**
   for quail, **100**
   Sonora, **54**

Salmon
   discussed, 84
   Fillet, with Black Bean Corn
      Salsa, **84**
   Paillard of, with Squash Salsa
      and Chipotle Crema, **83**
   pan-roasted, 154
   tamale of, 68

Salpicón, discussed, 44

Salsa
   Banana, **77**
   Black Bean, **16**
   Black Bean Corn, **16**, 84
   Chimayo Chile, **17**
   Fresca. *See* Salsa, Pico de Gallo
   Gazpacho, **19**, 154

Mango, **20**
Melon, **18**
Nopales, **17**
Pico de Gallo, **13**, 52, 61, 82, 86,
   112, 151
Pineapple, **18**
Roasted Corn, **14**
Roasted Serrano, **14**
Roasted Tomato and Mint, **13**, 52
Squash, **19**, 83, 154
Tomatillo, **13**, 44, 61

Sandwich, Grilled Cheese, **151**

Sassafras, 97

Sauce
   Ancho and Prickly Pear, **95**
   Desert Prickly Pear, **95**
   Green Chile, **26**, 68, 104, 120
   Guajillo, **49**
   habanero, 79
   Lobster, **79**
   Manchamantel, **28**, 117
      with tamales, 63
   Mark's Red Chile, **25**, 31, 88,
      102, 106, 114, 153
   Mole Verde. *See* Mole Verde
   Peanut Chipotle, **31**
   Ranchero, **28**, 148, 149
      in posole, 39
   Ravioli, **51**
   Red Chile, **25**, 85
      in posole, 39
   Red Chile Cider, **97**
   Red Mole. *See* Mole Rojo
   Smoked Tomato and Jalapeño,
      27, 68, 80, 82
   Sweet Red Pepper, **87**
   Tamarind Chipotle, **27**, 82, 83,
      120, 122
   Tomatillo Chipotle, **26**, 102, 113
   see also Pipián

Sausage
   andouille, in soup, 29
   cabrito and goat cheese, 155
   Chorizo, **152**
      with pheasant, 103
   Italian
      with pheasant, 103
      in soup, 29, 103
   Yucatán White, **152-153**

Scallop(s)
   Ceviche, **46**
   hash of, 82
   with lobster, in corn husks, 80
   in seafood stew, 88
   in soup, 37

Sea bass, 88
   in seafood stew, 88

Seafood Stew
   Caribbean, **89**
   Santa Fe, **88-89**

Señor Playboy, **8**

Shortcake(s)

Blackberry Cinnamon, **139**
Cinnamon, **139**
Shrimp
  brochettes of, 83
  Butter, **65**
  Chipotle, with Corn Cakes, **149**
  in cushions, 44
  dried
    butter of, 65
    discussed, 65
  in dumplings, 38
  salad of, 54
  in seafood stew, 89
  Stock, **65**
  in turkey stuffing, 105
Smoke, liquid, 27
Smoking, of foods, discussed, 27
Snapper, red
  in seafood stew, 89
  see also Huachinango
Sopes, **49**
  discussed, 49
  Wild Chanterelle, **49**
Sorbet, Gazpacho Salsa as, 19
Soup
  Black Bean, **32**, 96, 117
  Clam, with Sausage, **39**
  Green Gazpacho, **35**
  Roasted Corn, **36**
  Southwest Painted, **34**
  Yellow Squash, **34**
  Yucatán Lime, **36**
  see also Chowder
Spareribs, barbecued, 122
Squab
  Cumin, **100**
  discussed, 100
Squash
  summer
    in salsa, 19
    soup of, 34
  yellow, soup of, 34
Squash Blossoms, **52**
Squid, in seafood stew, 89
Steak
  Cowboy, **112**
  Tatare, Southwest Spicy, **47**
Stew, Green Chile, **149**
Stock
  lamb, **115**
  Mushroom, **102**
Strawberry, liquado, **9**
Sunburnt Señorita, **3**
Sundae, Cajeta Caramel, **136**
Swordfish
  Cumin, with Sweet Red Pepper
    Sauce, **87**
  en Escabeche, **45**

Syrup, Bourbon, **147**

T

Tacos, Pork, **120-121**
Tamale
  Black Bean, **62**
  Blue Corn, **65**
  Blue Corn Shrimp, **65**
  Carnitas, **63**
  Chicken, **61**
  Confit of Duck, **64**
  cooking, 60
  Currant and Canela, **70**, 97
  de Elote (fresh corn tamale), **61**,
    96, 104, 114, 120
  forming, 59
  Fresh Corn. *See* Tamale de Elote
  Goat Cheese and Mint, **70**
  Lobster and Salmon, **68**
  Mincemeat, **63**
  sweet, discussed, 70, 71
  Sweet Blackberry Blue Corn, **71**
  to make, 59-60
  White Truffle, **68**
  Wild Morel, **69**
  Yucatán Chicken, **62**
Tamalita, 61
Tamarind
  Barbecued Ribs, **122**
  liquado, **9**
  paste, 5, 9, 77
  pods, discussed, 5, 27
  sauce of, 27
Tamarindo, **5**
Tart
  Cajeta, **138**
  shell, 133, 138, **141**
  White Chocolate Buttermilk, **133**
Tequila, in cocktails, 3, 4
Texas Wild Game Co-operative,
  47
Timbales, Artichoke/Oyster, **99**
Tomatillo
  discussed, 13
  husks, 17
  in Queso Fundido, 52
  in salsa, 19
  in sauce, 26, 29, 30, 49
  soup of, 35
Tomato
  cherry, soup of, 34
  in dumplings, 38
  juice, 3
  in sauce, 25, 27, 28, 30, 49
  in soup, 36, 39, 46
  sun-dried, 14
  to smoke, 27
Tortillas, discussed, 44
Triple sec, 4

Trout
  Blue Corn, **85**
  Brook, **84-85**
Truffle, in tamales, 68
Tumbleweed shoots, 94
Tuna
  Grilled, **86**
  rellenos of, 86
Turkey, Yucatán Stuffed Wild,
  105

V

Vanilla
  beans, discussed, 135
  with seafood in corn husks, 80
Venison
  Carpaccio of, **47**
  chile-stew meat, 94
  discussed, 47, 94, 96
  Grilled
    with Ancho and Prickly Pear
      Sauce, **94**
    Texas Axis, **95**
  inside round, for carpaccio, 47
  leg, 96
  loin-end chops, 94
  for mincemeat, 132
  Roasted, **96**
  shoulder, 94, 96
  substituting for, 47
Venison Chile, **94**

W

Waffles
  Pecan Pumpkin, 147
  Pecan and Wild Boar Bacon, 96
    with Bourbon Syrup, **147**
Watermelon, cocktail of, 3
Waters, Alice, 36
Whitefish, trimmings of, for
  fumet, 77
Wood, Christine, 132

Y

Yerba santa, 61
  described, 31

Z

Zucchini
  in salsa, 19
  yellow, soup of, 34